Reflecting Narcissus

Reflecting Narcissus

A Queer Aesthetic

S T E V E N   B R U H M

University of Minnesota Press

Minneapolis

London

Parts of chapter 2 originally appeared as "Taking One to Know One: Oscar Wilde and Narcissism," *English Studies in Canada* 21 (1995): 170–88, and as "Reforming Byron's Narcissism," in *Lessons of Romanticism: A Critical Companion,* ed. Thomas Pfau and Robert F. Gleckner (Durham, N.C.: Duke University Press, 1998), 429–47. Part of chapter 3 originally appeared as "Blond Ambition: Tennessee Williams's Homographesis," *Essays in Theatre/Études théâtrales* 14, no. 2 (May 1996): 97–106; reprinted with permission. An earlier version of chapter 4 appeared as "Queer, Queer Vladimir," *American Imago* 53 (1996): 281–306; copyright 1996 The Johns Hopkins University Press; reprinted by permission.

Published by the University of Minnesota Press
111 Third Avenue South, Suite 290
Minneapolis, MN 55401-2520
http://www.upress.umn.edu

Printed in the United States of America on acid-free paper

The University of Minnesota is an equal-opportunity educator and employer.

Library of Congress Cataloging-in-Publication Data

Bruhm, Steven.
   Reflecting Narcissus : a queer aesthetic / Steven Bruhm.
     p. cm.
   Includes bibliographical references and index.
   ISBN 0-8166-3550-1 (hc : alk. paper) – ISBN 0-8166-3551-X (pbk. : alk. paper)
   1. Homosexuality in literature. 2. Narcissism in literature. 3. Literature,
Modern–History and criticism.   I. Title.

PN56.H57 B78 2000
809'.93353–dc21

00-041791

11 10 09 08 07 06 05 04 03 02 01 00   10 9 8 7 6 5 4 3 2 1

for
Peter Schwenger,
my favorite narcissist

We have discovered, especially clearly in people whose libidinal development has suffered some disturbance, such as perverts and homosexuals, that in their later choice of love objects they have taken as a model not their mother but their own selves. They are plainly seeking *themselves* as a love object, and are exhibiting a type of object choice which must be termed "narcissistic."

— SIGMUND FREUD, "On Narcissism"

I tell you, my dear, Narcissus was no egotist. . . . [H]e was merely another of us who, in our unshatterable isolation, recognized, on seeing his reflection, the one beautiful comrade, the only inseparable love . . . poor Narcissus, possibly the only human being who was ever honest on this point.

— TRUMAN CAPOTE, *Other Voices, Other Rooms*

I'm starting with the man in the mirror.

— MICHAEL JACKSON, "Man in the Mirror"

CONTENTS

ACKNOWLEDGMENTS

Of course, the author of a book on Narcissus and narcissism would love to claim that everything in it was conceived, written, and revised solely by him. But like the myth of Narcissus's solitude, nothing could be further from the truth in this case. Many people gave generously of their time, energies, and ideas; I thank them heartily. If I have forgotten to mention you, forgive me.

At the institutional level, I want to thank the Social Sciences and Humanities Research Council of Canada and Mount St. Vincent University for research grants. Without that generous support I could not have written this book. Also, the departments of English (and especially their secretaries) at Mount St. Vincent University and the Université de Montréal offered me help and advice while tactfully avoiding me when I appeared ready to burst into flames.

Advice, bibliography, critical engagement, and encouragement came from the following individuals: Catherine Burroughs, Glennis Stephenson Byron, Alvin Comiter, Richard Dellamora, Linda Dorff, Judith Halberstam, Elizabeth Hay Steinson, Jerrold Hogle, Natasha Hurley, Robert K. Martin, Richard Montoro, Michael Moon, Thomas Pfau, George Piggford, Tilottama Rajan, Eric Savoy (as always . . .), David Savran, Eve Kosofsky Sedgwick, Goran Stanivukovic, Larry Steele, Shelton Waldrep, Anne Wetmore, Anne Williams, and Ann Wilson. I hope you get your money's worth.

I appreciate my research assistants more than I can say. Peggy MacKinnon could find Godot if you asked her; and Reina Green, my chief laborer on the project, is simply the most conscientious reader I've ever met. Thanks for surviving the drudgery with good humor.

Finally, and most important, is my appreciation to Peter Schwenger, to whom this book is lovingly dedicated.

Introduction

REFLECTING NARCISSUS

In *Narcissism and the Novel* (1990), Jeffrey Berman argues that the "richness of the [Narcissus] myth is inexhaustible. Narcissus dramatizes not only the cold, self-centred love that proves fatally imprisoning, but fundamental oppositions of human existence: reality/illusion, presence/absence, subject/object, unity/disunity, involvement/detachment" (1). A field in which all the binarisms of contemporary culture and theory can be detected, narcissism is for Berman a seemingly endless treasure trove of tropic and theoretical meanings, which he traces in authors from Mary Shelley to Virginia Woolf. But let us stress that this trove is *seemingly* endless. When Berman gets to Oscar Wilde, the "inexhaustible" implications of the myth are suddenly exhausted by the category of homosexuality. Of Richard Ellmann's biography of Wilde, Berman writes:

> The biographer implicitly dismisses any attempt to trace back the tragedies of Wilde's adult life to early childhood conflicts. We learn nothing new, for example, about Wilde's relationship to his parents or the sources of his homosexuality. Nor does Ellmann analyze Wilde's fatal attraction to people who preyed upon him. In portraying a heroic Wilde who is more sinned against than sinning, Ellmann remains silent on the reasons for Wilde's complicity in his own victimization. (151)

The "reasons for Wilde's complicity in his own victimization" are to be located, naturally, in the psychological link between his narcissism and his homosexuality; by looking to Wilde's parents, argues Berman, we can find those all-important "sources," that necessary etiology that homosexuality seems to demand. The "cause" of Wilde's homosexuality, he argues, is an overbearing mother who dressed her son in girl's clothes. Lady Wilde's

> treatment of her son went far beyond the bounds of what was culturally acceptable, and in light of the current research on gender identity [that is, Robert Stoller's 1968 *Sex and Gender*], it is impossible to believe that Oscar Wilde's female childhood did not play a decisive role in his personality development.... To be dressed as a girl for years, to have one's masculinity mocked, to be raised as a replacement for another, to be taught that

1

appearance has no relation to reality: how can this not profoundly affect the child's imagination?...We can now understand better Oscar Wilde's gender conflicts and his identity confusion. The inability of his fictional characters to serve as healthy, joyful mirrors seems to reflect the novelist's own mirroring difficulty. (170–73)

And let there be no mistake: the "difficulty" and "confusion" of homosexuality are enveloped within the maternally induced condition of narcissism — "The image of perfect male beauty Wilde pursued in his life and embodied in [*Dorian Gray*] was the creation of a writer who was treated as his mother's feminized phallus" (175). Oscar Wilde, then, was creative *in spite of* his narcissism, not because of it (175).

I have quoted Berman at length here not to deride what I think is otherwise a very interesting study but to point to a phenomenon that one encounters repeatedly in treatments of narcissism, especially those whose methodologies borrow much from psychoanalysis. Regardless of the degree to which cultural critics and theorists may find the Narcissus myth a productive and generative fiction, they are always brought up short at the door of homoeros and at that moment revert to an easy pathologizing narrative that diagnoses and condemns the gay man (and sometimes the lesbian) for an antisocial, antisexual narcissism. As Ellis Hanson has written, "The term *narcissism* is, at present, enjoying a field day among conservative critics and journalists....Narcissism has become a catch-all not only for clinicians, among whom the term still retains a degree of descriptive power, but also for cultural critics who enlist its high-brow vagueness in a general condemnation of contemporary life" (1992, 23). This "descriptive power" deftly hinges sexual object-choice to ethical mettle, using "narcissism" to conflate homosexuality with egoism and selfishness and with self-delusion and excessive introspection. Moreover, it does so not only in "high theory" and "high art": the homosexual narcissist finds his way into contemporary popular culture. He may be depicted as the merely vain (the haughty and snobbish Leon continually foiled by Roseanne Connor), or he may be downright murderous (the Kenneth Halliwell who murdered Joe Orton, or Jame Gumb, who caresses his partially transexualized body in front of his video camera, erotically engaged by his own image).

Nor is such pathologizing contained within straight readings of culture. In *The Apparitional Lesbian* (1993), Terry Castle expresses her concern that, as an opera fan, she may be caught up by "the most narcissistic, and even absurd, of sapphic fan fantasies — that of being 'taken up' " by the desired diva (217). In *The Queen's Throat* (1993),

Wayne Koestenbaum attempts to resolve the same narcissistic tension by anatomizing the pleasure with which the opera fan both identifies with the diva and feels his distance from her. In *Homos* (1995), Leo Bersani makes the stakes of narcissism much more political as he argues the need for white, middle-class gay men to stop apologizing for the fact that they are white, middle-class, and male, but then tries to negotiate this need with the "more or less secret sympathy" gay males share with "heterosexual male misogyny," since such sympathy "carries with it the narcissistically gratifying reward of confirming our membership in (and not simply our erotic appetite for) the privileged male society" (64). Finally, in "The Mirror and the Tank," Lee Edelman catalogs the ways in which "narcissism" has been deployed by AIDS activists such as Larry Kramer to condemn a community that is allegedly more concerned about pursuing its physical desires than about fighting on the front lines for AIDS action (1994, 107–9). Indeed, to a remarkable degree gay and lesbian cultural theory has embodied wholesale the pathologizing narrative of narcissism. If the psychoanalytic paradigm that Berman uses against Wilde is premised on regressions, insulations, and perversions (literally: leaving the path), then it is reflected as well in late-twentieth-century queer self-representation. In other words, psychoanalysis not only posits mirror reflection as the lamentable symptom of homosexuality but provides the mirror for that reflection.

As a psychological diagnosis, narcissism arises at an interesting juncture in history, given its relation to sexual inversion. George Chauncey and David Halperin have both argued that the term "invert" was not, in the nineteenth century, synonymous with homosexuality, but rather "referred to a broad range of deviant gender behavior, of which homosexual desire was only a logical but indistinct aspect" (Chauncey, quoted in Halperin 1990, 15). However, in 1892 (the year after the publication of *The Picture of Dorian Gray*), the term "homosexuality" was introduced to the English language through Charles Gilbert Chaddock's translation of Krafft-Ebing's *Psychopathia sexualis* and distinguished homosexuality from inversion.[1] This differentiation, I want to suggest, had much to do with the use of narcissism as a taxonomic category, one that began to be associated not exclusively but predominantly with homosexual men. In his essay "The Conception of Narcissism," Havelock Ellis, that famous liberal advocate of tolerance for the "invert" (except, of course, for the "invert who flouts his perversion in [society's] face" [1897, 157]), observed that "after the middle of the nineteenth century, when sexual psychology was beginning to become a recognized study, we find —

under one name or another or under no definite name at all — various references which here concern us." These references turn out to be descriptions of the narcissistic "invert," the person who misdirects libidinal energy by turning it on him/herself. Indeed, Ellis was the first person to refer to a "Narcissus-like tendency" of autoerotics to become absorbed by their own image (1928, 355). But Ellis's vagueness about the "name" or lack of name under which one categorizes certain suspect behaviors opened up the possibilities for the designating of pathologies where before only moral crimes existed. Ellis himself discovered in his research of the early to mid-1890s that narcissism is a marked feature in both women and "feminine-minded men" (1928, 355), a behavioral type that had been identified for at least two hundred years in the form of the English molly. While Ellis only published this finding in 1898, he had gathered his data much earlier and may have withheld his "sympathetic" portrayal of homosexuality because of the public vitriol inspired by the Wilde trials. In volume 1 of *Studies in the Psychology of Sex* (1897), Ellis cites the case of a homosexual male who is "often impelled more by *amour propre* than sexual desire" (41). Thus, part of that famous articulation of the species that Foucault discusses (1978, 43) is that species's characterization and containment in the 1890s within the psychosexual framework of narcissism.

Freud's Fairy Tales

Following Ellis's pioneering work, his "Narcissus-like tendency" was translated in 1899 by the German psychiatrist Paul Näcke into *"Narcismus"* (quoted in Freud 1914, 73), which Freud used in his 1910 addendum to "Three Essays on the Theory of Sexuality" (1905).[2] In 1911, Otto Rank located narcissism in a decidedly homosexual context (Ellis 1928, 356), paving the way for Freud's full-blown essay of 1914, "On Narcissism: An Introduction," which concerns "the attitude of a person who treats his own body in the same way in which the body of a sexual object is normally treated" (1914, 73). Freud writes:

> We have discovered, especially clearly in people whose libidinal development has suffered some disturbance, such as perverts and homosexuals, that in their later choice of love objects they have taken as a model not their mother but their own selves. They are plainly seeking *themselves* as a love object, and are exhibiting a type of object choice which must be termed "narcissistic." In this observation we have the strongest of the reasons which have led us to adopt the hypothesis of narcissism. (88)

Freud contrasts this narcissistic object-choice with one he calls ana-clitic, in which the child takes the mother as a primary site of erotic attraction. The narcissistic invert, Freud suggests, identifies with the mother who had loved him to the degree that he loves as the mother had loved — which is to say, he loves another man, but a man who is really a projected self.[3] For Freud, as for Ellis, Näcke, and other early theorists of psychosexuality, homosexuality is not the exclusive domain of narcissism, but it is certainly the strongest test case. Thus Isidore Sadger concludes, "We can say of homosexuality that it is the Narcissistic perversion *par excellence*[;] ... the chief characteristic of inverts is their vanity, ... and they never forgive a wound to their Narcissism" (quoted in Ellis 1928, 364).

However, if narcissism as a behavioral signifier so markedly slips away from a stable referent — it appears "under one name or an-other or under no definite name at all" — then it begins to signal its own potential for disruptions, illicit affiliations, deviant meanings. For example, in "On Narcissism: An Introduction" (1914), Freud picks up Ellis's assertion that narcissism is evident in both (hetero-sexual) women and effeminate men and contrasts "normal" male sexual development with that of females. While both sexes embody a primary narcissism, that is, a unifying bond with the mother that recognizes no outside or otherness, the male child in puberty reroutes this overvaluation of the maternal onto another, sexual object. Thus, he is sexually marked by *anaclisis,* the "leaning up against" another, an other who was the mother but is now the socially palatable desired female. For women (and by implication homosexual men), however, a "different course is followed":

> With the onset of puberty the maturing of the female sexual organs, which up till then have been in a condition of latency, seems to bring about an intensification of the original narcissism, and this is unfavourable to the development of a true object-choice with its accompanying sexual over-valuation. Women, especially if they grow up with good looks, develop a certain self-contentment which compensates them for the social restrictions that are imposed upon them in their choice of object. Strictly speaking, it is only themselves that such women love with an intensity comparable to that of the man's love for them. Nor does their need lie in the direction of loving, but of being loved; and the man who fulfils this condition is the one who finds favour with them. (1914, 88–89)[4]

What follows from this statement is a remarkable twist in the binary distinction between those who are narcissistic and those who are not. Freud notes what fascination these beautiful women have for men

who desire them and then claims that "it seems very evident that another person's narcissism has a great attraction for those who have
renounced part of their own narcissism and are in search of object-
love" (89). Children, humorists, criminals, and anyone who holds on
to his/her "self-contentment and inaccessibility, . . . compel our interest by the narcissistic consistency with which they manage to keep
away from their ego anything that would diminish it. It is as if we envied them for maintaining a blissful state of mind — an unassailable
libidinal position which we ourselves have since abandoned" (89) —
a fascination that will be evidenced in my discussion of Lord Byron in
chapter 1. This fascination that straight men have in (narcissistically)
gazing at the narcissistically effeminate blurs the lines of narcissism
in an important way: it forges a strategic link between feminism and
gay male critique by exploiting the omnipresence of narcissism in a
heteronormativity. What Freud suggests here is that narcissism is less
the demarcating signifier between the hetero and the homo than a
phantasm that structures all desire.

It is that status as structuring phantasm that has already grounded
some queer critical interventions in Freud's psycho-normalizing narrative. Contrasting the gay and lesbian discomfort with narcissism
that I noted above, Michael Warner and Ellis Hanson have both
deployed narcissism as a tool of resistance rather than a delimiting
foundation of identity and diagnosis. Warner's brilliant 1990 essay,
"Homo-Narcissism; or, Heterosexuality," contrasts Freud's treatment
of primary narcissism with the argument in "On Narcissism" that
homosexuality is constructed later, "when the subject's original narcissism encounters 'the admonition of others and . . . the awakening of
his [*sic*] own critical judgement' " (192).[5] For Warner, this move from
a pathologizing dynamics of the enclosed family romance to larger social relations and "advanced ego ideal[s]" (193) breaks Freud's own
frame of reference and contradicts his claim that narcissism is regressive, a retreat to the desired identification with the mother. In Warner's
reading of Freud, "secondary narcissism does not preclude a recognition of alterity. Everybody undergoes — and indeed requires — the
kind of narcissism Freud describes. Everyone makes identifications
with others on the basis of ego ideals" (193). Now in all fairness,
Freud does say as much: "A strong egoism is a protection against
falling ill" (1914, 85); he goes on to suggest that "a human being has
originally two sexual objects — himself and the woman who nurses
him — and in so doing we are postulating a primary narcissism in
everyone" (88). Indeed, Freud thought the structural residue of primary narcissism could be therapeutically useful: in a footnote to "The

Psychogenesis of a Case of Homosexuality in a Woman" (1920), he writes:

> It is by no means rare for a love-relation to be broken off through a process of identification on the part of the lover with the loved object, a process equivalent to a kind of regression to narcissism. After this has been accomplished, it is easy in making a fresh choice of object to direct the libido to a member of the sex opposite to that of the earlier choice. (158)

But for Warner, such liberality mixed with condescension merely invites the question of how Freud can maintain the theory that homosexuality is regressive, a *special case* of narcissism. If we are all fundamentally narcissistic, what makes homosexual desire more regressive than any other?

To allow that a primary narcissism may structurally underlie all desire — hetero and homo — enables Warner to resist Freud's narrative at multiple points, the first being Freud's notion of homosexual narcissism as a reflexive interest in sameness:

> to describe homosexuality as *merely* a version of narcissism is counterintuitive. The homosexual, after all, is interested in others in a way that is not true of the narcissist in general. Ovid tells us that Narcissus rejects not just the girls who love him, but also the boys. Those boys, then, have an interest in other persons, if not in the other gender, and the myth of Narcissus does not collapse the two. What warrants the forgetting of this difference, which becomes a nondifference, sameness? Why should gender amount to alterity *tout court?* (193)

From here Warner moves to the second and more central part of his critique: "If normal development leads from autoerotics to narcissism to heterosexuality, how would heterosexuality transcend its sources in narcissism more than homosexuality does?" (195). The answer, says Warner, is simply convenience: in "On Narcissism," Freud thinks it possible both to identify with and to desire a gendered image. The homosexual male, in that case, can both identify with and desire the father, thus giving rise to Leo Bersani's earlier discomfort that we might want to be the Father at the same time that we want to fuck the father; simultaneously, the homosexual male can identify with the mother out of his desire for her, thus adopting the "negative axis" of desiring the phallus with her. However, in "The Ego and the Id" (1923), Freud suggests that in "normal" male development the child identifies with (not desires) the father only and desires (not identifies with) the mother-substitute; Freud chooses the father as the object of identification simply in order to simplify his argument. Warner quotes the footnote in which Freud admits,

> Perhaps it would be safer to say "[that the child identifies] with the parents"; for before a child has arrived at definite knowledge of the difference between the sexes, the lack of a penis, it does not distinguish in value between its father and its mother....In order to simplify my presentation I shall discuss only identification with the father. (1923, 19, 31; quoted in Warner 1990, 195)

This arbitrary identification with the father renders Freud's theory of homosexual narcissism a mere smoke screen for the arbitrariness of all gender identification and desire, thus effecting through narcissism Warner's deconstruction of narcissism.

For Warner, the location of homosexuality within narcissism serves a larger political program of constituting as normative heterosexual identity and its entitlement to power:

> The central imperative of heterosexist ideology is that the homosexual be supposed to be out of dialogue on the subject of his being. Imagining that the homosexual is narcissistically contained in an unbreakable fixation on himself serves two functions at once: it allows a self-confirming pathology by declaring homosexuals' speech, their interrelations, to be an illusion; *and more fundamentally it allows the constitution of heterosexuality as such.* (1990, 202)

Warner detects a particularly narcissistic self-serving in heterosexuality's need to posit a homosexual narcissism against which it can define itself. For Ellis Hanson, that straight narcissism, and its reliance upon the narcissistic homosexual, can be seen to underlie more formal, rigidly defined political structures and informs Theodor Adorno's discussion of fascism. Writes Hanson:

> Adorno saw in the psychoanalytic concept of narcissism, and the pre-oedipal in general, both a way of describing the authoritarian personality and a position from which to launch a critical assault on fascism; that is, he found in narcissism a theory of fascist propaganda as well as a theory for its subversion. Adorno collapses the distinction between the narcissist and the authoritarian subject whose position is secured through a repression of narcissism. (1992, 25)

To the degree that the primal horde Freud describes in "Totem and Taboo" (1913) and "Group Psychology and the Analysis of the Ego" (1921) enacts "a regression to a prehistoric epoch when men surrendered individuality and freedom to the rule of an omnipotent and unloving 'primal father'" (Hanson 1992, 26–27), fascism is pre-oedipal and narcissistic, merely replacing an "unloving" father with a loving one in order to encourage "mass identification" (27). Adorno then uses the collapsed distinction to perform a (for Hanson, queer) reading of Franz Kafka, whose unapologetic representation of his own infantile regression "becomes a metaphor for this larger political relationship of a charismatic leader to his followers.... In this way, the autonomous ego, which finds its archetype in the authoritarian subject, has come to resemble the very narcissism against which it defined itself" (31). And this move toward "a dialectical demystification of ... conservative sexual politics" that diagnoses narcissists in order to pathologize and contain them is *the* intervention of the Freudian left: Hanson's essay concludes, "those who are vilified under the category of narcissism ... are held up to the patriarch as an ironic mirror of his own oppressiveness and valorized as a site of radical change" (43).

In Warner's and Hanson's provocative and trenchant deployments of Freudian theory, narcissism becomes a tool or weapon that critiques hegemonic culture by betraying the narcissism that lies within and subtends it. In this sense, the suspicion of narcissism as delimiting, self-delusive, and potentially dangerous can be used to represent straight culture to itself. But such a use depends for its strength on the same suspicion of narcissism that gave rise to its use within sexology in the first place. It is only because there is "something wrong" with Narcissus that he can be used to shame straight culture. Such a strategy is what Eve Kosofsky Sedgwick has described as the "universalizing impulse" that informs representations of homosexuality — the critical idea that the homosexual (here the homosexual narcissist) merely represents the larger dynamics of a given culture (Sedgwick 1990, 1). In this use of Narcissus as parodic mirror, there is no particularity to his desire; we're all queer here. But the story of Narcissus is also a love story — indeed, were it not a love story it would not be pathologizable — and we would do well to figure him within dyads of the erotic as well as within synecdoches of larger culture. To be sure, Warner and Hanson do note Narcissus's erotic possibilities: Warner in the passage on Ovid I quoted above and Hanson in his discussion of Irigaray, who he claims rescues narcissism for a lesbian eros. Still, the critical thrust of both articles depends upon narcissism as "charge," as a resistance to the sexological discourse that it remains contained within.

Earl Jackson attempts a different strategy. One of the few gay critics not to apologize for narcissism, Jackson devotes a portion of his book, *Strategies of Deviance,* to reading Freud's "On Narcissism" with a "radical and deviant literalness" (1995, 40). By accepting Freud's premise that homosexuals have suffered some disturbance in their libidinal development, Jackson says, we can locate gay male eros more firmly in the pleasure principle (a libidinal Imaginary)

than in the stultifying, moralizing strictures of the reality principle (inscribed as it is within the Symbolic order) (40). The primary
mechanism to characterize this pleasure principle Jackson calls "intersubjective narcissism," which locates in the body of the same-sex lover
a simultaneous confirmation and annihilation of the ego:

> In the body of the other, the gay male recognizes his (somatic) like and
> object of desire; in the look of the other, he sees himself as object of desire.
> The other's desire and the other's look are means by which he can reconsti-
> tute himself as transitory ego ideal, confirmed in the "annihilation" of the
> other's desiring look. From the perspective of the anaclitic subject, gay male
> sexual behavior would endanger and disperse one's "identity" as subject
> rather than actualize it. (30–31)

Following Leo Bersani's argument in "Is the Rectum a Grave?"
(1988), Jackson maintains that it is precisely that annihilation of the
ego that sets up (or sets off) gay sexual subjectivity as a political dis-
ruption because it celebrates the very violations of the phallic ego by
which the straight man claims his power. Indeed, at times Jackson
can barely contain his utopian joy:

> Gay male lovemaking is a pulsation of inter-ruptions of subjectivity, of
> inter-irruptions into the subject's somatic extension of his imaginary self-
> hood by the subject whose object he has ec-statically become. Subjectivity
> within male coupling is episodic, cognized and re-cognized as stroboscopic
> fluctuations of intense (yet dislocated, asymmetrical, decentered) aware-
> ness of self-as-other, self-for-other, via interlunations of psychic and sexual
> exuberance. If the heterosexual male imaginary includes a defense against
> ejaculation as loss of self, risk of nonmeaning, or abyss of meaning, gay
> male sexuality (with the anal drives restored) is a circulatory system of
> expenditure and absorption, taking/giving and giving/taking. (33)

For Jackson, a certain reading of Freud's narcissism aligns with what
he calls a "negating affirmation": the gay man's joy of surrendering
masculine patriarchal entitlement in order to engage a pleasure that
is outside the patriarchal, a pleasure accessible only to the narcissistic
subject, not the anaclitic one.

For Jackson, the anaclitic subject — by which he means the
heterosexual male — has "domesticated and subordinated" his "polymorphous perversities ... under the genital organization in the service
of reproduction" (91). In so doing, he has "stabilized, unified,
and sublimated" his "narcissistic operations" (91). Conversely, "the
nonsublimated, narcissistic subject's [viz., the homosexual's] identifications involve ego ideals whose artificiality, transience, specificity,
contingency, and multidirectionality of address inhibit a uniform progression or coherent teleological structure that would culminate in a

patriarchal superego" (91). I find Jackson's use of this narcissistic paradigm exciting and rich, and a good deal of what I read later in this book will exploit a similar model of narcissistic suspension, doubling, and dissolution. However, while his polemical statements carve out the terrain of straight versus gay productions and receptions of culture, they give one pause in their assumptions about the gay man's access to a privileged aesthetic, one that is perforce debarred from straights. Is all gay male lovemaking episodic and stroboscopic? Does it always exuberantly recognize a self-as-other and a self-for-other, thus remaining free from those more conventionally narcissistic tendencies of power and self-gratification? And what of the gay man who sires a child, especially with a lesbian? Has he, have they, domesticated the perversities to serve reproduction, or does he/do they maintain a narcissistic decentering that remains multidirectional? If one can note a universalizing tendency in Warner's and Hanson's treatment of narcissism, one can see the opposite in Jackson: a minoritizing location of narcissistic aesthetics within gay cultural production and erotic practice. Jackson's book is too theoretically informed by poststructuralist theory to want to espouse an identity politics, but it does anyway. All of Jackson's cultural examples are self-identified gay men (Oscar Wilde is in an appellational gray zone, but Jackson puts him in bed with Derek Jarman as evidencing the same phenomenon, and so he becomes gay *avant la lettre*) who employ strategies of deviance in their (self-)representations. Thus, it is significant that Jackson continually uses the adjective "gay" rather than "queer": his is a theory produced by and located in homosexual men only. The minority speaks from the margins yet continually fortifies the boundaries that ghettoize it.[6]

Refracting Narcissus

It should come as no surprise that discussions of narcissism tend toward either a universalizing model — where a narcissistic structure is located within straight modes of desire so that the homosexual functions mostly as a disruptive parody of the larger culture — or a minoritizing model where the object-oriented narcissistic ego authorizes a specifically gay identity whose boundaries it delimits at the same time that it wants to explode them. No surprise, since the same dynamic is written into the original Ovidian myth, to which Freud alludes in his discussion of narcissism. In that myth we see the depiction of self-enclosure, the beautiful youth in love with himself to the exclusion of the outside world. Ovid's Narcissus is his own minority, his own subculture, as he categorically rejects all others who want contact with him and posits the beauty of the reflection — his own beauty — as the sole object of his attentions. Yet in that myth we also see a generalizing across subjects: Narcissus's infatuation with his own image is replayed in Echo, who is the auditory complement to Narcissus's visual replications, for she can only repeat what has already been spoken; the male and female youths who desire Narcissus do so in vain, thus replicating his inability to have the object of desire, even though the youths can be said to "cause" Narcissus's inability to love, since they petition Nemesis to avenge them; and Tiresias, who has embodied both sexes and their attendant knowledges, repeats Narcissus's own connection with the mythic Androgyne, the perfect Adam who originally contained both sexes (more on this in chapter 2). Ovid's Narcissus evinces neither a universalizing equation of sexual object-choice and egoism nor a minoritizing celebration of the love of beauty, but rather both simultaneously. The tale holds up a mirror within itself that allows a shuttle between oppositions, a shuttle that begins to demarcate the "queerness" of Ovid's text. It is that shuttle, that rich overdetermination that makes Narcissus something more than narcissism, that I want to explore in this book.

The replication of a (primarily homoerotic) trope across the auditory field of (the primarily heterosexual) Echo has authorized a history of problematic readings of Narcissus in both ancient and modern texts. While Ovid is probably the first writer to give us a complete chronicle of Narcissus, he is also the first to add the story of Echo to what, before him, was a same-sex narrative. Louise Vinge's exhaustive study, *The Narcissus Theme in Western European Literature up to the Early 19th Century,* lays out the earliest fragments of the myth, noting that in the Greek sources, like the story of Conon, "Narcissus is loved exclusively by men. The homosexual element has not, as in Ovid, been mixed with female passion" (1967, 20). Havelock Ellis detected the same homoeros in the Greek versions, reading desire metonymically into a dildo:

> In a fragment of a comedy by Kratinos there is an uncertain phrase which Meinke [as quoted by Athaneus] reads as "the olisbos of Narcissus." The olisbos, as we know, was primarily an instrument for the sexual gratification of women. But there is reason to believe that even in the days of Greek myth it was recognized that such a device could have masculine use *per anum,* and there is a story of Dionysius in point. (1928, 348)

As I will discuss more fully in chapter 1, the Greek homoerotic versions of the myth have vied with that of Ovid as the definitive tale to which later writers and critics allude, but even in this shadowy pas de deux, one thing is clear: the early sources of the myth are not about configurations of sexuality per se (Vinge's reference to the "homosexual" above is an unfortunate anachronism), nor about the moral preferences that a given culture might attach to these sexualities. As Vinge forcefully and repeatedly reminds us, the early Narcissus tales are not moral exempla on the folly of self-love, stories of "this is what happens when": "Ovid makes no moralizing generalizations on the basis of the story. He tells a story which is at the same time curious and tragic without applying any didactic points of view" (19). Nor are they about the tragedy of a boy who preferred same-sex objects to a culturally privileged heterosexed desire: these early tales make no ethical distinction between rejected male or female lovers or between masculine or feminine reflections in the pool. Rather, the stories demonstrate the angry play of the gods, the seductive traps of specular beauty, and the gorgeous poignancy of metamorphoses into nature.

I am suggesting, then, that Ovid's introduction of Echo to a myth that circles around same-sex erotic desire sets up a queerly disruptive paradigm in which Narcissus's love for another man is replicated in the desire of a woman doomed to the same doubling imperative, a replication that is dazzling and confusing in the way it both conflates and separates desiring subjects, desiring objects, objects and subjects of desire. It is that instability, that unreadability of the tales' multiple resonances, that provoked Christianity's simplifications of the Narcissus story into a moral allegory against *vanitas,* one whose cultural legacy is still with us today. The second-century satirist Lucian was the first to use the Narcissus myth to moralize on the transience of worldly beauty and to show what happens when we fall in love with the corporeal world. Vinge writes, "When, as far as one can see, Narcissus appears for the first time in a Christian context, his reflection is thus made to illustrate *Vanitas,* the emptiness of outward, perishable beauty" (36). Significantly, this *vanitas* gets figured in the form of a *woman,* who becomes the reflected image in Narcissus's pond. Clement of Alexandria, Lucian's near contemporary, equates the vanity of women before their mirror with the self-delusions of Narcissus at his pool (36), and Alexandre de Paris's 1180 account of Narcissus in the *Roman d'Alexandre* suggests that the vain lad actually saw a female in the pool (64). I will discuss more fully in the next chapter the history and significance of this cross-gendered reflection, but the following observations seem appropriate here: first, that the history of the Narcissus myth since at least the twelfth century is as much an attempt to efface or obliterate homoerotic desire as it is the desire to anatomize and decry it; second, that this homoerotic desire cannot, in the history of the Narcissus myth, be separated from figurations of women as either subjects or objects of desire — nor should women's desire, as it is figured within male economies, be kept separate from considerations of male narcissism and the degree to which these considerations invoke or repress male homoeroticism; and, third, that we need to be careful about heterosexualizing the story of Narcissus into a narrative of gender relations and female exclusions (examples of which will be found frequently in this book). For to place the daughters of Echo in the hermeneutic foreground of the tale is to invoke and replicate the Christian Neoplatonic tradition of condemning her as the figure of worldly vanity; her restoration to the center of the narcissistic male text may serve as many antifeminist agendas as feminist ones. If the Ovidian text can be used to criticize Narcissus's misogyny (and Freud certainly treats Narcissus in this way), its historical manifestations risk reinscribing that misogyny by resurrecting the woman from her original abjection in order to make her figure as worldly vanity.

To efface the homoerotic by discounting Narcissus as delusional; to efface the homoerotic by transforming Narcissus into woman; to efface the homoerotic by promoting it as the necessary other against which heterosexuality can be invented: these are the markers of the historically diachronic Narcissus that have rendered him pathetic, delusional, and so very useful. By refusing the eros of the other, Narcissus has made it easy for us to refuse him. But as the work of Judith Butler — and the whole Freudian enterprise — makes clear, the repudiation of desire instrumentally structures desire, so that the denial or rewriting of Narcissus's homo-desire does not guarantee its disappearance. Quite the contrary. As Butler argues, Freudian thought makes clear that gender identity is formulated around the threat of injury and castration: the male fears he will be castrated, the female fears she will not. Thus, adopting a sexed subject-position requires the repudiation of unacceptable desires, the banishing of them to the unconscious where their presence as threat (their status as abject, in Julia Kristeva's language) is continually necessary for the constitution of the subjectivity that repudiates them. In the tradition of Lacan, Foucault, and Leo Bersani, Butler writes that "the law is not only that which represses sexuality, but a prohibition that *generates* sexuality or, at least, compels its directionality" (1993, 95). Normative sexuality may be constituted by the repudiation of threatening or taboo desires, but "Sexuality is as much motivated by the fantasy of retrieving prohibited objects as by the desire to remain protected from the threat of punishment that such a retrieval might bring on" (100). If this is the case, if Narcissus's same-sex image lurks behind or within the reflected other as the phantasm of desire, then we need to tease out that image, seduce it, lure it to the surface to see how it both constitutes and troubles normative gender.

I am suggesting, then, that a politically aesthetic resistance — a queer reading — of Narcissus needs to begin by reconsidering Narcissus as the figure who *rejects*. This rejection, I have been arguing, begins in the very notion of a stable gender that the Freudian enterprise, according to Warner, has made *the* signifier of alterity. As Narcissus rejects Echo and the boys who want him, he rejects not only the dictate to desire another (a socially prescribed and approved other) but also the drive to stabilize a range of binarisms upon which gender in Western culture is founded. Each of the chapters that follow centers on one of those binarisms as it has come to be associated with the "problem" of Narcissus: solipsism versus communality in chapter 1; surface versus depth in chapter 2; regression versus growth in chapter 3; madness versus sanity and self-obsession versus democracy in chapter 4; and sterility versus signification in chapter 5. Because Narcissus is seen to prefer the first term of the binarisms over the culturally privileged second, his rejections have made him utterly rejectable: the sad delusion he is made to perform stabilizes a culture that attaches itself to the "healthy" and "productive," if only by rejecting Narcissus's rejections. But Butler's "logic of repudiation" forces us to return to that figure of Narcissus as rejecting and rejectable, that figure of Narcissus who insists on seeing and desiring an other who is the same, and to ask what effect his rejections *and his affirmations* have on the cultural discourses that frame them.

To that end I have structured this book around signal moments in the invention of Narcissus and his relation to normative eros. We shall begin at the end of the eighteenth century when Neoplatonic discourses began to collide with the awareness that sodomitic desire itself (rather than act) was a prosecutable offense. This collision is especially problematic for Narcissus, given that Neoplatonic discourse itself had designated all poets Narcissus by demanding that the poet search the beauty of the soul within his own body to determine Truth in Poetry. That the poet's self, the poet's beauty, should become the object of his desiring gaze invites a crisis of narcissistic desire in the figurations of sexuality: the poet must always and never be a narcissist. This aporia, this mandatory yet condemned self-desire, becomes the crystallizing problem in the chapters that follow. Neoplatonism, Symbolism and sexology, Freudian psychoanalysis, the Modernism of the Cold War, and the 1970s "me" generation all made narcissism crucial to self-knowledge — and it is of course self-knowledge to which discourses as varied as Neoplatonism, psychoanalysis, and Mc-Carthyistic surveillance all tend — yet these discursive regimes needed to repress the eros of this self-knowledge while depending on it for the "truth." With an eye to historical specificity, each chapter identi-fies the abyss into which the homoerotic narcissist is plummeted, yet which he uses to make trouble, since his own desire, his own identity, is constructed on the aporia of the other he sees/wants, the other who is himself.

While it is the project of this book to render a queer Narcissus leg-ible within certain historical, philosophical, and political discourses, such a queer reading demands the very rejection of a *knowledge* we might want to claim in order to interpret Narcissus, to diagnose him, to straighten him out. And it is this imperative to hermeneutic re-jection that, paradoxically, is inscribed both in the Ovidian and the psychoanalytic versions of the tale. While it is Tiresias who declares that Narcissus "[w]ould . . . long years and ripe old age enjoy / . . . 'If he shall himself not know' " (Ovid 1986, 61), it is Tiresias who him-self knows, who knows himself, who knows himself as other, and who knows the otherness of self, having inhabited a woman's body for eight years before being changed back into a man. This androgynous knowledge, which will come to figure so richly in Plotinus and Ficino, depends on having two sexes and abandoning one, returning to the position of patriarchal seer from which he can then speak to some degree "as woman." And curiously, it is this androgynous knowledge that Narcissus must not have, but the lack of which also generates in him the longevity of his desire: as long as the beautiful youth does not know, he can be in love. Love may have its genesis in oneself, as Oscar Wilde knew, but it ends in revelations. Unlike Earl Jack-son's gay narcissist, who "cognizes" and "re-cognizes" his subjectivity with an "intense awareness," queer Narcissus refuses knowledge and re-fuses it, as much plagued by the fleeting chimera of self-knowledge as he is constituted by it. And while such attraction to an impossible self-knowledge should make him the poster boy for psychoanalysis, his vicissitudes of knowledge also control (at least partially) the very direction psychoanalysis would take: the move in Freud from the talk-ing cure to analysis interminable, from linear revelation to mirror transference, from the analyst's voyeuristic looking on to his/her nar-cissistic implication within the analysand's representational process (a phenomenon I return to in chapter 5); and on to Lacan, for whom the whole Freudian thing must be rethought through return — obses-sively, desirously, narcissistically — to the mirror stage, from which we can then theorize our place within the Symbolic that, like Narcissus's pool, grants us a signifier of our own presence and displaces that presence in the granting. Thus "knowledge" in queer Narcissus inexorably deconstructs the "gay" imperative to "know thyself" — Narcissus's presence destroys the illusion of self-presence yet inscribes queer desire where presence might be.

Thus, to the degree that psychoanalysis and psychoanalytically based queer theory articulate the way in which the human subject is constituted through rejection and repudiation, they govern and direct the readings that follow. Psychoanalytic theorists from Freud to Butler illuminate the way that repudiation constitutes the law of the forbidden, the desired and desirable, the other that continually seduces the subject as Narcissus is continually seduced by Narcissus. Yet, because Freud is as psychonormalizing and clinical as he is speculative and radical, because psychoanalysis has delimited the range of significations for Narcissus at least as much as it has opened them up, because it often smells in homosexual narcissism a suspect odor it would not detect in other forms of desire, I am refusing Freud the status of master-narrator in these chapters. Like much contemporary queer discourse, this book uses psychoanalysis against itself, cognizant of its historical inflections and limitations, suspicious of its agendas. But rather than merely betray a kind of Nabokovian crankiness toward Freud, I'm more interested in teasing out Freud's own discursive contradictions regarding Homo-Narcissus. And these contradictions, I am suggesting, both precede Freud — inasmuch as they are inscribed in Neoplatonic self-anatomizing, psychoanalysis *avant la lettre* — and outlive him, in those more recent psychological theories that revisit, revise, or even reject Freud. I am interested in a Narcissus who is framed by psychoanalysis but who at the same time exceeds it.

Narcissus's excesses: he loves, he loves another, he recognizes, he dies, he enters the other, the other enters him. The result, a metamorphosis:

> And then the brandished torches, bier and pyre
> Were ready — but no body anywhere;
> And in its stead they found a flower — behold,
> White petals clustered around a cup of gold! (Ovid 1986, 66)

No body anywhere, but another body in its stead — a metaphor, a displacement, perhaps a work of art, perhaps even the preciosity that heralds the birth of camp? The story of Narcissus is most suggestive in the way it gathers up significations — gender transformations, homo-othered desire, self-other identifications, self-knowledge that is self-destruction/self-apotheosis — and attempts to contain them within an artistic signifier, a signifier that all too readily betrays its overdeterminations. With this in mind, I have chosen texts that not only were produced within those signal moments of the invention of Narcissus that I mentioned above, but also articulate particular, and particularly historical, definitions of art and artistic production. The works I read here cohere into no one historical period, genre, or school. Rather, each work provides a meditation on a particular problem associated with Narcissus and aesthetics. But more to the point, I have wanted to avoid limiting my discussion to a coherent body precisely in order to get to that sense of excess that Narcissus embodies, that phenomenon of transgressing borders, of making trouble for laws, of reappearing phantasmatically through (and because of) repudiation. While I do not want to suggest a seamless, complete, and representative history, I do want to trace from Romanticism onward the use of Narcissus as the definitive trope of cultural production: the production of "art" from Neoplatonism to pornography and the Gothic, the production of masculinity from Decadence to French feminism, the production of the *literary* signifier from Symbolism to Kristevan psychoanalysis. And what I hope to make clear here is the degree to which Narcissus can be contained within none of these discourses while at the same time he subtends them all: I read him within men who are self-proclaimed homoerotic (Oscar Wilde, Tennessee Williams), men whose relation to homoeroticism is understood to be periodic or tangential (Lord Byron), philosophical (Hermann Hesse), panicked (Samuel Taylor Coleridge, perhaps André Gide), noncommittal (Peter Straub), or even hostile (Vladimir Nabokov). I am interested in the way Narcissus's queer desires forge a bond between producer and receiver (looker and looked upon, analysand and analyst, storyteller and audience). That bond has a homoerotic charge that reflects, refracts, and distorts social relations from the family romance (chapter 3) to nationalist political nostalgia (chapter 4). Narcissus is both the white-petaled cup of gold and the phallus, but the phallus in its psychoanalytic sense: Narcissus is the centralizing, unifying trope whose presence only bespeaks his absence, whose self-identification can only engender the slippages of desire, and whose mystifications within the masculine order cannot belie the spectral traces, the vestiges of the penis as an organ of pleasure. Narcissus belongs to no one historical category or political identity, but he does metamorphose and mirror them all.

Thus, I suspect the choice of particular texts here is governed more by personal idiosyncrasy than anything else — but in a book about gay male narcissistic pleasure, this seems inevitable (and desirable). Having said that, let me contain my own discussion and admit where I am not reading Narcissus: in lesbian representation. I have three reasons for this. The first is quite practical, having simply to do with the limitations of what can be contained within one focused, book-length study. The other two are more substantive. While this book forges some links between homoerotic men and heteroerotic women, the definitive tropes of lesbian representation both before and within psychoanalysis seem to me different from that of Narcissus. As Diana Fuss and Mary Jacobus make clear, lesbianism in Freud is theorized on a linear trajectory of development and falling back, in which the butch dyke does not assume the (appropriately narcissistic) place of converting her desire for the mother into an identification but rather falls back from this development into an identification with the father. It is that identification with the father and his phallus — Freud's lesbian is not narcissistic enough — that allows Sue-Ellen Case to posit a butch-femme aesthetic based on a parodic assumption of the paternal phallus, one that remains outside the narcissistic register of one's attraction to sameness.[7] Finally, and perhaps most important for my purposes, I have wanted to return to some historical texts (prior to Stonewall, prior to queer theory) to interrogate the place of queer Narcissus within the male-authored history of Anglo-American literature (and my confinement to the literary signifier is in order to talk with some accuracy about theories prior to the cinematic). In doing so I am following Judith Butler's notion of the critically queer where a certain performance of gender (drag for her, Narcissus for me) magnifies "the regulated productions of hyperbolic versions of 'man' and 'woman.' " For Butler, "The resignification of norms is thus a function of their *inefficacy,* and so the question of subversion, of *working the weakness in the norm,* becomes a matter of inhabiting the practices of its rearticulation" (1993, 237). By this practice, to reflect Narcissus is to place him not only at the phallicized center of a male cultural hierarchy where the male image is glorified (and it does do that; Narcissus is a queer man, and I don't apologize for my attraction to phalluses); it is also to place him within a specular optic that submits his phallic oneness to division, multiplication, and a melancholia that is always homoerotic. It is in that reflected division that Narcissus's queerly disruptive work can begin.

Chapter 1

NO EXIT:
ROMANTIC MALE NARCISSISM

Could Freud *not* have been thinking about British male Romanticism when, in *Civilization and Its Discontents* (1930), he described narcissism? It is for him "a protection against suffering through a delusional remoulding of reality" and "an intention of making oneself independent of the external world by seeking satisfaction in internal psychical processes" (80–81), namely, works of art (82) and feelings of sexual love (83).[1] Such a catalog has certainly provided critics with a rich spectrum for the diagnosis of the Romantic male, beginning with Peter Thorslev's location of a murderous "narcissistic sensibility" in Manfred's love for Astarte (1965, 50), to Thomas Weiskel's claim that Romantic desire is "fundamentally narcissistic" (1976, 144), to Anne K. Mellor's recent categorization of "masculine Romanticism." In *Romanticism and Gender* (1993), Mellor writes:

> when we look closely at the gender implications of romantic love, we discover that rather than embracing the female as the valued other, the male lover usually effaces her into a narcissistic projection of his own self. . . . [A] fundamental desire of the romantic lover [is] to find in female form a mirror image of himself, what Shelley in his essay *On Love* called the "anti-type." . . . In matters of love, these poets frequently, and narcissistically, idolized female mirrors of themselves, mirrors inevitably shattered by their biographical experience of female otherness. (25–26)

Unable to sustain an existence apart from male psychological and visionary energies, the Romantic woman inexorably dies (as in the case of Astarte, Lamia, or Elizabeth Frankenstein) or evaporates into nothingness (the visionary maiden of *Alastor* or *Endymion*), with no embodied self or desire of her own.

Mellor's allusion to Shelley's *On Love* is worth lingering on, for it goes to the heart of one of Romanticism's primary aesthetic manifestos. Shelley writes:

> if we feel, we would that another's nerves should vibrate to our own, that their beams of their eyes should kindle at once and melt into our own, that lips of motionless ice should not reply to lips quivering and burning

20

with the heart's best blood. This is love. This is the bond and the sanction that connects not only man with man, but every thing which exists. We are born into the world, and there is something in us which, from the instant that we live, more and more thirsts after its likeness. It is probably in correspondence with this law that the infant drains milk from the bosom of its mother; this propensity develops itself with the development of our nature. We dimly see within our intellectual nature a miniature as it were of our entire self, yet deprived of all that we condemn or despise, the ideal prototype of every thing excellent or lovely that we are capable of conceiving as belonging to the nature of man. (Shelley 1977b, 473–74)

Elsewhere, in the "Discourse on the Manners of the Ancient Greeks Relative to the Subject of Love," Shelley extends the point to suggest that the love object only exists as it is perceived; it is always already a narcissistic projection. The lover's mind, he says,

selects among those who resemble it, that which most resembles it; and instinctively fills up the interstices of the imperfect image, in the same manner as the imagination moulds and completes the shapes in clouds, or in the fire, into the resemblances of whatever form, animal, building, etc., happens to be present to it. (Quoted in Notopoulos 1969, 408)

In an epistemological universe since Berkeley, perhaps *all* vision is by definition narcissistic; all gender relations are egotistical.

I would like then to begin a reconsideration of Romantic male narcissism on the grounds that such narcissism has been the basis of artistic productivity from the late eighteenth century at least until Modernism. My point here is not to deny that such Romantic narcissism effaces and destroys the represented woman; to the degree that Romantic male narcissism acts itself out within heterosexual relations in the literature, it is certainly a justifiable target for feminist critique. And as I noted in my introduction, the patriarchal practice of figuring Vanity as woman allowed Christian moralists to exploit the Narcissus paradigm in ways that would meld homophobia with misogyny. But to call Shelley's condition (and that of the other "masculine Romantics") "narcissistic" is to impose an anachronistic psychological diagnosis on a culture that not only called such egotism by a different name (self-love) but, more important, used the Narcissus myth in ways different from those employed in the twentieth century. Thus, I want to take a different tack here, one that formulates itself through two questions. The first is, What effect did "narcissism" *as an aesthetic manifesto* have on the self-representation of creative men in the period? For unlike the Ovidian Narcissus who is ignorant of the identity of the reflected other, Romantic male authors purposely exploited the implications of looking at — and looking into — oneself. And the second question is related: How did this consciously embraced narcissism, this self-representation, collide with the dangerous and volatile field of same-sex relations within the homosocial spectrum? In other words, what happens when a poet tries to craft love-language by looking into the pool of desire and seeing a man looking back at him?

The Uses of Narcissus

As Louise Vinge has argued, the aesthetic doctrines of August and Friedrich Schlegel — clearly sources for the British male Romantics[2] — made conscious and celebratory the Narcissus image as a paradigm of creativity. August's famous 1798 proclamation, "Dichter sind doch immer Narcisse" (quoted in Vinge 1967, 305), and his 1800 sonnet "Narcissus" make clear that narcissism is consciously and intellectually embraced as an image of subjectivity and introspection. Here is the sonnet in German and in translation:

> O Nymphe! sprach Narcissus zu der Quelle
> Du Spiegel! Bett des fern und nahen Lieben!
> Du Tafel, wo sich Schönheit eingeschrieben,
> Und meiner Wünsch' unüberstiegne Schwelle!
> Nicht thöricht mehr umarmend deine Welle
> Will ich die zarte Mahlerei dir trüben,
> Lass mich in mich sie fassen, bei dir drüben,
> Indem ich weinend dich gelinde schwelle.
> Doch wenn ich nun ganz in dich ergossen:
> Wer weiss, ob ich dies Bild in mir nicht misse,
> Und wieder mich aus mir hinweg muss sehnen?
> Er sag'st, und sein Leben war entflossen,
> Doch neight, nicht mehr Narcissus, die Narcisse
> Den schwanken Stiel noch stets zum Bach der Thränen.
> (1971, 332)

> O Nymph! said Narcissus to the spring
> You mirror! Bed of distant and near loves!
> You tablet, where beauty inscribes itself,
> And impassable threshold of my wishes!
> No more foolishly embracing your wave
> Will I your tender painting muddy,
> Let me, across from you, grasp it in myself,
> While, weeping, I gently swell you.
> Yet when I now completely overflow myself in you:
> Who is to say that I would not miss this picture,
> And again would yearn to find a way out of myself?
> He said, and his life flowed away,

There leaned no more Narcissus but the narcissus's
Wavering stalk forever by the brook of tears.[3]

This mirror of reflection is also a tablet of inscription, a moment of epiphany and creativity. Schlegel's brother, Friedrich, makes the same point in prose. In *Lucinde,*

> the eye sees in the mirror of the river only the reflection of the blue sky, the green banks, the swaying trees, and the form of the gazer lost in contemplation of himself. When a heart full of unconscious love finds itself where it hoped to find another's love, then it is struck with amazement. But soon man lets himself be tempted again, and deceived by the magic of self-observation into loving his own shadow. Then the moment of graciousness has come, then the soul once more constructs its shell, and blows the last breath of perfection through its form. The spirit loses itself in its translucent depths and, like Narcissus, rediscovers itself as a flower. (1971, 105–6)

As Vinge explains, Romanticism revises narcissism and the moral that Christianity extracted from Ovid: "a changed attitude to the individual and to self-knowledge gives the Narcissus myth its new content. . . . It becomes the symbol of the creative genius to come to know the deepest spiritual forces within himself. One no longer sees aberration, arrogance, and fatal isolation in the observation of the reflection, but rather an approach to truth and a genuine love of God and man" (313). And, obviously, this romance of the truth is carried on in extremely erotic terms; it is a marriage proposal akin to the one that concludes Shelley's *Epipsychidion.*

But this truth, this *Gottähnlichkeit,* as it is called in *Lucinde,* exacts a price. Schlegel's romance occurs between Lucinde and Julius, who see themselves in each other; August Schlegel's Narcissus addresses not himself or the man in the pool but a water nymph, someone who is *drüben,* which is to say "across" or "over there." The sonneteer does not so much look vertically down at himself as horizontally; the nymph is across the pool at the same time as she is down in it. And, significantly, through this optical distortion the nymph also becomes othered in terms of gender. Similarly, Shelley's praise of the Neoplatonic search for beauty confines sexual intercourse to the "highest emotions" (Notopoulos 1969, 410) rather than the "diseased habit" of man-boy love (411); and, finally, all the critical discussions of Romantic narcissism that I have been able to uncover view the spectacle of Narcissus at the pool solely in heterosexualizing terms: Narcissus is always in relation to a female figure, and the resulting power asymmetries always result in her destruction.[4] Such a heterosexualizing is

part of a long history of mythic revision that seeks, consciously or unconsciously, to repudiate the same-sex dynamic within the myth and
thus to violently reject the possibility of queer eros. In their attempts
to normalize Narcissus and make him Act Right, practitioners and
critics of Romanticism have deformed the myth and vacuated it of an
entire continent of meaning. Narcissism may originally be a tableau
of same-sex desire, but the multiple refractions of the story since
Ovid, refractions culminating in the enterprise of Romanticism, re-see
Narcissus through a more drastically othering, normalizing optic.

To look into the Schlegels' use of Narcissus is to look into a hall
of mirrors whose reflections recede into an abyss of meanings and
contexts. But it is precisely these reflections, these twists and deforma-
tions, that constitute what gets written into — and out of — Romantic
male desire. Late-eighteenth- and early-nineteenth-century narcissism
represents the coming together of two traditions, the Platonic and
the Ovidian, each mirroring the other as it refracts it. The Platonic,
popularized in England by the seventeenth-century Cambridge Neo-
platonists, underlies Shelley's desire to find the spiritually true, the
ideal beauty, in the other (and it is because this Platonic ideal can
never be fully embodied in human form that the Arab maiden of
Alastor is abandoned, and Astarte is no longer allowed to live in this
fallen world). As articulated by Diotima in the *Symposium,* the path
to truth begins with the contemplation of physical beauty "existing
alone with itself, unique, eternal, and all other things as partaking of
it" (Plato 1987, 94). This absolute truth, moreover, is not to be seen in
representations and simulacra, but is the real. "Do you not see," Diotima asks Socrates, "that in that region alone where he sees beauty
with the faculty capable of seeing it, will he be able to bring forth
not mere reflected images of goodness but true goodness, because he
will be in contact not with a reflection but with the truth?" (95).
Moralizing Narcissus before the fact, Diotima privileges the optic of
absolute truth over reflected beauty, implicitly condemning the beauty
in worldly things in general and manly physical eros in particular.

This suspicion of manly beauty and physicality directly unites the
Platonic and the Ovidian in the writings of Marsilio Ficino, the
fifteenth-century Florentine philosopher whose Neoplatonism held
currency in nineteenth-century London.[5] In his 1469 commentary on
the *Symposium,* Ficino asks why, in the Platonic progression to the
absolute, men so often follow the wrong aim and attach themselves
to the wrong beauty. The answer, he says, can be found in Orpheus's
record of Narcissus. The soul, as part of but lesser than the truth of
God, is tempted by "shadows" or reflections of divine beauty; it is "so

captivated by the charms of corporeal beauty that it neglects its own beauty, and forgetting itself, runs after the beauty of the body, which is a mere shadow of its own beauty" (1985, 140). This pursuit, he says, is the "tragic fate of Narcissus" and thus the "pitiable calamity of men." Quoting Orpheus (in italics), Ficino argues that the soul of Narcissus *"does not look at his own face,* that is, does not notice its own substance and character at all," but rather "admires in the body, which is unstable and in flux, ... a beauty which is the shadow of the soul itself" (140). And so "the soul, in pursuing the body, ne-glects itself, but finds no gratification in its use of the body. For it does not really desire the body itself; rather, seduced, like Narcissus, by corporeal beauty, which is an image of its own beauty, it desires its own beauty" (141).[6] The paradoxes here are manifold: Narcissus is simultaneously too narcissistic (he admires his own beauty) and not narcissistic enough (he does not look intently enough at his own face to see his soul); he loves the beauty of the body (a reflection, a synecdoche for absolute truth) yet does not love Beauty (the whole of which the body is a part); he desires the body yet "does not really desire the body," desiring instead a beauty that is somehow different from the body — and it is the beauty of this "body" that may lead Narcissus, as it did Plato's countrymen, to that murderous "error" of sodomy (Ficino 1985, 135) rather than to the love of the absolute truth. With Ficino, then, we see the conjoining of the Ovidian and the Platonic as a praise of disembodied love and a caution against car-nal desire, but in this conjoining we feel the tremulousness of using beauty to deny beauty, of gazing upon the male face to elide the male face, of using the erotics of Narcissus against himself.

Nor was Ficino's discomfort the only one the Romantics would inherit. We can also locate the tendency to vacuate the myth of its homoeros by looking at another source of the story, that of Plotinus. In the first book of the *Enneads,* Plotinus argues that it is the nature of the soul to rise toward the good; it ascends "until, passing in the ascent all that is alien to the God, one sees with one's self alone That alone, simple, single and pure." "That," the vision of goodness, truth, and beauty that one can only ever see "alone," by oneself, is achieved through a long and lonely process of adjusting optics:

> Go back to yourself and look; and if you do not see yourself beautiful, then, just as someone making a statue which has to be beautiful cuts away here and polishes there and makes one part smooth and clears another till he has given his statue a beautiful face, so you too must cut away the excess and straighten the crooked and clear the dark and make it bright, and never stop "working on your statue" till the divine glory of virtue

shines out on you, till you see "self-mastery enthroned upon its holy seat."
(1966, 1.6.9, p. 259)

While the passage here clearly echoes Diotima's emphasis on the gradual ascent of the soul, the statuary beauty of that soul is not the only
thing Plotinus straightens out. As A. H. Armstrong indicates in an explanatory note to this passage, the phrase "working on your statue"
is an allusion to the *Phaedrus* 252D7, "but in Plato it is the lover
who works on the soul of his beloved, fashioning it into the likeness of the god they once followed together" (259).[7] In the *Phaedrus,*
the lover remakes his beloved into an image of his highest ideal —
Narcissus becomes Pygmalion, or vice versa — whereas in Plotinus
the other (body *and* soul) is removed from the philosophical picture,
except to the degree that the self addresses its self. Plotinus here employs a version of narcissism but only to get rid of a dangerously
carnal male-male eros. This move is startling when we compare it to
the late nineteenth century; whereas fin de siècle psychology would
equate narcissism with male homosexuality, Neoplatonism invokes
self-loving narcissism to *replace* the other-invested homoeroticism of
Greek desire and thus employs the paradigm of same-sex desire to
displace same-sex desire.

But if a selective reading of Plato could be wedded to the myth
of Narcissus to represent the quest for the spiritual ideal within the
self, what was to be done with the whole problem of eros? If Shelley's
translation of the *Symposium* and his commentary on it were directly
linked to his self-appointed role as advocate of free love, where could
the Romantics place Narcissus as a desiring, erotic, enraptured figure? And how are we to read the sexuality of Schlegel's sonnet or of
Lucinde? Once more a negotiation of the Platonic and the Ovidian
served the Romantics well. We remember that, in *On Love,* Shelley
defined erotic desire as perfect sympathy, the "thirst" after a "perfect likeness," a physical and psychic "correspondence" that (in the
"Discourse on Manners") "most resembles" the lover's own mind.
The language of love here, that whole enterprise condemned as Romantic male narcissism, finds its source in the speech of Aristophanes
in the *Symposium*. In his definition of love, Aristophanes constructs
the fabulous myth that all people were originally a "rounded whole"
with four hands, four legs, two faces, etc. (Plato 1987, 59). Because
of their formidable strength, Zeus separated them into the bodies we
now recognize and left them to seek out the other half from which
they have been severed. "[T]his was our previous condition when we
were wholes," Aristophanes suggests, "and love is simply the name

for the desire and pursuit of the whole" (64). And while Aristophanes' speech is clearly satiric and by no means the last word on love in the *Symposium,* he does provide the lens through which the Romantic lover sees himself: like Aristophanes' lover, the Romantic male perpetually feels the loss of his wholeness and seeks that wholeness in a narcissistically reflected complement, the other that is simultaneously part of himself. And while Ficino may insist on seeing this quest in solely spiritual terms (75), Aristophanes is clear that his myth is about physical, erotic desire — physical precisely because it is narcissistic.

For critics of Romanticism, Aristophanes' speech is the foundation for the poet's disastrous relation to women. Notably, Aristophanes asserts that there were once *three* sexes, yet the myth has become useful only for the third, that of the hermaphrodite who provides the paradigm of heterosexual desire in the *Symposium* and for the narcissistic brother-sister incest theme in Romantic literature.[8] But Aristophanes himself says little about those men who proceeded from the hermaphrodite, other than that they are "lovers of women" and usually "adulterers" (Plato 1987, 62). Rather, most of Aristophanes' story is concerned with men who are searching for their other *male* half, a quest that is usually homoerotic:

> Whenever the lover of boys — or any other person for that matter — has the good fortune to encounter his own actual other half, affection and kinship and love combined inspire in him an emotion which is quite overwhelming, and such a pair practically refuse ever to be separated even for a moment. It is people like these who form lifelong partnerships, although they would find it difficult to say what they hope to gain from one another's society. No one can suppose that it is mere physical enjoyment which causes the one to take such intense delight in the company of the other. It is clear that the soul of each has some other longing which it cannot express, but can only obscurely hint at. (63)

Shelley's translation[9] (and Ficino's commentary) notwithstanding, Aristophanes' tale includes the physical and the homoerotic: physical enjoyment is certainly not forbidden to the lovers; it is simply not to become the sole purpose for loving outside the control of the will.[10] Moreover, "Some people say that they [the lovers who find each other] are shameless, but they are wrong. It is not shamelessness that inspires their behaviour, but high spirit and manliness and virility" (62). The ideal of same-sex union here is also articulated in the *Phaedrus,* where the images are even more suggestive of narcissism. Here the beloved

> does not know and cannot explain what has happened to him; he is like a man who has caught an eye-infection from another and cannot account

for it; he does not realize that he is seeing himself in his lover as in a glass....He is experiencing a counter-love which is the reflection of the love he inspires, but he speaks of it and thinks of it as friendship, not as love. Like his lover, though less strongly, he feels a desire to see, to touch, to kiss him, and to share his bed. And naturally it is not long before these desires are fulfilled in action. (1985, 64)

This outburst of lovemaking, if an outburst it is, may not befit the philosopher in Plato's scheme, but Socrates himself argues that for soldiers the consummation of physical desire "is no mean prize" (65). Their very desire to seek the beautiful results in their partial attainment of it through a fuller, richer military valor (as evidenced by Plato's Theban band, gays in the military writ large). In this reading, male-male love is not the antithesis to truth but is necessary to its attainment. The principal meaning of "narcissism" in this homoerotic psychological profile, then, is not in self-absorption but in the seeking out of the other — the beautiful boy whose desirability leads to higher truth.

Surrounded by the anti-Platonism and homophobia rampant in Georgian England,[11] the Romantics inherited a philosophical argument whose eros was simultaneously compulsory and forbidden. What was to be done? Call again upon Narcissus, but re-see him at source. Whereas the Ovidian Narcissus clearly falls in love with another man and is enraptured by him, Romanticism (and its critics) rejects Ovid's version for another, more recognizable one, that of Pausanias. In Pausanias's version, the errant boy looks into the pool and sees himself, but, like the Narcissus of the Schlegels and German idealism, this Narcissus *knows* the reflection is himself; that he should not recognize himself strikes Pausanias as silly and unbelievable. So, in his own proto-Romantic act of revisioning, Pausanias recasts the story:

> Narkissos had a twin sister; they were exactly the same to look at with just the same hair-style and the same clothes, and they even used to go hunting together. Narkissos was in love with his sister, and when she died he used to visit the spring; he knew what he saw was his own reflection, but even so he found some relief in telling himself it was his sister's image. (1971, 376)

Almost paraphrasing the kind of creative love Shelley describes in *On Love* (not to mention the narcissism of Manfred with Astarte, Laon with Cythna, William with Dorothy...), this version had popular currency in eighteenth-century fictions and aesthetic tracts. According to Vinge, "The euhemeristic version of Narcissus' love as a love of his dead twin sister was ... presented in several authoritative works in the 18th century," including the works of Abbé Banier, Benjamin Hederich, and Denis Diderot, and was considered "a more correct and true story than Ovid's invented fable. It was so wide-spread that it can be considered well-known" (266). Well known, Vinge argues, but not significant, for "Despite the fact that the Greek versions, particularly Pausanias' twin sister version, are commoner in encyclopaedias and handbooks in the 18th century than in previous centuries, they do not have any effect on the literary treatments of the theme of that century. The information which is used," she concludes, "is still ultimately derived from Ovid" (313).

Obviously, I take such a statement to be too categorical. While the Ovidian version of the myth *is* the primary source for our image of Narcissus, Pausanias's version offers the normalizing, heterosexualizing paradigm that serves a number of needs for the early nineteenth century. First, it genders the reflection female and thus easily encodes a body/soul division that allows the tale to be used for the Neoplatonic exploration of ideal truth in a world of forms. Second, it places such desire in a by now normative and compulsory hetero-gendered context, so that the "real meaning" of the myth — illusion, vision, desire, truth — need not be obfuscated by questions of "unnatural" or "bestial" practice. And that this revision should occur at a historical moment — the late eighteenth and early nineteenth centuries in Europe — when one could be hanged not only for sodomitic *acts* but for sodomitic *desires*[12] strikes one as a historically necessary maneuver: to the degree that narcissism is a useful Neoplatonic allegory of creativity *and at the same time* a cautionary exemplum of the sterility of male-male sexual desire, it must be reworked, redeployed, and sanitized. In other words, the diagnostic investment that medieval moralists had in making the reflection female in order to condemn it as Vanity here inverts to a blessed assurance that the heterosexed other is desirable, metaphysical, an other to be sought rather than eschewed. The heterosexed narcissism of Pausanias can replace the homosexed narcissism of Ovid and in so doing combine the salubrious effects of the imagination with socially acceptable gender behavior. Thus, rather than Pausanias having "no effect" on late-eighteenth- and early-nineteenth-century literature, he is working overtime, behind the scenes, to reformulate the significance of narcissistic eros. And in so doing, he echoes a repudiation of the homoerotic that Narcissus had inaugurated in his rejection of his male suitors, a repudiation that will replicate itself, mirrorlike, through the history of the myth, its revisions, and its criticism.

But as I stated in my introduction, Judith Butler has made clear that the repudiation of desire is productive of desire itself; it is in the rejection of that which is forbidden to the self that the self is actually constituted, making the repudiated thing an object of simultaneous desire and prohibition. As Butler puts it, "the law is not only that which represses sexuality, but a prohibition that *generates* sexuality or, at least, compels its directionality" (1993, 95). What effect might this logic of repudiation have on canonical Romanticism? If Narcissus's sister appears in the pool to protect Narcissus from retrieving the prohibited object behind her — that is, his face, the face of another man, a desired and desiring man — then how might such a heterosexed transposition and its narcissistic repudiations affect the Romantic male poet? There is, perhaps, no more fitting subject for an analysis of reflections, desires, repudiations, and the fear of punishment than Samuel Taylor Coleridge.

The Picture of Little S.T.C.; or, The Lover's Dissolution

Coleridge's "The Picture; or, The Lover's Resolution" (1802) is a study in repudiation. The poem opens with the speaker forcing his way through a thick forest in order to free himself from loving Isabel, a woman whom he has rejected (or who has rejected him?). He boasts:

> Onward still I toil,
> I know not, ask not whither! A new joy,
> Lovely as light, sudden as summer gust,
> And gladsome as the first-born of the spring,
> Beckons me on, or follows from behind,
> Playmate, or guide! The master-passion quelled,
> I feel that I am free. (1969, lines 6–12)

The quelling of his master-passion, the repudiation of his desire, is achieved through a kind of splitting where the speaker imagines a youth to represent his alter ego. As Raimonda Modiano writes, this youth becomes for the speaker "the most extreme form of his fantasy." He is "a facet of the narrator's own personality, the 'fool' within him which the narrator is trying to exorcise through self-analysis" (1985, 91). Narcissus-like, the youth looks into a pool and sees his beloved reflected there until she scatters flowers on the water and her image dissolves. The youth is told sardonically to

> Go, day by day, and waste thy manly prime
> In mad love-yearning by the vacant brook,

Till sickly thoughts bewitch thine eyes, and thou
Behold'st her shadow abiding there,
The Naiad of the mirror! (lines 107–11)

The speaker, conversely, is off to better things, rejecting the Narcissus figure of desire and taking himself into a deeper, even more remote part of the wood where Love has never been. He is resolved (the "resolution" of the poem's subtitle) to give up love and to remain alone. But in the wood he finds the titular "picture," a birch-bark drawing of a sleeping child in a domestic scene, made by his beloved Isabel, which he will take to his bosom as a memento of her. His resolution fails, and he uses the picture to direct himself back to her. This scene contrasts markedly with that of the youth at the pool, Modiano says, for the picture is a real object, made by a real woman, thus instructive of a healthier, more proper object cathexis. Jean-Pierre Mileur is not so sure of the authenticity of the drawing, arguing that "It is never made clear that there is a real woman, that she was not the naiad to which she is compared" (1982, 86). But his moral imperative is the same: visionary maidens are to be given over for flesh-and-blood community, and this giving over performs Coleridge's critique of Romantic imaginative projection. Thus, for critics of the poem, "The Picture" documents a "gradual process of discovery, namely that only encounters with human beings matter" (Modiano 1985, 93). By repudiating Narcissus, "the speaker realizes what Narcissus failed to see: that representation is not Being, and that passion directed toward the phenomenal self produces a destructive Phantom" (Kessler 1979, 67).

But is it the case that the poem pits visionary narcissism against Coleridgean realism to find the former wanting? Is this poem really about straightening Narcissus out and having him behave properly, as Modiano and Kessler suggest? Geoffrey Yarlott argued against such a linear, salvational reading in 1967 when he pointed out that "the poem actually depicts . . . a lover trying *without success* to 'emancipate himself from Passion' for, when towards the end he discovers that the maid has dropped a picture (deliberately?), he at once forgets his resolution and hastens off after her with this new pretext for *renewing* the relationship" (39). And if we look closely at the speaker's new resolution, can we deem it any less narcissistic than what the youth was doing at the pool? The new resolution:

fit it is I should restore this sketch,
Dropt unawares, no doubt. Why should I yearn
To keep the relique? 'twill but idly feed
The passion that consumes me. Let me haste!

The picture in my hand which she has left;
She cannot blame me that I followed her:
And I may be her guide the long wood through. (lines 180–86)

The speaker repudiates narcissism, giving up the picture so that it does not "idly feed" his consuming passion, but the rationalizations that follow are staggering: "She cannot blame me that I followed her" because, even though the picture was "dropt unawares," it inflames and entices me. Perhaps it was even dropped deliberately, so that I would find it. Even though I am deep in the wood where no one ever goes (that is the point of my being here), she will expect me to be here and to find her artwork. And she will be impressed by my sensitivity when I return it to her. And from this favorable impression I will become "her guide" (Does she need one? Hasn't she traversed the area by herself?). The speaker's projections and assumptions, in other words, are as deliriously teleological as those of the youth: I found her picture = She loves me = We will be partners for life. Is the worship of the "watery idol" by the youth (line 85), then, really all that different from the fetishization of the drawing? Or does the trajectory from representation to desire operate in exactly the same way in the two desiring males? If, as the psychoanalytic tradition of Lacan, Kristeva, and Butler suggests, desire is always metonymically rerouted to seek in fantasy a full pleasure, completion, and wholeness (the Lacanian concept of the phallus), doesn't the primary narcissistic effect of Isabel's maternal, domestic picture speak to the same psychological dynamic as the specular reflection of the m/other in the pool?[13] Both are beatific, feminine tableaux that momentarily and narcissistically heal the desiring male.

It might be a more accurate reading of the poem, then, to question what kinds of narcissism are being pitted against each other. For if the "Gentle Lunatic" staring in the pool encodes one aspect of the Narcissus myth — the boy who is erotically cathected on an other, one of his own creating — then the speaker surely encodes a second aspect of Narcissus: the vain, solipsistic character who refuses all intercourse with others. As Edward Kessler puts it, "Both the poet's persona and Narcissus come to nature in order to escape human passion" (1979, 66). Instead of privileging the older, more mature, and knowing figure over the younger, impetuous one, the poem seems to imagine two narcissisms that it then deploys against each other to "cure" each. The older, wiser male seeks a solitude where the pangs of love and the need to envision lovers will never reach him; thus is the erotic Narcissus repudiated. But so is this solipsistic Narcissus rejected when, at the poem's close, the speaker enacts a youthful erotic cathexis and renews his pursuit of his love object. Indeed, his earlier repudiation of the love-struck visionary youth requires that he *envision* him, that he conjure him and the "stately virgin" out of his own narcissistic spring so that they may be rejected. In other words, his "resolution" is such that it must deconstruct its own integrity in order to be useful. In a way not dissimilar to the Ovidian myth, then, one image of Narcissus collapses into the other here, and, at best, we are left with an Ancient Mariner–type repetition-compulsion whereby he will seek out (yet again) his desired object. Just as Freud in "Homosexuality in a Woman" (1920) could use narcissism to direct the libido "properly," so can Coleridge use narcissism(s) to "cure" narcissism(s). The speaker may have "quelled" his master-passion — in the sense of subduing it — or he may be drawing on the more archaic meaning of "quell," as in "to flow" or "to bubble up," as in the German *Quelle,* the "spring" to whom Schlegel's Narcissus directs his lament.

Coleridge's deployment of Narcissus as a *useful* creation — as well as a deluded, immature one — gestures to a similar bifurcation in his larger metaphysical theory of creativity. While I do not have space to lay out Coleridge's entire idealist theology, let me sketch a tendency as it relates to narcissism. Like Bishop Berkeley, Percy Shelley, and perhaps even Ovid, Coleridge knew that "Nothing can become an object of consciousness but by reflection, not even the things of perception" (quoted in Shaffer 1968, 197). This compulsory yet unattainable objectivity presents obvious dangers for one's relation with the object-world. In a letter of 21 February 1825, Coleridge toyed with the image of a "self-conscious Looking-glass" which could only *reflect* reality, not create it, but know it was doing so. Such recognition, pace Narcissus, would be necessary to lead the perceiving self toward that spiritual, Neoplatonic ideal of Being. Coleridge continued the fantasy by imagining "two such Looking-glasses fronting, each seeing the other in itself, and itself in the other" (Coleridge 1956, 414). Such multiple reflections, he suggests, would bring the subject to the realization that the sensual world entraps him and closes him off from the possibility of higher truth.[14] This limited perception Coleridge called "Self-Love," which he contrasted to the Self that Loves, a self that must not be imprisoned by the reflections of its own Lockean, empirical sensations. It is this Self-Love, obviously, that characterizes the youth at the pool in "The Picture." One only moves out of the prison, in Coleridge's scheme, through another, different kind of narcissism: reflection leads to truth if it is combined with an exercise of willful self-denial in adherence to duty. The self must continually look at the self (and here we remember Ficino) but never see itself, only the truths of beauty that lie beyond (which is exactly, is it not, the crime of Ovid's Narcissus at the pool?). Just as Coleridge's famous definition of the "secondary imagination" makes it "an echo of the former . . . yet still identical with the primary" (Coleridge 1987, 167), so does his entire metaphysic depend upon mirror reflection: he once wrote, "from my very childhood, I have been accustomed to abstract, and as it were, unrealize whatever of more than common interest my eyes dwelt on, *and then by a sort of transfusion and transformation of my consciousness to identify myself with the object*" (quoted in Lowes 1927, 130). The creative narcissism of this optic Coleridge loved to call the "*fontal mirror* of the idea" of Being, a phrase that combines the narcissistic pool and the mirror (quoted in Hamilton 1983, 202).[15]

Now while Narcissus may be useful for Coleridge's sexless Neoplatonism, the poet also makes it clear (as had his German predecessors whom I have already discussed) that there is no exit from narcissism: indeed, Coleridge renders the narcissistically reflected sensual body *necessary* in order to reject it. Given Judith Butler's discussion of the logic of repudiation and the status of what has been abjected in constituting the identity that rejected it, we can return to "The Picture" and watch it unravel the very Neoplatonism it employs (not to mention the heteroeros that frames the broad movement of the poem). For it becomes clear in the poem that while Isabel is the manifest object of desire, she is invoked, visualized, and mediated by a third party: the erotic, desiring youth at the pool and the reclining boy in the picture. In the context of Coleridge's use of German sources, the poem employs the Schlegelian optic of looking across the pool to see the desired object, but that desired object is now restored to its original Ovidian masculinity, even though such masculinity is depicted as desiring a female other. Schlegel's "Nymph" is not Coleridge's "watery idol" but rather the desiring youth looking for a watery idol. Though the male youth conjures the woman as his object of desire, it is the youth whom the speaker conjures and with whom the speaker will ultimately identify. In psychoanalytic terms, the poem registers the speaker's desire for the youth's desire. Nor is the youth the only male he desires. In a poem that ostensibly condemns the youth's conjuring of the image in the pool, how are we to read the speaker's *self*-representation in the following lines?

> Here will I seat myself, beside this old,
> Hollow, and weedy oak, which ivy-twine

Clothes as with net-work; here will I couch my limbs,
Close by this river, in this silent shade,
As safe and sacred from the step of man
As an invisible world — unheard, unseen,
And listening only to the pebbly brook
That murmurs with a dead, yet tinkling sound. (lines 49–56)

This time it is not the languid virgin who is envisioned but the languid self, composed and contextualized as an enviable third person. This moment differs from the youth at the pool only in terms of the gender of the reflection: in bifurcating himself into subject and object, the speaker engages the kind of same-sex narcissism that the Romantics both exploited and tried to get rid of. Like the erotic youth whose sexuality the speaker is trying to emulate yet repudiate, the speaker holds a desiring male imago as the central phantasm in the poem. Each is a desiring male, each looks into a mirror to see his own reflection there, and each disingenuously reads that reflection as a heterosexed desire. Yet each is awash in desire for a male other who is the male self.

As the speaker falls into the image of the youth at the end of the poem, and the youth is absorbed by the speaker (and then, both collapse into the image of the *boy* in the picture, whose desire for the m/other they then imitate), we see the act of identity and identification that this poem is really about. As Butler argues, identifications are often for the purpose of a fantasy, that of "recovering a primary object of a love lost — and produced — through prohibition" (1993, 99). That lost object, I am suggesting, can only be seen in a Romantic male optic as a desiring and desired male other whom the Coleridgean subject desires to possess and to be possessed by. After all, don't the poem's opening ambiguity — the "master-passion" that "Beckons me on, or follows from behind" (line 10) — and the poet's desire both to "follow" Isabel and to "be her guide" (lines 185–86) place the speaker in both the active and the passive role? Don't these further collapse him into the youth he was repudiating, as he desires what that youth desires? For this quest to identify with a male need not be only the oedipal assumption of a sexed subject-position: the speaker is not necessarily identifying with the youth only in order to imitate his heterosexed desire. As Butler writes, "To identify is not to oppose desire. Identification is a phantasmatic trajectory and resolution of desire; an assumption of place; a territorialization of an object which enables a temporary resolution of desire, but which remains desire if only in its repudiated form" (1993, 99). In Butler's logic of repudiation, the male's identification with masculinity proceeds on the grounds of the *desire* for that masculinity, to *have* it as well as to *be* it. One becomes a man not only to be able to desire women other than the mother but also to desire men whose identity one is partially (never fully) transuming. Identification with masculinity returns the speaker to the heterosexual exchange he had previously rejected (this is not, after all, a "gay" poem), but it also and inevitably vitalizes the homoerotic spectrum of masculinity that normative Romantic aesthetics had so vigorously foreclosed. As Butler says, "certain identifications and affiliations are made, certain sympathetic connections amplified, precisely in order to institute a *dis*identification with a position that seems to be saturated with injury or aggression" (100), a position like compulsory homo-narcissism in Romantic desire.

If, as I have been arguing, Romantic male desire is structured by a same-sex narcissism that it must continually repudiate, then what effects does that repudiation have on the self-representation of a man like Coleridge whose eros was always contested and volatile? How did it affect a man who could define his friendship with Thomas Poole in such Aristophanic and Socratic language as this: "to see you daily, to tell you all my thoughts in their first birth, and to hear your's, *to be mingling identities with you,* as it were" (Coleridge 1956, 249; emphasis added)?[16] What happens when, in Judith Butler's terms, the prohibitions against homo-narcissism "become objects of eroticization, such that coming under the censure of law becomes what Freud called a necessary condition for love" (1993, 110)? For Coleridge, the repudiation of sexual desire was necessary for the Neoplatonic search for ideal Being in the Self, but it brought with it a price: that of an eroticized self-consciousness. In a notebook entry of June 1810, he wrote that the Catholic practice of forbidding priests to marry brought with it not only a *"perpetual Burning"* of heterosexed desire, but also significantly an "ungratified Priapism of the inward man" (1957, 3899). The problem here is not on my (externalized) fixation for the woman I desire but on my inner erection, my constant erotic fascination with my own phallus. And if Jacques Lacan was right to suggest that a man's excessive attention on his phallus actually renders him feminized, then such a fear must taint "The Picture." The narcissistic youth sees a *female* image in the pool, one whose disappearance is replaced not with the male face but with none at all, only "Each wildflower on the marge inverted there, / And there the half-uprooted tree" (lines 101–2); without his feminine other — or is it his femininity? — he disappears. And this is not the only moment of effeminized maleness. Love itself is gendered male in this poem, yet it suffers a role-reversal in the natural landscape. Nature issues a phallicized penetration as

> the low stumps shall gore
> His dainty feet, the briar and the thorn
> Make his plumes haggard. . . .
> With prickles sharper than his darts bemock
> His little Godship, making him perforce
> Creep through a thorn-bush on yon hedgehog's back.
> (lines 29–31, 43–45)

In a contest of phalluses, Dame Nature's is clearly sharper and more powerful than the detumescent male's, who is rendered feminine by contrast. And when the speaker is finally "pricked" by love, when he delivers over narcissistic solitude for narcissistic desire, he exits the poem by adopting the position of Echo pathetically and expectantly in search of her desired lover, who has only given her the slightest hint that he may reciprocate before he vanishes into absence.

In perhaps the finest poetry in "The Picture," the reflected woman's image is destroyed by flowers she has plucked and dropped into the water:

> Then all the charm
> Is broken — all that phantom world so fair
> Vanishes, and a thousand circlets spread,
> And each mis-shape the other. Stay awhile,
> Poor youth, who scarcely dar'st lift up thine eyes!
> The stream will soon renew its smoothness, soon
> The visions will return! (lines 91–97)

I'd like to conclude my speculations on Coleridge by holding this moment against one from Butler's *Bodies That Matter* (1993):

> The breaking of certain taboos brings on the spectre of psychosis, but to what extent can we understand "psychosis" as relative to the very prohibitions that guard against it? In other words, what precise cultural possibilities threaten the subject with a psychotic dissolution, marking the boundaries of livable being? To what extent is the fantasy of psychotic dissolution itself the effect of a certain prohibition against those sexual possibilities which abrogate the heterosexual contract? Under what conditions and under the sway of what regulatory schemes does homosexuality itself appear as the living prospect of death? (98)

When the youth sees himself othered as female, his projected image destroys the specular moment by plucking "[t]he heads of tall flowers that behind her grow" (line 88). That the self is dissolved through a castration image should alert us to the poem's anxieties about submission to the laws of desire where desire itself is both required and forbidden. But that the castration should take place from "behind" may also alert us to an anal geography that is another facet of the poem's worry: to the degree that the female figure is the gazer's femininity that refuses to cathect on an other (an actual woman), "homosexuality itself appears as the living prospect of death."[17] And for a poet who declared himself as having a "feminine" spirit, such reflection might be all the more threatening (Coleridge 1956, 430). Similarly, when the speaker sees himself othered as the youth (who is then othered as the female), we see an attempt to shore up a dissolving self, first through a resolution *not* to desire, and then to identify with the other's desire. Yet, as the *OED* makes clear, "resolution" is etymologically linked to "dissolution," a link displayed in the poem by the psychotic self-multiplications by which the self is misshaped, centrifugally dispersed, and obliterated. And driving all of this is a "master-passion" that must both be sought and repudiated, a passion which either "Beckons me on, or follows from behind" (line 10). Homo-Narcissus provides the "boundaries of livable being" precisely by threatening dissolution: he marks the teleological progress of heterosexed desire, yet he constantly abrogates that desire by remaining beautifully, terrifyingly, perhaps even sublimely same-sexed.

Byronic Narcissism: Heathcliff, I *Am* Nellie!

In a canonical and post-Freudian reading of narcissism, Romantic poetry like Coleridge's "The Picture" at best describes the Neoplatonic search for ideal Being as represented by the visionary maiden and at worst documents the systematic projection and destruction of the female other needed to constitute the male psyche. Narcissism makes the personal egregiously political in its orchestration of power relations. And nowhere does the madness and badness of Narcissus become more dangerous to know than in Byron's Manfred, whose delusions of grandeur take him a step beyond the youth at Coleridge's pool to assume a "real" woman into his own ego and thus to obliterate her. He says of his sister Astarte:

> She was like me in lineaments — her eyes,
> Her hair, her features, all, to the very tone
> Even of her voice, they said were like to mine;
> But soften'd all, and temper'd into beauty; . . .
> I loved her, and destroy'd her! (1980–91,
> 2.2.105–17)

To this self-representation of Byron's gender relations many, including Lady Caroline Lamb, Claire Claremont, and John William Polidori, would agree. But what if this destruction of the representation of the female is itself a repudiation of something else, as in Coleridge's pool the reflected and dissolved female gestures to male effeminization? What if the following apocryphal anecdote, first recorded by Edward Stevenson and then quoted by Louis Crompton, is authentic? In it Byron claims to have said, "I expected a while ago to write a drama on Greek love — not less — modernizing the atmosphere — glooming it over — to throw the whole subject *back into nature, where it belongs....* But I made up my mind that British philosophy is not far enough on for swallowing such a thing neat. So I turned much of it into 'Manfred' " (quoted in Crompton 1985, 371; emphasis added). Had Byron written this play, it might have been a strategic repudiation of his own scandalous (heterosexed) relationship with Augusta Leigh. Yet it also raises the specter of homo-narcissism we find in some of Byron's other narratives on same-sex love: *Childe Harold*, the travelogue more about the poet's psychological fixations than about European vacation spots, inscribes Robert Rushton and John Edleston, two boys with whom Byron had once been in love, into the foreground of the poet's consciousness; and the poem sequence addressed to Thyrza, initially read as Byron's complaint over a lost female love, is now accepted as having been written for Edleston after his death in 1810. If these poems, which awakened Byron to declare him famous, are actually founded on homoerotic rather than "ideal" and "pure" — that is, heterosexed — attachments, then we may locate in Byron the same complex of repudiations and cathexes that we have seen elsewhere in the period, but which Byron redeploys in order to circumvent the destructive panic and self-deception operative in Coleridge.

An interrogation of such redeployment of Romantic panic might begin with one of Byron's earliest pieces of Romantic drag, the stanzas to Thyrza. For the queer reader, the very nomenclature already resonates with the homoerotic: Thyrza is a female biblical name belonging to Abel's wife. And Abel is, of course, the brother of Cain, a figure who speaks in the Byron canon for the author's constructed literary persona, a figure who doubles Abel at the same time that he destroys him. These queer energies — my lover is the wife of my brother-enemy, a homoerotic triangle stretching from Ann Radcliffe's Gothic to David Cronenberg's *Dead Ringers* — are then redoubled by Byron's ascription of the name to Edleston, the young chorister of humble birth whom Byron had adored at Cambridge, whose reputation had been clouded by rumors of "indecency" (Byron 1973a, 257) and who died of consumption in May 1810. The titular poem, "To

Thyrza," is a conventional elegy for a man about whom Byron had candidly written, "I certainly *love* him more than any human being" (1973a, 124), and, as Crompton notes, finds its place in a tradition of elegies ranging from *Lycidas* to *Adonais* to Tennyson's *In Memoriam*. But unlike these other love lyrics to dead men, "To Thyrza" registers the early Byronic materialism, the suspicion of a metaphysics that would ensure Edleston's everlasting life either in heaven or on earth. The speaker has loved the boy "in vain," for "[t]he past, the future fled to thee, / To bid us meet — no — ne'er again!" (lines 7–8). And while the poem moves toward a conventional elegiac *consolatio*, employing Platonic ideals of pure and virtuous love as instruction for heavenly reward, it resists its own optimism by the emphasis on the limitations of the physical: "Oft have I borne the weight of ill, / But never bent beneath till now!" (lines 43–44); and by the use of the conditional: "If rest alone be in the tomb, / I would not wish thee here again" (lines 47–48); "if in worlds more blest than this . . . " (line 49), the boy's love "fain would form my hope in Heaven" (line 56). One thinks here of Wordsworth's great expression of doubt in the midst of his "Tintern Abbey": "If this / Be but a vain belief . . . " (lines 50–51). Like the earlier "Epitaph on a Friend," Byron's poem is remarkable for inscribing a refusal of past and future, for negating the supposed consolations of a heaven-earth relationship. It rejects the consolations of Neoplatonic idealism that Shelley and Coleridge would hold on to with varying degrees of success. Instead, it emphasizes the corporeal intensity and vulnerability and ultimately the loss of the relationship between lover and beloved.

But if the poem charts a desire whose mise-en-scène is in the temporal and the embodied rather than the transcendent and spiritual, then it also rejects the Romantic, Neoplatonic repudiation of the body and restores it to the focus of the elegy. That focus — the nature of embodied, erotic transaction — is narcissistic in conventional ways. While the poem begins with the usual bewailing of a life cut short and the equally standard inscription of sorrow by the poetic speaker left behind, it then takes a rather audacious turn:

> And didst thou not, since Death for thee
>   Prepar'd a light and pangless dart,
> Once long for him thou ne'er shalt see,
>   Who held, and holds thee in his heart? (lines 13–16)

The note struck here is reminiscent of Byron's poem to the living Edleston, "The Cornelian," in which the boy's virtues are gathered together — or reductively appropriated — in the line, "I am sure, the giver lov'd *me*" (line 8; emphasis added). Here we sense that familiar Romantic narcissism, an egocentrism of which Byron is perhaps the most famous example, only this time its "victim" is a male, not a female. In this grieving love lyric we are no longer in the register of the subject's own virtues, nor are we even to consider the speaker's sorrow for the loss of the subject's virtues; rather, we are to consider the *speaker*'s virtues, his desirability as it is prosopopaically imagined through the dead subject (or shall we now say "object"?). This is a strategy we find repeatedly in Byron's consolation poems: in "Epitaph on a Friend," written to an unknown person also of lower birth, the speaker imagines how the "gentle spirit" of the dead boy will "hover nigh" to "read, recorded on my heart, / A grief too deep to trust the sculptor's art" (lines 11–15). And later in "To Thyrza," the speaker asks "who like [himself] had watch'd thee here? / Or sadly mark'd thy glazing eye / In that dread hour ere death appear?" (lines 17–19). Rather than bemoan the loss, the poem seems instead to celebrate the intensity with which the loss is felt and the intensely individual subject that such loss constructs. Crompton writes that when Byron "held the stricken boy in his arms and broke down himself, he felt whole at last: Euryalus had rescued Nisus" (191). Like the visionary youth in "The Picture," the speaker has narcissistically appropriated the prismatic array of desires to focus on himself and his intense lovability rather than on the loss of the other. What death has put asunder, clinical narcissism joins together.

Yet for the lover of Greek culture, Narcissus is a multifaceted character whose erotic energies are not easily fixed. When the elegies' speaker looks into himself, he sees himself reflected not through a female figure (as in Pausanias and the Coleridgean youth) but in relation to another man. This relation to a decidedly male other may point to another source of the Narcissus myth, that of Conon, a Greek contemporary of Ovid whom I noted in my introduction. In Conon, the spurned male lover Ameinias kills himself because Narcissus will not return his love. This unrequited desire for another gets replicated in the desire for the self: "When Narcissus saw his own face and figure in a spring he became in a strange way his own lover as the first and only one" (quoted in Vinge 1967, 20). According to Vinge, Conon "does not say whether Narcissus recognizes himself but does not seem to reflect on this matter. His Narcissus seems to die in confusion because he cannot reach the person he loves, not in conscious awareness that he sees himself" (20), and so this tale, like Ovid's, effects that curious blend of the universalizing and the minoritizing: Narcissus's self-love is simultaneously the cause of another's desire and the punishment for another's desire. Thus, if Narcissus is normalized and straightened out here, it is because he learns from the desire of *another man* how his own desires should be structured. And if we hold this version against the terms laid out by Aristophanes and the *Phaedrus,* we find an intermingling of male lovers, a transference of the lover into the beloved where it becomes impossible to distinguish between desires. Like the Greeks, Byron's strategy in the elegies is to meld the perceiver with the perceived in a way that audaciously rebukes Coleridge's — and history's — moralizing of the Ovidian story, for wasn't the "crime" of Ovid's Narcissus that he could not tell the difference between himself as a desiring subject and himself as a desiring object? Byron sees this melding not as heterosexed destruction but as homoerotic desire.

Such obfuscation of subject and object is, for Shelley (as for Coleridge, Schlegel, and Schelling), the very heart of Romanticism. For Byron's "To Thyrza," it defines the boys' erotic life together, a life where "Affection's mingling tears" (line 28) replicated the "whisper'd thought of hearts allied" (line 31), as the magnetism of erotic bonds displays itself in the "pressure of the thrilling hand" (line 32). For Louis Crompton, this "affection" is the expression of closeted emotion that is the central thrust of Crompton's study. And if this "thrilling" is taken in its eighteenth-century meaning of "[a] subtle nervous tremor caused by intense emotion or excitement... producing a slight shudder or tingling through the body; a penetrating influx of feeling or emotion" (*OED*), the "thrill" of the erotic touch is not a (narcissistic) isolation of the Byronic lover as much as a closed-circuit communication of pleasure that moves through the lover and the beloved and that transforms subject and object into subject and subject.[18] The lorn speaker's "heart-drops" of "Affection" gush over — which is to say, the beloved's sorrows for the world are picked up, appropriated, and continued by the lover as part of the continuum of male-male interpsychic communication. And this interpsychic communion continues after death: the speaker requests, "Impart some portion of thy bliss" (line 51), and "Teach me — too early taught by thee!" (line 53). The speaker here becomes both agent and recipient, both "forgiving and forgiven" (line 54) for the improper emotion of despair (and perhaps other improper emotions?). The speaker is always alone yet always connected, always a lover and always beloved, always complete and always in process, always erotic and always desiring eros; his is the "pulsation of inter-ruptions of subjectivity, of inter-irruptions into the subject's somatic extension of his imaginary selfhood by the subject whose object he has ecstatically become," to return to Earl Jackson's discussion of affirming negation. Thus, the poem becomes not only about loss and frustration, as Coleridge's had been, but also about transference and communion as they are inscribed in "narcissistic" desire. And in this sense, Ovid's boy leaning over his image in the pool is recast as Conon's Narcissus identifying with Ameinias, or Aristophanes' man looking for his other male half. Byron's is a scene of desire for another man, an intense appreciation of beauty and love that is unwitting — and uncaring — of its source in the perceiver.

In fact, if Byron's homo-narcissism inscribes any kind of frustration, it is the frustration of those who watch from outside the closed circle of narcissistic bliss. The speaker describes this union as one that the world cannot penetrate: "Ours too the glance none saw beside; / The smile none else might understand" (lines 29–30). That communication, furthermore, exists even after the boy is dead. In "One Struggle More and I Am Free," the speaker leads a superficial existence that "smiles with all, and weeps with none" (line 12), as if the social life of surfaces were a game and narcissism really the condition of pondering depths and secrets. These secrets, he explains to the dead lover in "If Sometimes in the Haunts of Men," intermingle the lover and the beloved and exclude the outside world: "I would not fools should overhear / One sigh that should be wholly *thine*" (lines 15–16). What we learn here, perhaps, is a lesson in our own narcissism. As Byron betrays his "open secret" (to use D. A. Miller's sense of the term),[19] as he tells us he has a secret he won't tell us, he establishes in us an ambivalent relation to his narcissistic disclosure/ enclosure. As we read the Thyrza lyrics, we are made aware that we are looking in on the Byronic union, yet we are kept outside it. We find out that the narcissist is condemnable not only because he stares at himself but because he demands to be *stared at,* commanding a gaze that wants to interpret but cannot, because the gazer exists outside the circle of erotic knowledge. The narcissist demands that we stare at him — and what Romantic figure was stared at more than Byron? — if only in order to demonstrate that we cannot know what we are seeing: "none saw beside"; "none else might understand." And it is perhaps this thwarted dialogism that Byron's personal physician, John William Polidori, had in mind when he cast his former employer as a vampire, Lord Strongmore. As Polidori's hero, Aubrey, watches the mysterious, Byronic, and narcissistic Strongmore,

> the very impossibility of forming an idea of the character of a man entirely absorbed in himself, of one who gave few other signs of his observation of external objects, than the tacit assent to their existence, implied by the avoidance of their contact: at last allowed his imagination to picture some

thing that flattered its propensity to extravagant ideas. He soon formed this person into the hero of a romance, and determined to observe the offspring of his fancy, rather than the individual before him. (1994, 34–35)

If narcissism is the state of staring at another in order to be thrown back on one's own desires, then perhaps it is the reader, or Byron's phobic contemporaries, whom the Thyrza sequence constructs as narcissistic.

Thus, Byron is "queer" not merely in the sense that he entertained a love for boys, a love both "violent" and *"pure"* in all its Socratic ambiguities (Byron 1978, 24; emphasis in original). Moreover, his queerness resides not only in the fact that he lived in a homoerotic closet whose narcissism drew the blinds to keep out prurient onlookers. Rather, Byron is queer in that he forces us to reevaluate our very notion of what Romantic male sexuality might be. Earlier, I quoted Judith Butler to ask what happens when the prohibited object becomes eroticized for its very prohibition. One answer to that question, clearly, is the Gothic. Contemporary queer theory, following Eve Kosofsky Sedgwick, has posited male sexuality in Romanticism as governed by the "transmutability of the intrapsychic with the intersubjective" that leaves "two potent male figures locked in an epistemologically indissoluble clench of will and desire" (1990, 187). This transmutability is what Sedgwick calls the terrorism of homosexual panic, the fear that a man might know another man too well, that he might get inside him psychologically and otherwise. In both *Between Men* (1985) and *Epistemology of the Closet* (1990), Sedgwick locates this paranoid terrorism at the turn of the nineteenth century, when the intersubjective agencies of sentimentalism, the rise of the bourgeois family, and the proliferation of capitalist homosocial bonds coalesced to place men in a strikingly magnetic, strikingly panicked relationship to one another. Thus, as Otto Rank made clear in his early essay on the double, the narcissistic love of oneself gets transferred in dreamwork, and in fiction, into a doppelgänger, the feared and loathed other of one's own desires.[20] But as Sedgwick's discussion makes clear, this panic is that of a straight sexuality, a regime self-imposed by men who vehemently *want* to keep other men at arm's length. Byron undoes the paranoid terrorism of the panic: his closet transforms the intersubjective into the narcissistic not to threaten erotic identity but to celebrate it. In "Thyrza" I become my lover and my lover becomes me within the (almost) impermeable confines of a closet that the cold world cannot know. I long for you and you long for me and we do so like no other. This is Romantic subjectivity and bourgeois individualism to be sure, but it is also the historical development of an "identity" space that one can exploit in the service of pleasure. In a way very different from paranoid terrorism, it takes one to know one.

It is precisely this kind of democratizing, valorizing reading of homoerotic desire that Jerome Christensen warns us about when reading Byron. For Christensen, "Lord Byron learned his homosexuality from books — old books" (54). It is significant, Christensen argues, that the "Greek love" about which Byron read led to an investment of "sexual desire only in Greek boys." Byron does not figure his "pure," Platonic relationship to Edleston as lacking or unfulfilled, Christensen argues, because for Byron sexual desire was a political act, directed toward those Greek boys whom he wanted to liberate: in other words, Byron "entered" Greece in order to free it; Greece acted as a site where " 'liberation' . . . can be rendered as feeding back just those classically 'Greek' principles that supply the rationale for imperial rule" (55–57). Thus, he concludes, Byron's Greek jargon "artificially creates a body of traders . . . forming the basis for and boundaries of association" (61). In this reading, homoerotic narcissism differs little from hetero-narcissism in that it still deploys a power differential: this time it is class rather than gender that structures desire, but such desire is still a power trip for the Romantic male. But Christensen assumes here that "sexual desire" can only be measured by genital contact, that the aristocratic body to which Byron's penis and orifices belong tells all about his relations with the boys he "loved." This seems to me far too restrictive a register for the kind of diagnosis the critic ultimately makes; it begs the question of what kind of homosexuality Byron learned from Plato and how it might figure in his representation of homo-narcissism. For while Christensen argues that "Greek love" could mobilize imperialistic class differences in the powerful Byron, Michel Foucault reads Plato in exactly opposite terms: Foucault argues that it is the effect of male-male love in general and of Aristophanes' definition in particular to posit a mirror-equality between lovers, one that "abolishes the game of dissymmetries that structured the complex relations between man and boy" (1985, 233). For David Halperin, this abolition is replayed in Socrates' relationship to Alcibiades and thus marks the whole tenor of Platonic, homoerotic love:

> Plato all but erases the distinction between the "active" and the "passive" partner — or, to put it better, the genius of Plato's analysis is that it eliminates passivity altogether: according to Socrates, both members of the relationship become active, desiring lovers; neither remains a merely passive object of desire. (1990, 132)

Byron effects a similar breakdown of power relations as he describes himself as both *"Padrone"* and *"amico"* to the Greek boy Nicolo Giraud, an "oscillation" that, for Christensen, "would remain a constant threat to the stability of the Byronic poetic subject" (59). And we remember as well Byron's giving up his bed to his ill last love-object, Lukas Chalandrutsanos, a "weakness," said Pietro Gambra, that "rose only from a noble source and a generous aim — his pity for the innocent unfortunate" (quoted in Moore 1961, 180–81). Thus, if Byron did learn his sexuality from "old books" (and indeed which of us hasn't?), then perhaps what he learned is not the pathologizing eradication of difference — which we have come to designate as "narcissism" in the gay male — or the exercise of class power. Instead, what we see in Byron's homoerotic works is the way his classical sources and their queer narcissistic *frissons* inform and code his own same-sexual expression, one that rewrites the implications of eradicating difference.

Such a consideration of power relations and their political imperatives can be detected in Byron's early meditation on heroic and erotic love, his translation of the Nisus and Euryalus episode from the *Aeneid*. A depiction of a soldier and his boy-lover en route to sacking Troy, this poem again gestures to Byron's narcissism in the form of his egomaniacal penchant for boys whose inferior age and social status magnified his superiority and influence. And in this sense, it echoes what Jerome Christensen has identified as Byron's imperialistic accession over the Greek boys he was claiming to liberate. Yet the poem also echoes Socrates' speech in the *Phaedrus* by emphasizing the equalizing effects of love into erotic oneness: "In peace, in war, united still they move; / Friendship and glory form their joint reward, / And, now, combined they hold their nightly guard" (lines 16–18). If Greek — and indeed Byronic — love turns on asymmetries in age and status, Byron's borrowings from Virgil here document the interchangeability of lover and beloved, of two becoming as one. When the young Euryalus is captured, Nisus ponders whether he should "rush, his comrade's fate to share!" (line 334) and "die with him, for whom he wish'd to live!" (line 338) or whether "His life a votive ransom nobly give" (line 337). The choices here are to change places with the beloved or to die with him, but either way the noble lover shares the beloved's disempowerment. Both love and war destroy power asymmetries, and, as Nisus kills his beloved's murderers, he too is mortally wounded:

> Thus Nisus all his fond affection prov'd,
> Dying, reveng'd the fate of him he lov'd;

Then on his bosom, sought his wonted place,
And death was heavenly, in his friend's embrace!
(lines 397–400)

The poem then ends with a declaration of the soldier/lover's valor and fame, a peroration that feels somewhat facile and hubristic — what we conventionally call narcissistic — in its trading of human life for everlasting fame. But if we read the story through the *Phaedrus,* it becomes a magnetic site for the fragments of narcissistic desire: the man's desire for the beautiful boy transforms into an equalizing erotic bond whose effect is the protection and love of the other through an interchangeability with the other. Narcissism — what gets transferred in homosexual panic into paranoid terrorism — is here a mutually embracing and politically efficacious union.

If "Nisus and Euryalus" flirts with the erotic interchangeability of men and its implications for military valor, Byron's dramatic fragment *The Deformed Transformed* begins to analyze that relationship fully. Begun in 1822 and left unfinished, *The Deformed Transformed* presents the hunchbacked and unloved Arnold, who escapes his cruel mother and flees to the forest. Here, at a fountain, he sees his own ugliness and, like Frankenstein's monster in a similar antinarcissistic moment, decides to kill himself. He is halted by a Stranger, modeled on Goethe's Mephistopheles, who conjures a string of beautiful male bodies out of the same fountain in which Arnold had seen himself and transforms him into the beautiful and strong soldier Achilles; the Stranger then assumes Arnold's own rejected body and accompanies him as a doppelgänger. Arnold and the Stranger head off to assist in the battle of Rome in 1527, where Arnold meets the hapless Roman maid Olimpia, falls in love with her, and attempts to win her love. The play breaks off with some suggestion that Olimpia momentarily returns his affections, but that she eventually becomes attracted to the Stranger, who wears Arnold's form, because he is more interesting and witty. When Arnold learns this, he kills Olimpia. In some ways the play follows the conventional narcissistic paradigm as Freud would outline it: the subject's development begins with the narcissistic identification of the reflected self as a way of manufacturing self-love (the vestiges of primary narcissism), which then gets transferred onto the other — the female Olimpia. Moreover, like "The Picture," *The Deformed Transformed* bifurcates the male into the self-loving, narcissistic "monster" and the active male in search of a female other. Heterosexual desire is the mature fruition of a desire that begins as eros for oneself. However, the projected

Othello-like slaying of Olimpia suggests that Arnold never really worked through his primary narcissism and that such retardation results naturally in narcissistic self-loathing and misogyny. *The Deformed Transformed,* then, is Mellor's masculine Romanticism fully and sardonically brought to light.

Yet if we look closely at the first act, which documents the transformation (an act critics agree represents the only real energy and interest in a play that quickly falls into cliché), we see the degree to which homoeroticism structures a number of Byronic agendas in Arnold. Let's consider for a moment the parade of pretty boys that gets trotted out before Arnold: the "fair" Caesar (1.1.197), the "lovely" and "beautiful" Alcibiades (212), the "broad brow," "curly beard," and "manly aspect" of Mark Anthony (230–31), the shade of Demetrius Poliocretes, "Who truly looketh like a demigod, / Blooming and bright, with golden hair, and stature" (246–47), indeed the "Glory of mankind" (256), and finally the winner, Achilles, "The god-like son of the Sea-goddess, / The unshorn boy of Peleus, with his locks / As beautiful and clear as the amber waves / Of rich Pactolus" (266–69). George Steiner contends that, as Arnold chooses "the radiant form of Achilles," "it requires no Freudian to note the covert relation between Achilles' heel and Byron's own deformity" (1963, 211). Nor, I would argue, does it require a Freudian to note the homoerotic overtones that Byron infuses in Arnold's desire for Achilles, the lover of Patroclus, in a line like this one: "I gaze upon him / As if I were his soul, whose form shall soon / Envelope mine" (282–84). The queerly charged potential of being enveloped by Achilles' body is inscribed in the source for Byron's play, Joshua Pickersgill's 1802 novel, *The Three Brothers.* In this novel, the "various men distinguished for that beauty and grace" are paraded in front of Arnauld (who becomes Arnold in Byron's version), and "Arnauld's heart heaved quick with preference" (quoted in Robinson 1970, 180). This heaving preference, this thinly coded cruisy desire, enacts a double movement: it conflates the love of another with the narcissistic love of self, and it makes this love of "beauty" intensely physical, corporeal. Indeed, the only character to be rejected out of hand is Socrates, who, mental beauty aside, has a body so ugly that "I had better / Remain that which I am" (219–20).

In Plato and Virgil, this desire for the physical is a manly desire that risks effeminizing in its consummation. This effeminizing in the desire for male identification was a marked fear for Coleridge, and Byron's fragment gestures to the same anxiety. As Arnold pants for the possibilities before him, the Stranger consistently genders him female in his desire: "you are far more difficult to please / Than Cato's sister, or than Brutus' mother, / Or Cleopatra at sixteen" (1.1.198–200); he calls Arnold impatient "As a youthful beauty / Before her glass. *You both* see what is not, / But dream it is what must be" (288–90). By constructing Arnold as female, and as narcissistic, Byron hints not only at the history of representations of the Narcissus reflection as vain woman, a history I noted earlier, but also at a certain representation of the eighteenth-century sodomite as narcissistically female. As early as 1632, Henry Reynolds had suggested that the narcissistic boy, pace Aristophanes, was weakened, unmanly, effeminate (Vinge 1967, 185). By 1662, Louis Richer had conflated Ovid's and Pausanias's versions of the myth so that, when the Narcissus of his *L'Ovide bouffon* looks into the water, he sees himself, but himself transformed *into a woman* (Vinge 1967, 191). Such compulsory heterosexualizing is the case also for Rousseau, whose narcissistic Valère is represented in a portrait as female (Vinge 1967, 278). Narcissus does not imagine the reflection to be female, a compulsory heterosexualizing as in Pausanias and the Romantics; rather, Narcissus *becomes* a woman, identifying rather than desiring. These Continental moments have their English counterparts, of course, on the Restoration stage, with which Byron was extremely familiar. As Randolph Trumbach has pointed out, "the fop's effeminacy...came [in the 1720s] to be identified with the effeminacy of the then emerging role of the exclusive adult sodomite" (134), and if we think of Sir Fopling Flutter, John Harvey, or Colley Cibber's Sir Novelty Fashion, we can place Byron in a tradition that associates the feminine with the sodomitic. And that tradition, as Linda Dowling has demonstrated, is predicated on the widely held eighteenth-century equation of the Hellenistic (and homoerotic) with "civic incapacity," the product of "aimless and self-regarding egoism" (9). Yet Byron's appropriation of such narcissistic "femininity" is an attempt to undo the phobic and persecutory associations of male-male love with narcissistic softening. First because, in contrast to Coleridge's fear of the feminine, Byron's scene strikes one as parodically campy, a queer appropriation rather than an identity crisis. And, second, if narcissistic desire "feminizes" Arnold, it does so only to embolden him, in that he *becomes* the Achilles he beholds: his cruising, Socratic, yet "feminine" desire for a manly self provides him access to that self. My point is not to applaud an appropriation of the feminine that then destroys the feminine; rather, it is to posit in Byron a conscious transgression, one that effectively contradicts the foundations of Georgian homophobia. Indeed,

Arnold's transformation situates him in that proto-Victorian war-
rior ideal that Dowling says replaced the effeminate and debilitated
and came to constitute in the late nineteenth century a homoerotic
masculine ideal.

Part 1 of *The Deformed Transformed,* then, dramatizes a homophilic narcissism that exploits Greek tropes of male possession to
demonstrate the ways in which the asymmetries of power, status, and
age break down as one man is enveloped by another; moreover, it
dramatizes the jubilant erosion of the self-other division upon which
the Romantic egotistical sublime — Mellor's "masculine Romanticism" — is founded. To this end, Achilles serves as an apt figure for
Arnold to transume and to be enveloped by, not only because he is
beautiful and strong but because, as Foucault tells us, it was common Greek practice "to talk about the relationship of Achilles to
Patroclus . . . to determine what differentiated them from one another
and which of the two had precedence over the other (since Homer's
text was ambiguous on this point)" (1985, 195).[21] In other words,
one could not tell who in this dyad was the active lover and who was
the passive beloved. Such interchangeability, achieved through narcissism, allows Byron to reimagine the potentially panicked relation
between men. Instead, he imagines a transmutation between men that
is erotically welcome rather than terrifying or paranoia-making. He
has opened up a space for a queer reading of Romanticism that exploits the dissolution of the self-other boundary and that revises that
boundary from a threatened and policed border to a homoerotically
inviting space. Thus, Arnold is on the mark when he punctuates his
union with Achilles by proclaiming, "I love, and I shall be beloved!
Oh, life!" (1.1.420).

If the ecstasy of being beloved as one loves accurately describes the
homophilic narcissism of the play's first part, it also modifies what
will become heterosexed passion in parts 2 and 3 (although such a
binary opposition between homo- and hetero-identity was not operative for Byron). As Arnold "becomes" Achilles, the play changes
registers from a consideration of the monstrous, homophilic, "queer"
hunchback to the overtly masculinist tyrannical soldier:[22] for Byron,
to be enveloped by masculinity is not only homoerotic but also terrifyingly productive of masculine ideologies. With this transformation,
the queer discourse — that which is critical of such masculinist, heterosexual ideologies — is transferred onto the Stranger, now called
Caesar,[23] who becomes the critical foil for Arnold's marauding endeavors. These endeavors continue and complete Byron's sexual
allegory by demonstrating the ways in which military masculinity

depends upon the expression of both misogyny and homophobia: misogyny, in that the siege on Rome is an attempt to drive out the "Harlot" of Catholicism (2.3.26) that has rendered Rome "an hermaphrodite of empire," a "*Lady* of the Old World" (1.2.9–10), and whose femininity has weakened its glory; homophobia, in that corrupt Rome is an ideal target for destruction — "scarce a better to be found on earth, / Since Sodom was put out" (1.1.502–3) — and that one of Rome's representatives to be attacked is Benvenuto Cellini, the Florentine sculptor and goldsmith charged as a "dirty sodomite" (quoted in Dynes 1990, 208). Rome becomes a fitting site for the deployment of such masculinity as its very founding depended upon the murder of one twin brother by the other, Romulus's slaying of Remus. And here we see the inversion of the (homo)sexual politics of Byron's earlier lyrics: whereas the Cain-like Byron becomes the victim mourning his dead "wife" Edleston, here the hypermasculine figure recapitulates the slaying of the twin and the destruction of the feminine. Moreover, what Arnold destroys here is precisely the figuration of effeminate sodomy that moments earlier had given him the identity he now claims. Reminiscent of the repudiation of Narcissus at Coleridge's pool, Arnold severs the erotic possibilities of sameness and symmetry, invoking a compulsory differentiation that becomes, both politically and psychologically, a brutally split and splitting subject. And as the erotic narcissist becomes the pernicious paranoid, Byron makes a startlingly candid critique of his own masculinist heroism, one that contradicts the image of himself that he worked so hard to construct.

For Byron, this is a critique of the alleged narcissism of masculine Romanticism, but narcissistic masculinity only in its heterosexual register (Romantic critics distinguish between genders but rarely between sexualities). Byron renders unto Caesar, the queer, aloof, dispassionate hunchback, the last word on narcissism and its relation to eros:

> you would be *loved* — what you call loved —
>   *Self-loved* — loved for *yourself* — for neither health
> Nor wealth — nor youth — nor power — nor rank nor beauty —
>   For these you may be script of — but *beloved*
> As an Abstraction — for — you know not what —
>   (pt. 3, text of fragment, 61–65)

"You are jealous," Caesar charges Arnold, jealous "of Yourself" (pt. 3, text of fragment, 69–70). Like the masculine Romantic, Arnold loves, but that love recognizes no external object, no other. Even the final line of the fragment betrays a masculine desire that is at once poignant and sardonically pathetic in its narcissism: "You have possessed the woman — still possess," says Caesar to Arnold; "What need you more? — / To be myself possest — ," answers Arnold, "To be her heart as she is mine" (pt. 3, text of fragment, 99–101). For Byron, one must *deserve* love if one is to be beloved; one must *do* the activity of making oneself worthy of love. To be beloved (the passive receptivity of the Greek model) is to be the lover, the active pursuer. Whereas the erotic union of Arnold and Achilles had produced an immediate *jouissance* — "I love, and I shall be beloved! Oh, life!" — the heterosexual union is always doomed to be thwarted, partial, asymmetrically disrupted, as Arnold continually bemoans his own egotistical inability to be egoless. What the play may ultimately argue, then, is not that homoerotic narcissism is a perversion of "natural" heterosexual desire; rather, like the universalizing critique of heterosexuality that Michael Warner locates in Freud, the play offers a paradigm by which heterosexual desire itself can be deformed and transformed.

But don't we run the risk here of suggesting that homo-narcissism is a "good" thing whereas hetero-narcissism is "bad"? Doesn't a queer rereading of Narcissus inexorably plunge us into the well, our love of our own image causing us to see merely what we want to see? Judith Butler warns us against the "ideal of transforming all excluded identifications into inclusive features" — resurrecting all of our repudiations and integrating them back into our self-definitions — as a "return to a Hegelian synthesis" that is ultimately "a romantic, insidious, and all-consuming humanism" (1993, 116). Indeed, in our search for a queer Narcissus, there does appear to be No Exit, in that Romanticism demonstrates how the projected other is always and only ourselves — autoerotic, rather than homoerotic. But it is perhaps here that Coleridge's poem is queer by implication, Byron's drama queer by design. In Coleridge, the treatment of homo-narcissism leaves us with a vague dis-ease (or celebration) over the instability of male heterosexual definition; it renders *all* gender relations narcissistically circular. Byron's play is much more direct: his hunchbacked queer speaks his critique without positing a specious solution; he deploys self-loving narcissism as a critique of Romantic humanism, one that decenters any "gay" reclamation of Byron at the same time that it authorizes a queer one. And that Byron's play should collapse into fragments at the end is the perfect final critique. His illness gained in service to the Greek war prevented him from finishing, but in a way this play could never be finished, is "unfinished" in Balachandra Rajan's sense of the term (1985). Its self-congratulating critique of self-love is its final irony as it deploys the mechanics of heterosexist self-construction against itself, and like the effeminized/repudiated male in Coleridge's pool, it "vanishes" into "fragments," "mis-shaping" and thus performing the very dissolution of masculine self-narrative that it has become the queer project to critique.

Chapter 2

REVERSE OF THE MIRROR:
SYMBOLISM AND SEXOLOGY

Among the many bon mots to outrage Edward Carson, the pros-
ecuting attorney at the second and third Oscar Wilde trials, was
Wilde's response to the question, "Have you ever adored a young
man madly?" Wilde quipped, "I have never given adoration to anyone except myself" (Hyde 1948, 129). For the late-twentieth-century
reader, the witticism is itself a kind of evidence, but evidence for what?
Narcissism, to be sure, but of what sort? Self-aggrandizement? Certainly. Self-preservation (in the Freudian sense of protecting the ego
from persecution)? Definitely. Wilde is, after all, on trial for acts of
gross indecency punishable under the Criminal Law Amendment Act
of 1885 that made private sodomitic acts as legally egregious as public
ones. But there is also medical, psychosexual evidence in the retort,
for Wilde would become one of the prominent case studies in the
major treatises on narcissism: Havelock Ellis is referring to Wilde
when he scoffs at the invert who "assumes that because he would
rather take his pleasure with a soldier or a policeman than with their
sisters he is of a finer clay than the vulgar herd" (1897, 157). Max
Simon Nordau, writing the year Wilde was tried, charges that "Wilde
has done more by his eccentricities than his works.... What really de-
termines his actions is the hysterical craving to be noticed, to occupy
the attention of the world with himself, to get talked about" (1968,
317).[1] (Wilde here would agree: "there is only one thing in the world
worse than being talked about, and that is not being talked about"
[Wilde 1987, 2].) And only ten years after this 1895 testimony Freud
would begin to theorize narcissism as *the* psychological condition of
the male homosexual who is searching for himself in a sexual object. Thus we can detect in Wilde's line the "evidence" that could
prove not only immorality but degeneracy, a medical disease whose
erotic manifestations were synecdochic of a larger condition rather
than constituting the "condition" itself. And if we contrast Wilde's
insouciant eloquence to the "narcissism" we have seen anachronisti-
cally but no less brutally imposed on Byron, we get a clearer sense

54

of the ethical and judicial stakes: Byron's narcissism may have been every bit as cultivated a pose as Wilde's, but it was also the fallout of an epistemological inevitability, a compulsory optic that situates the self at the center of late-Cartesian perception. One was narcissistic in Byron because one had to be, and so narcissism was as much resignation as transgression, the label cast on the figure who could not honestly claim to be part of the larger social other. But in Wilde there is no such sense of defeat or resignation: his narcissism, like his genius, is declared, consciously aware that it is overdetermined, that it will signify in multiple, complex, and even dangerous ways.

It is my contention in this chapter that the overdetermination of Wilde's narcissism — its contradictory status of being at the same time clearly readable and impossible to specify — is part of a larger hermeneutic crisis that Wilde cultivated, that was endemic to the deployment of the Narcissus story, and that continues to trouble us today in our queer recuperation of "Wilde." In one sense, Wilde's narcissistic response to Carson is legible precisely because it exploits the superficial; it focuses on the surface of the self that Wilde's aphorisms and epigrams are famous for asserting (the most delightful, from "Phrases and Philosophies for the Use of the Young": "In all unimportant matters, style, not sincerity, is the essential. In all important matters, style, not sincerity, is the essential." Or, "Only the shallow know themselves." Or, "To love oneself is the beginning of a lifelong romance" [Wilde 1980, 851–82]). Narcissus here is a surface image whose original, unlike Ovid's, knows himself and who underwrites a whole tradition of queer Wilde criticism. Yet, as Wilde's critics make obvious, the superficial in Wilde, that which begs to be read on the two-dimensional plane of *surface,* is always implicated in a *depth* model that late-nineteenth-century culture brought to bear on Wilde (through the burgeoning field of psychoanalysis as well as through the Romantic legacy of what would get called the unconscious) and, perhaps more important, that Wilde brought to bear on late-nineteenth-century culture (in his rejection of bourgeois superficiality and vulgar materialism). This depth model, existing as it does within and against Wilde's love of surfaces, is particularly productive for queer critics who are searching for some articulation of queer desire and of a "subjectivity," no matter how relative or contingent, in the late nineteenth century. In what remains one of the finest readings of *Dorian Gray,* Ed Cohen's inaugural essay, "Writing Gone Wilde: Homoerotic Desire in the Closet of Representation" (1987), Cohen begins with an analysis of the discourses volleyed at Wilde (thus following Foucauldian practice and suspicion of the "depth model" in

The History of Sexuality, vol. 1 [1978]), yet quickly moves to an analysis of "a theory of 'innate difference' similar to the third-sex theories" (75) and then to an analysis of "what *lurks behind* Wilde's manifestly straight language" in *Dorian Gray* (75; emphasis added). From this it seems that the concept of "depth" becomes essential if we are to theorize desire and the articulation of closeted subjectivity at all. The tendency to add that third dimension — the psychological depth of subject and text — is evidenced as well in Jonathan Dollimore's "Different Desires: Subjectivity and Transgression in Wilde and Gide" (1991). Here Dollimore explores Wilde's love of artifice and surface and its use in "de-moralizing" and "dis-spiriting" André Gide by destroying his paralyzing adherence to Protestant sincerity (49).[2] Dollimore's brilliant deployment of Wildean surface against Gidean depth (of "proto-structuralism" against "essentialism") leads him to define why Wilde and Gide together intrigue him:

> In different ways their work explores what we are now beginning to attend to again: the complexities, the potentials and dangers of what it is to transgress, invert and displace *from within;* the paradox of a marginality which is always anterior to, or at least intimate with, the centre. (63)

Indeed, I would argue that the recent increase in the use of psychoanalysis in queer methodology is part of the renaissance Dollimore is suggesting: to the degree that Judith Butler can be taken as the bellwether of queer studies, her emphasis in *Bodies That Matter* (1993) and *The Psychic Life of Power* (1997) on Freud, the logic of repudiation, and the phantasmatic becomes a significant corrective to the tendency she saw in some readers of *Gender Trouble* (1990) to privilege the surface of drag over the social and psychic structures that frame drag, to privilege performance, in other words, over performativity. Thus, to read Wilde, as to read certain tendencies in queerness, is to adopt the position of Schlegel's sonneteer or the Coleridgean speaker in "The Picture": we are directed to look *across* a flat surface to see the desiring figure, a figure who is often the projection or representation of our own desires. But that very projected figure is itself looking *down, in, behind*. Optical models collide here as a hermeneutic of surfaces comes axiologically to clash with a hermeneutic of depth — psychoanalysis, the figurations of desire, the epistemology of the closet. What Romanticism *represents* as the paradigm of Narcissus the Wildean aesthetic can be said to *perform*.[3]

As I outlined in my introduction, "narcissism" as a psychosexual condition came into existence through explicit theorizing at the end of the nineteenth century. Like the pose of Narcissus itself, the psychological diagnosis moved from a kind of surface tableau (a descriptive picture of what narcissists *do* and whom they prefer as determining what defines them) to a more dynamic narrative of desire — *how* their eros moves, shifts, inflects, distorts. Gregory Bredbeck detects in sexology a "fetishization of narrative," a "desire to subject its 'scientific observations' to an explanatory . . . principle" (1994, 61–62). And primarily, the narrative is one of *regression:* as the Narcissus allusion passes from Havelock Ellis through Otto Rank to Freud, one detects various fairy tales of return, of collapsing back, either into a primary narcissistic love of the self, as in "On Narcissism: An Introduction," or the related but significantly different return to identification with the mother and the imitation of her desire for other young men, as in Freud's discussion of Leonardo da Vinci (more on this in chapter 3). Nor is this regression gender-specific: as I noted earlier, Diana Fuss argues in "Freud's Fallen Woman" that the very psychogenesis of lesbian sexuality is, according to Freud, a fall back to earlier cathexes and immature object-relations. Although Wilde was a key figure in many major sexological texts — he is a test case for both Havelock Ellis and Max Simon Nordau — one can detect only flickers of the regression narrative in the discourse surrounding Wilde (a discourse that would emerge fully fledged in Otto Rank's analysis of *Dorian Gray*). Yet I want to argue that it is precisely this regression narrative and its relation to the surface/depth binarism that structure Wilde's use of the myth in the 1890s. And I want to substantiate this claim by reading Wilde's sexological (and sexy) discourse in the context of another prominent theory of Narcissus, the poetics of Symbolism.

(De)Generating Literature

Symbolism is, of course, the very aesthetic of narcissism. Arising out of the French *l'art pour l'art,* whose titular grammar doubles back on its own image, Symbolism became the late-nineteenth-century mode for exploring the innate properties of poetry itself. Baldly contesting "responsible" projects like Zola's realism, Dickens's reformism, and the century's overall stress on the importance of being earnest, Symbolism instead held its own product as the object of its process: it meditated on the laws, sensualities, and effects of poetry itself. Hence it became the manifesto for "Decadent" writers like Joris-Karl Huysmans whose influence on Wilde is clear in *Dorian Gray*. Symbolism's process was to employ a language that would not coarsely and flatly name its object but would create a sort of tone painting, a field of sensual gestures and effects pointing to that object that could only exist in the reader's imaginative experience. Understandably, Narcissus could be extremely useful here. Stéphane Mallarmé's "Hérodiade" (1951), Paul Valéry's "Narcisse parle" and "Fragments du Narcisse" (in *Poems* [1971]), and perhaps most importantly André Gide's "Le traité du Narcisse: Théorie du symbole" (trans. "Narcissus: A Treatise on the Theory of Symbolism" [1953]) foreground the importance of narcissistic reflexivity and the antisocial in thinking about the perfect artwork, the work that must exist solely for its own sake. Little wonder, then, that Max Simon Nordau could write in his 1892 medico-moralizing jeremiad *Degeneration* the following diagnosis of the Symbolists: "They had in common all the signs of degeneracy and imbecility: overweening vanity and self-conceit, strong emotionalism, confused disconnected thoughts, garrulity (the 'logorrhea' of mental therapeutics), and complete incapacity for serious, sustained work" (1968, 101). Narcissists *avant la lettre,* the Symbolists were sterile, jejune, regressed.

Thus, 1892 seems to be a significant year for the molding of Narcissus into a homosexual artist: it sees the publication of Gide's "Traité," Nordau's *Degeneration,* and significantly for Wilde, the introduction into English of the term "homosexuality" through Charles Gilbert Chaddock's translation of Krafft-Ebing's *Psychopathia sexualis.* Yet while Nordau pits himself against the mostly French writers of the end of the century (Gide excluded), a comparison of his concept of "ego-mania" with Gide's use of the Narcissus image is instructive: both writers link Narcissus to artistic creativity, and in similar ways. To see how these two texts, appearing in the same year (1892, a year after *Dorian Gray*), handle the Narcissus figure, let us set up their arguments as mirror images:

Gide, "Le traité du Narcisse"	Nordau, *Degeneration*
Trapped in the industrially ravaged landscape of the late nineteenth century, Narcissus pines to know the nature of his soul. He needs a mirror, and a mirror image, to separate himself from that which he is not. As he gazes into the stream, the reflected landscape changes, becoming rich, fecund, generative. Narcissus knows that these are only	Those who have coined the term "fin-de-siècle" are plagued by a disposition to "feverish restlessness and blunted discouragement," seeing in their day the collapse and fall of the human race (2). Because "it is a habit of the human mind to project its own subjective states" (2), men have turned to art and politics to reflect a sick exhaustion, one that indulges the

forms, imperfect because they change, imperfect because they are striving toward some deeper, more ideal state that they have lost.

To understand this state, Narcissus dreams of Paradise, a garden characterized by its lack of division, its lack of imperfection, its lack of lack. "Everything in it crystallized into a necessary flowering, and everything was perfectly what it ought to be" (7).

Here, Adam exists. "Single, still unsexed" (8), he sits at the center of Paradise where all things exist for him. But the perfection outside him informs him that Paradise is *not* him, that he knows this other but not himself, that he is a slave to the external. And so, breaking a branch from the "logorithmic tree" of perfection and symmetry, he introduces division into Paradise and becomes a "terror-stricken, self-duplicated hermaphrodite" who feels "surg[ing] up within him, at the same time as a new sex, the anxious, uneasy desire for that other half, so like himself" (9). Heterosexed desire enters Paradise, condemned to replicate itself in ways that should fulfill it but that instead only increase its sense of fragmentation and alienation.

Aware of the compulsory fragmentations of desire, Narcissus returns to the pool and continues to gaze, but does so in order to instruct himself that all forms are fleeting, that "Paradise has always to be remade; it is not in some *ultima Thule*. It dwells under appearances.... Everything is striving after its lost form" (10), a form that gets confused with the real Paradise when Narcissus insists on putting himself, his pride, his own form at the center of his perception. And Gide punctuates the fable with an extremely

self in its degeneration rather than contributing to the laudable virtues of duty and reason, the "traditional views of custom and morality" (5). Base impulses are attended to, crime is glorified, selfishness is de rigeur. And nowhere is this degeneration more evident than in fin-de-siècle art and its producers, the "ego-maniacs" who are unable to perceive any impressions other than their own internal ones.

The genesis of such egomania, and of degeneration itself, can be glimpsed in the history of art. The plastic arts originally rose out of the desire to imitate Nature. "Imitation is without doubt one of the first and most general reactions of the developed living being upon the impressions it receives from the external world" (323). Moreover, this desire to imitate, to form a mirror model of the external, is programmed into and "a necessary consequence of the...nervous system. Every compound movement must be preceded by the representation of this movement, and, conversely, no representation of movement can be elaborated without at least a faint and hinted accomplishment of the corresponding movement by the muscles" (323). The artist "forms for itself a representation" of the movement of a thing and then "transform[s] the representation into a movement resembling it" (323). Often, though, the activity of imitation is undertaken to relieve some emotion generated by the object being imitated. This points to a higher purpose in art, one beyond imitation: the artist "creates a work of art, not for its own sake, but to free his nervous system from a tension" (324).

This privilege of utility over Symbolist reflexivity extends to one more realm, "the objective end of moralizing footnote warning us that "Truths lie behind Forms" and that "The rules of morality and aesthetics are the same. Every work which does not manifest itself is useless and for that very reason, bad. Every man who does not manifest himself is useless and bad" (11–12). Thus Narcissus is once more bifurcated into the subject who contemplates the truth of what is beyond or outside him (and who accepts "subordination" to this otherness [11]) and the poet who "tends to prefer himself to the Idea that he manifests" (12), who installs his own form in the place where consciousness of the other should be.

acting upon others" (324). To be worthy of the name, the artist should aspire "to impart his own emotions to those of his own species, just as he himself participates in the emotions of those of his own species. This strong desire to know himself in emotional communion with the species is sympathy, that organic base of the social edifice" (325). And the best kind of art to produce this social effect is not the mere "sensually-beautiful," which appeals only to organic nerve organization, but the "intellectually beautiful," which awakens feelings of "altruism" and self-abnegation in service to the higher ideals of "concepts and judgments" (328).

While one might expect the author of *Corydon* (1950) and *Si le grain ne meurt* (*If It Die* [1935]) to voice a position entirely opposite to that of Nordau's conservative, reactionary normalizing, the two are actually strikingly close in their analyses (*Corydon* and the autobiography, we must remember, come much later in Gide's life, after Wilde's demoralizing of him). For both writers, "The artist himself divines the idea behind the structure, and its inner principle and connection, intelligible but not perceivable, in the form, and discloses it in his work to the spectator" (Nordau 1968, 333).[4] Yet, for each writer, Narcissus interposes his own body between his creative gaze and the artistic object he would create. His insistence on seeing himself rather than the larger truths that lie beyond him results in a stultified, impotent art that focuses on the physical rather than on the metaphysical. Such art obfuscates the deeper meaning — in Gide, idealism, in Nordau, social sympathy — to which art should lead. And in both cases, Narcissus is *the* figure for this artistic impotence, even though Nordau does not name him as such; in both cases, the tendency to put oneself at the center of the artistic optic is what destroys art itself. Like the narcissist in Neoplatonism, this poet refuses to manifest himself as Idea, thus refusing the dictates of a productive culture. This refusal, this impotence, is for Nordau the connecting link between the artist and the homosexual; the degenerate, a type so obviously incarnate in artists like Oscar Wilde, "has desires which are contrary to the purpose of the instinct [the sexual appetite], *i.e.*, the preservation of the species" (260).[5]

Yet if the broad outlines of Gide's and Nordau's arguments lead to the condemnation of Narcissus's egomania, they also make clear the inescapability of the narcissistic ego and the narcissistic body. In Gide's "Traité," it is precisely the perfection of artistic form and the pristine unity of Paradise that force the poet and Adam to desire more. The absence of lack, it seems, produces lack, the desire for desire, which in the larger movement of the work is what impels creativity. This creativity can only be accomplished if the poet stares at his own form, if he desires to duplicate himself and represent himself to himself through his splitting into self and form. Similarly in Nordau, the human organism is physiologically programmed to imitate, to seek knowledge and pleasure through the imitation of external form. The artist appropriates and replicates within himself the movements in the external world (what could be more narcissistic?) and then further replicates that movement in the production of plastic art. While both Gide's idealism and Nordau's "intellectually-beautiful" art gesture beyond the double, narcissistically inflected (male) body, they inscribe that body at the center of the creative process. Narcissus as a surface-lover may not be sufficient to the production of responsible, ethical art, but his love of surface — his love of himself — in replication is certainly a necessary ingredient in creativity.

In both theorists of narcissism and art, the figure of Narcissus presides over an axis of creativity whose poles are progression and regression: Narcissus is necessary for creativity yet risks collapsing back into a preference for himself and his own body as a form he will mistake for the numinous, the beyond-form. But here we begin to see the slipperiness that art introduces into medicine, for the possible movements along that axis are quite different in the two writers. For Max Nordau, the degenerate is preoccupied with himself, and this is his major folly, the prime symptom of his disease; were he to abnegate himself for the greater cause of altruism and social sympathy, he would be much happier, much healthier, much more productive. In Gide, conversely (perversely?), it is only the contemplation of self that can lead to the knowledge of the truth, to something beyond the self. As Wallace Fowlie has argued, Gide's fascination with "mirrors" and "self-portraits," the whole phenomenon of *dédoublement*, is the key to his quest for "living authentically" (1979, 250). Despite Gide's prissy and authoritative footnote telling the artist not to prefer himself, he then completes the "Traité" by forcing the artist to prefer himself, to gaze upon himself as the only possible means of recognizing himself as the form, as that which is not to be preferred. Thus, Fowlie suggests, the mirror becomes Gide's way of negotiating the central contradiction of his later life — his worldly hedonism versus his aestheticism — a contradiction structured on the bifurcated and self-contesting images of Narcissus at the pool. As one might expect, this ambivalence is simplified in Nordau: whereas Gide posits the surface as a necessarily risky, potentially regressive optic that also pushes one forward into the morally acceptable, epistemologically tenable state of artistic productivity, in Nordau, the privileging of narcissistic surface is seen to cause the patient to regress. Nordau's binaristic thinking stably equates narcissism with surface with regression,[6] whereas, in Gide, narcissistic surface dismantles its equation with regression at the same time that it promotes it.

Gide's ambivalence about the placement of Narcissus in his ethical-aesthetic treatise may be the product of his own precious lingering over the text, his obsessive return to the surface of the page during composition. On 9 July 1891, Gide wrote to Paul Valéry: "I am irked about my *Traité du Narcisse,* which I did not write fast enough and which is therefore difficult in coming" (Mallet 1966, 74).[7] Or, as Helen Watson-Williams has argued, Narcissus's double movement may be an aspect of the tension between contemplation and action, self-subordination and self-affirmation, that Gide will return to throughout his life (1967, 38). Or, as Richard Ellmann suggests, the ambivalence is part of Gide's satire of Symbolism, for his Narcissus is forced to sacrifice physical act for contemplative idealism (lest he end up desperate, fragmented — that is, sexual — like Adam) while he would clearly prefer to enact his desires and live in a world of beautiful, incarnate form (1973, 93). What does seem sure is this: Gide's "Traité" continues the link between Narcissus and creativity that extends at least as far back as Schlegel, and his overt reference to the hermaphroditic Adam separating himself into desire constitutes heterosexuality where homosexuality was and where, especially for Gide, homosexuality will come to be.[8] The "Traité," emerging at the same time as Nordau's medicalizing of egomania, brings into sharp focus the ways in which Narcissus, art, and (homo)sexuality can connect, even though Gide's special blend of earnestness and timidity prevented him from exploring that connection fully. Such exploration would be left to his Mephistophelean contemporary, Oscar Wilde.

The Mirror Has Two Faces; or, Knowing from Behind

While it would be lovely to think that Wilde's most direct (although by no means only)[9] address to Narcissus, his short prose poem "The Disciple," influenced and demoralized Gide, this is probably not the case: as Patrick Pollard reminds us, the "Traité" was mostly completed by the time Gide first met Wilde in November 1891. Nor is there direct evidence that Wilde read Gide's piece before writing his own (Ellmann 1973, 93). But the two works share aspects that go beyond abstract, late-Symbolist manifestos for art. Let us read the prose poem in full:

> When Narcissus died the pool of his pleasure changed from a cup of sweet waters into a cup of salt tears, and the Oreads came weeping through the woodland that they might sing to the pool and give it comfort.
>
> And when they saw that the pool had changed from a cup of sweet waters into a cup of salt tears, they loosened the green tresses of their hair and cried to the pool and said, "We do not wonder that you should mourn in this manner for Narcissus, so beautiful was he."
>
> "But was Narcissus beautiful?" said the pool.
>
> "Who should know that better than you?" answered the Oreads. "Us did he ever pass by, but you he sought for, and would lie on your banks and look down at you, and in the mirror of your waters he would mirror his own beauty."
>
> And the pool answered, "But I loved Narcissus because, as he lay on my banks and looked down on me, in the mirror of his eyes I saw my own beauty mirrored." (Wilde 1980, 844)

As Ellmann contends, the point of Wilde's fable is that there are no disciples: "People are suns, not moons" (1973, 94), always generating their own light, never reflecting others. But just as Gide's treatise can be read within late-nineteenth-century medical discourse, so can Wilde's fable. In a marvelously suggestive reading, Gregory Bredbeck places the tale within the language of sexology to argue that Wilde inverts the received morality of the tale by inverting the subject-object relation: like Gide in his depiction of the contemplative, Wilde turns the gazer into the gazed upon (1994, 54). For Bredbeck, this inversion is significant because it connects to the larger language of inversion in the period, specifically in the way homosexual desire arises out of an initial desire *for* the mother. As Freud suggested in 1910, the homosexual's short-lived desire for the mother (what he calls the "anaclitic cathexis" — that is, "leaning up against" another) becomes an identification with the mother in a narcissistic cathexis. Sexual inversion is then a *re*version to an earlier mode of desiring (thus playing on the regressive axis that I have been tracing in this chapter); it is a mode whose primary relations are anaclitic, requiring an other, rather than being narcissistic, centered primarily in the self. As Nordau maintained, the degenerate artist falls backward into a circular attention on the self. But for Bredbeck, this presence of the anaclitic within the narcissistic is the deconstructive lever in Wilde's tale. At the same time that "The Disciple" enacts an anaclitic cathexis by "leaning up against" other cultural meanings — the classical tale, the language of sexology, the primacy of Narcissus within that language of sexology — the tale also displays (dis-plays) the privilege given by compulsory heterosexuality to the anaclitic. It flaunts its narcissistic circularity; it is filled with in-jokes and references to Wilde's life and associates; and it suggests the very narcissistic underpinnings of all sexuality, not just the homosexual (67). This refusal to privilege either the narcissistic or the anaclitic, Bredbeck concludes, is germane to Wilde's definition of camp since it refuses to recognize a "proper" object-choice or "right" cathexis and reclaims the perversity of the polymorphous (69).

Bredbeck's discussion is fascinating and suggestive, for its use of a yet-to-be-developed language of "anaclitic" cathexes addresses the very issues of narcissism that were plaguing Gide in his treatise, issues regarding Narcissus's focus on himself as a way of leading to something other or as a way of leading back to the self — a dialogue between creation and generation. These same issues nagged Wilde in the early 1890s and were overtly contemplated in *Dorian Gray* and *Teleny* as questions of optics, of looking at desired/desiring male bodies. Such a question of optics is the main thrust of the tale that seeks to instruct the Oreads in their misunderstanding: they assume that while Narcissus would only see himself in the pool, the pool was somehow capable of a different optic, able to see itself in Narcissus rather than Narcissus in it. What Wilde does here is extend the principle we saw in Romanticism to include all gazers: the subject does not become an object (as in the feminist critiques of Romantic male narcissism), the gazer does not become the gazed upon (as Bredbeck argues), but rather all gazers are made into desiring and desired subjects. The Wildean Narcissus can only see himself reflected in a surface, yet that surface itself is a Wildean Narcissus. Wilde does not transgress an anticipated psychoanalysis here so much as he transgresses Neoplatonism, the kind Gide is exploring in his treatise. Wilde imagines a kind of double mirror of the sort we saw Coleridge consider in "The Picture," a double mirror that does not allow the reflected image to be subordinated to the "Truth" that supposedly lies behind the image. There is no "behind" that is not itself a narcissistic reflection. The tale is a paean to image and form themselves, without the moralizing distinction of the "depth" within or behind which the Truth is thought to exist.

Yet, while the tale closes off the possibility of a Neoplatonic surface-depth dichotomy, it presents surfaces in a way that implicates them in the notion of depth. For as in Schlegel and Coleridge, the optic of the prose poem is vertical as well as horizontal; one looks up or down into, as well as at or across. In other words, the beauty of surface is not diametrically opposed to the soul but is contiguous with it, for the pool knows something of its soul by looking at it through the desiring gaze of Narcissus. Indeed, Wilde's Narcissus rewrites mythic history to see the focus on image as the essential truth, not an illusion at all. The Neoplatonic, Gidean Narcissus who is encouraged to look at the body in order to get to the soul is here refigured as a Narcissus who looks at the body in order to create the soul, for the only way to heal the soul is through the senses, as Henry Wotton tells Dorian Gray, and the only way to heal the senses is through the soul. Which puts art as a sensual experience in a very important place. In another short story, "The Nightingale and the Rose," the nightingale kills herself to create a red rose for the student to give to his beloved. This rose, an image of Wildean art as perfect as Narcissus, blooms thus: "Pale was it, at first, as the mist that hangs over the river — pale as the feet of the morning, and silver as the wings of the dawn. As a shadow of a rose in a mirror of silver, as the shadow of a rose in a water-pool, so was the rose that had blossomed on the topmost spray of the Tree" (Wilde 1980, 294–95). The "real" rose, like all of nature in "The Critic as Artist," is created by similes to artistic roses or, more specifically, roses that exist only as representations in mirrors and pools, which is to say, roses *that are representations of themselves, roses that are both originals and copies with no hope of distinguishing between the two.* The beautiful representation here gestures to a profound truth in desire, but, pace Gide, the form itself is the internal truth, the truth that lies within (or is it beyond?). Thus, Wilde's Narcissus refuses his placement on the moralizing scale of truth/illusion, subject/object, self/other, and form/soul and pulls the soul out of the depths (*de profundis*) to place it within the space separating two facing mirrors.

While we can glimpse in "The Disciple" the complexities of surface narcissism and its relation to creativity, a relation whose structures may forecast the language of psychoanalysis, we can see these issues more fully contemplated in Wilde's larger fiction. *The Picture of Dorian Gray,* which has already attracted more than one discussion of narcissism,[10] offers us a look at the multiple uses of the myth, both in its ethical and its aesthetic considerations. Through the character of Dorian, himself called a Narcissus early in the novel, Wilde creates a narrative of ethical dissolution proceeding from narcissism;

and in marked contrast, he explores through the artist Basil Hallward the artistic, creative aspects of narcissistic desire. But in both
of these characters, the relation of homoeros to narcissism is cryptic
and metonymic; as Ed Cohen points out, we all "know" the novel
is "about" homosexuality, but we are not sure how we know (1987,
75). And so, I want to read the novel as a mirror image of another
Wildean treatment of narcissism, the pornographic novel *Teleny; or,
The Reverse of the Medal.* I call this novel "Wildean" rather than
"Wilde's" because I want to emphasize the relation of its subject
matter to Wilde's oeuvre, rather than discuss its authorship, which
is still in dispute.[11] What is interesting about the pairing is that, like
Gide's "Traité" and Nordau's *Degeneration, Dorian Gray* and *Teleny* foreground Narcissus in their consideration of artistic creativity,
but whereas the "Traité" and *Dorian Gray* keep their homosexuality
muted, *Teleny* makes sexuality, a sexuality rooted in narcissism, one
of its central concerns.

Like Coleridge's "The Picture," *Dorian Gray* and *Teleny* depict series of rejections or repudiations, but what these 1890 texts reject, initially anyway, is the now-conventional equation of homo-narcissism
with psychic cruelty, impotence, and thanatos. Both Dorian and
Camille Des Grieux, the narrator of *Teleny,* begin their erotic es-
capades by meeting mirror images of themselves. Dorian Gray is little
more than the pretty boy on Basil Hallward's and Henry Wotton's
erotic runway until he confronts the painting:

> When he saw it he drew back, and his cheeks flushed for a moment with
> pleasure. A look of joy came into his eyes, as if he had recognized himself
> for the first time. He stood there motionless and in wonder, dimly conscious
> that Hallward was speaking to him, but not catching the meaning of his
> words. The sense of his own beauty came on him like a revelation. He had
> never felt it before. (1987, 24–25)

For Eve Sedgwick, the beautiful portrait of the beautiful boy invokes,
through its classical allusions, the Greek aesthetic of the male body
on display, a body that can be looked at without shame; the portrait, she says, presents "a body whose surfaces, features, and abilities
[are] the subject or object of unphobic enjoyment" (1990, 136). This
body, moreover, is the one we have been constantly returning to in
Ovid: "Once, in boyish mockery of Narcissus, [Dorian] had kissed,
or feigned to kiss, those painted lips that now smiled so cruelly at
him" (Wilde 1987, 105). Narcissus here is a scene of erotic instruction; it wrenches epistemology out of the closet and claims to instruct,
through delight, the pleasures of self-knowledge.

While the portrait in *Dorian Gray* merely gestures to the desire for the other, *Teleny* literalizes the dual status of the male body as "subject or object"; it presents the body of René Teleny both as an object of Camille's erotic desire and as a narcissistic projection of himself. "[W]e are alike in looks as well as in tastes" (1986, 136), René observes to Camille, and in their first meeting Camille is aroused by Teleny's "magnetic hand, which seems to have a secret affinity for [my] own" (33). Elsewhere: "we had but one head and one heart" (169). Indeed, the novel quickly betrays its mythic and psychosexual basis, as we are told that Teleny's fascinating erotic power resides in that familiar image of the pool: he has eyes "as unfathomable as the dim water of a well" (69), a well not dissimilar to that of Narcissus. This narcissistic imagery then culminates in an undifferentiated blending, an obfuscation of self and other. Camille remembers:

> The image of Teleny haunted me, the name of René was ever on my lips. I kept repeating it over and over for dozens of times. What a sweet name it was! At its sound my heart was beating faster....I stared at myself within the looking-glass, and I saw Teleny in it instead of myself; and behind him arose our blended shadows, as I had seen them on the pavement the evening before. (46)

Unlike the true narcissist — or perhaps *precisely* like him — Camille sees another's face in his reflection. Like the pool in "The Disciple," like Gide's Narcissus in the "Traité," the desired object is at the same time an erotic other and a desiring self. In fact, the love of sameness is essential to the pedagogy of lovemaking itself. Camille explains while reflecting on their mutual masturbation:

> The most skilled of prostitutes could never give such thrilling sensations as those which I felt with my lover, for the tweake is, after all, only acquainted with the pleasures she herself has felt; whilst the keener emotions, not being those of her sex, are unknown to and cannot be imagined by her....The quintessence of bliss can, therefore, only be enjoyed by beings of the same sex. (167)

The quality of sameness here is highly functional. In pornographic convention — and, indeed, in the heterosexual scenes of *Teleny* — desire is always instructed, a product of imitation. (One need only think here of the writings of the Marquis de Sade or Cleland's Fanny Hill and her tutelage.) But for a homosexual subculture, there are no overtly imitable models; there is no convention from which to imagine a sexual behavior combined with and inseparable from identity. The philosophy of Neoplatonism to which Wilde's work owes such a debt displaces male homoerotic desire into tropes of friendship, the disembodied, transcendent negotiations of the male citizens. But sexual pleasure always depends to a degree on sexual knowledge, a knowledge that, in this text, must begin in the self and in the registers of sameness.[12] What the text accomplishes here, at least temporarily, is a divestment of the moral implications of narcissism that were beginning to take shape at the end of the century. We see instead what Jacques Lacan will call the "flutter of jubilant activity" by which the child identifies itself and/as its other in the mirror stage (1977, 1), a desire that, outside Lacan's analysis, renders all desire always already homoerotic. In *Dorian Gray* and *Teleny,* homoerotic desire is jubilantly framed as a sameness in the other, an otherness in the self, and such surface sameness bespeaks the depth of erotic desire.

So far so good, if you are a queer reader looking to recuperate narcissism at the end of the nineteenth century. But it is not long before both texts lock into place the disastrous psychological trajectory that ruins the narcissist and those around him. In an extremely influential psychonormalizing reading of *Dorian Gray,* Otto Rank hypothesizes that homosexual narcissists channel their infatuation with their own youthful image into the pursuit of same-sex liaisons and that this channeling is the result of the fear of aging and death. Thus the narcissist, he claims, is characterized by a "defective capacity to love" that "arises from his narcissistic fixation on his own ego" (1971, 72). The egoism that psychoanalysis can detect in the homosexual — and that Nordau was sure he could find as well — is a defense mechanism against death that projects itself out into the figure of the double or doppelgänger (73). Such is, of course, the process in Dorian Gray: moments after he has the flush of self-recognition — the flush of auto-homo-narcissism — Dorian complains, "I am jealous of everything whose beauty does not die. I am jealous of the portrait you have painted of me. Why should it keep what I must lose?" (26). The rest of the story, the construction of the painting as doppelgänger that haunts and destroys Dorian, is too familiar to rehearse. And this doubling, whose mechanics work their torture on Freud's Schreber (and which has been thoroughly theorized by Eve Sedgwick in *Between Men*), invades the narcissistic other-desire of Camille and René Teleny. When Camille gives his lover an antique cameo whose features seem to each lover to be those of the other, René portentously bemoans: "you are, perhaps, my *Doppelgänger*? Then woe to one of us!... In our country [Hungary] they say that a man must never meet his *alter ego,* it brings misfortune to one or both" (136). The slip from "one of us" to "one or both" is not accidental: René stabs himself, Dorian-like, at the end of the novel, and Camille attempts to drown himself, Narcissus-like, in the river. Camille is saved only by a wandering stranger, a man who occupies "My own image. A man exactly like myself — my *Doppelgänger,* in fact" (183). Both texts, then, seem to follow a psycho-logic whose normalizing ethical weight is clear: narcissism is ultimately an escape from the fear of death into (homo)sexuality, where one validates oneself by observing one's own image (Rank 1971, 83). But self-recognition is inevitable — for Dorian, for Teleny, for Narcissus, for Gide's Adam — and the result is tragedy: death, madness (and in Adam's case, compulsory unsatisfactory heterosexuality); it is a lesson each of these works would appear to teach, a lesson that schools the subject beyond his regressive, infantilizing fascination with surface and into a more forward contemplation of the internal and the True.[13]

Self-recognition: the glorious and salvific end of psychoanalysis, the oedipal-Shakespearean literary virtue, the sine qua non of Western metaphysical maturity, and the abjected yet inexorable tragedy of the narcissist. For Otto Rank, this moment of self-recognition is also the moment at which the narcissist recognizes that he cannot obtain the object he desires, that his passion is destined not to be fulfilled, that what is at the center of his desire is death, not love (77). Such insight concludes Dorian's first meeting with the finished portrait: "now, as he stood gazing at the shadow of his own loveliness, the full reality of the description flashed across him. Yes, there would be a day when his face would be wrinkled and wizen, his eyes dim and colourless, the grace of his figure broken and deformed" (25). Like the Narcissus in Gide, Dorian sees reflected beauty — "the shadow of his own loveliness" — to herald not complete perfection but desire and fragmentation, the kind that for Rank will degenerate into "the defective capacity to love." Dorian complains:

> "I wish I could love," cried Dorian Gray [to Lord Henry], with a deep note of pathos in his voice. "But I seem to have lost the passion, and forgotten the desire. I am too much concentrated on myself. My own personality has become a burden to me. I want to escape, to go away, to forget." (205)

And with this self-knowledge — a knowledge of the desire to escape the self, a knowledge whose contents are themselves inescapable — the self-adored becomes the self-loathed. The picture of Dorian Gray becomes not an erotic self-affirmation — no jubilant activity or mirror assumption — but rather a haunting doppelgänger, a constant reminder of sin and eros gone wrong. In the latter part of the novel, Dorian becomes increasingly afraid of the portrait and of anything that might reflect him to himself. Like his Parisian double in the infamous "yellow book" (Huysmans's *A Rebours*), Dorian assumes a "grotesque dread of mirrors" (127). His decision to destroy the portrait follows from a horrifying reflection:

> The curiously-carved mirror that Lord Henry had given to him, so many years ago now, was standing on the table, and the white-limbed Cupids laughed round as of old. He took it up, as he had done on that night of horror, when he had first noted the change in the fatal picture, and with wild tear-dimmed eyes looked into its polished shield.... Then he loathed his own beauty, and flinging the mirror on the floor crushed it into silver splinters beneath his heel. It was his beauty that had ruined him. (220)

Dorian destroys the otherness of the reflected image in much the same way that he will drive a knife into the painting. And these acts of destroying the other ultimately destroy the self, as Dorian falls dead before the freshly restored portrait. The narcissist meets his palpably moral end but does so by reuniting the division between the self and other that narcissism had facilitated. Surfaces, the dual facing mirrors, are collapsed into a triumphant depth model as Dorian melds *into* the painting, a movement into a third dimension of soul that his life has been dedicated to forgetting.

In a curious way, though, it is not narcissism that causes the death of Dorian Gray so much as the end of narcissism, that crucial moment when the boy flings himself into the drowning pool because his erotic bond with the other male can no longer be sustained. As we remember, Tiresias prophesied that Narcissus would "long years and ripe old age enjoy... 'If he himself not know'" (Ovid 1986, 61). For Otto Rank, self-knowledge leads the narcissist to despair and self-loathing and inevitably to his own death, since the object of desire is recognized as being unattainable, but such a reading depends for its power solely on the idea that narcissism is self-contained, solipsistic, and primarily *about* the self. Rather, self-consciousness in Ovid (as in Gide and even in Lacan) generates desire as Narcissus stares at and desires him*self*, whom he perceives to be an*other*. In *Teleny,* the object-relation or object-cathexis echoes the Ovidian image of Narcissus as a boy in love with another boy; in so doing, *Teleny* enacts another Wildean repudiation of the moralizing trope of depth. Self-consciousness is deployed in this novel not to arrest the radical moral ambiguity of the tale and thus to placate Victorian sensibility but rather to illustrate it as a kind of foreign invasion, an extraerotic or extranarcissistic interruption of homo-narcissism's *physical* components. As we have just seen, the erotically invested Camille looks Narcissus-like into his mirror and sees his lover looking back. But presently, "the servant tapped at the door; this recalled me to self-consciousness. I saw myself in the glass, and found myself hideous, and for the first time in my life I wished myself good-looking — nay, enticingly handsome" (46). The process here is fascinating: unlike Dorian Gray, whose own self-consciousness interrupts the narcissistic *jouissance* he has with the painting on first meeting, Camille utilizes narcissism precisely in the service of *jouissance;* and unlike Gide's Narcissus and Adam, who see themselves reflected and thus desire an other to make them whole, Camille *first* sees the other that makes him whole and only later wishes to retrieve the vision in himself, to be as "entranced" with his own good looks as he and Narcissus are with their lovers'. In this novel, the narcissist does not replicate himself through homoerotic desire *but rather constructs a self out of homo-erotic desire,* a desire that at least partially reflects the desire in/for oneself. And in that homo-narcissistic mirroring, the precious self-knowledge that, in heteronormative psychoanalysis, disciplines and punishes Narcissus here divests depth of the privileged position it has in Western metaphysics and ethics. More Ovidian than Symbolist-medical, Camille basks in the narcissism of the other-love until a human voice wakes him and he drowns in self-consciousness. And it is the surface, superficial self whose narcissistic reflection engages the queer narcissist in a desire for the other and whose narcissism is always constituted by the desire for the other.[14]

This critical contradiction in the function of self-consciousness gets us, perhaps, closer to understanding what Wilde means by his use of Narcissus and the normalizing self-recognition that has accompanied the myth since at least the beginning of the Christian era (Vinge 1967, 35). Elsewhere Wilde tells us that "there is no fine art without self-consciousness, and self-consciousness and the critical spirit are one" (1980, 56). The Schlegelian echoes here form a critical aporia, one that plagued Coleridge: the narcissist is too fixated on, too conscious of, himself and at the same time he does not know himself nearly well enough; he needs to plumb his depths further instead of . . . well, whatever it is we are sure he is doing. But unlike Schlegel (although perhaps not unlike Coleridge), the wash of homoeroticism is never far away from this self-consciousness. As Henry Wotton watches Dorian develop, he marvels that

> the lad was premature. He was gathering his harvest while it was yet spring. The pulse and passion of youth were in him, but he was becoming self-conscious. It was delightful to watch him. With his beautiful face, and his beautiful soul, he was a thing to wonder at. (57)

As in "The Disciple," beautiful faces and beautiful souls combine to give the definition of homoerotic desire as Wilde plays off both surface and depth. Narcissism's same-sex desire refuses to fix itself at the polar sites of surface or depth, deformity or beauty, good or bad, identity or otherness. Narcissism shuttles the subject over all points on the map of desire, suggesting not that narcissism is necessarily virtuous in some simple way but that it cannot be stably confined by the Symbolist-medical pathologizing of Wilde's contemporaries.

To the degree that the narrative of Dorian Gray attempts to halt the vacillations of the narcissistic paradigm by having Dorian erotically cathect on the image of his own body and take it as a sexual object, it announces the theory of narcissism that psychoanalysis will work out as the master-narrative for the twentieth-century queer man. But, as I have been suggesting, this is not the only thing the novel does, despite the fact that such a normalizing narrative worked so well as evidence against Oscar Wilde in his trials. The ambiguity that seems to shroud the issue in this novel gets clarified by Wilde's treatment of the most innocuous and innocent of the characters, Basil Hallward. Dorian's narrative may pose the ethical problem of homo-narcissism by emphasizing the surface desire at the expense of soul, but Basil's narrative considers the *aesthetic* possibilities of homo-narcissism, possibilities that I take to be of greater interest to Wilde precisely because they combine the creative with the erotic. Dorian Gray's portrait is an erotic site not only for Dorian but for Basil as well, and if Dorian can only penetrate himself with the phallic knife at the end, Basil has other, more nuanced modes of entering the young man. As Ed Cohen argues, the painting represents for both Basil and Lord Henry the ever-present, ever-concealed "symbolic displacement of the erotic onto the aesthetic" (1987, 77), and, given the fascination that both Gide and Nordau have brought to narcissistic aestheticism and symbolism, we might ask how Basil's artistic temperament is coded as both narcissistic and homoerotic. In a gesture back to Schlegelian Romanticism, Basil, the character with whom Wilde most closely identified,[15] considers the painting of the portrait a narcissistic act. As Lord Henry encourages him to exhibit the painting at Grosvenor, Hallward explains why he can't: " 'I know you will laugh at me,' he replied, 'but I really can't exhibit it. I have put too much of myself into it' " (2). He continues:

> every portrait that is painted with feeling is a portrait of the artist, not of the sitter. The sitter is merely the accident, the occasion. It is not he who is revealed by the painter; it is rather the painter who, on the coloured

canvas, reveals himself. The reason I will not exhibit this picture is that I am afraid that I have shown in it the secret of my own soul. (5)

While the painting bifurcates Dorian into body and soul (a split that Wilde argues is deadly to both), it enacts another bifurcation, one reminiscent of the Coleridgean speaker imaging his male other at the pool. The painting shows not only the (hideous, murderous) secrets of Dorian's soul but also the (erotic, desiring) secrets of Basil's. The painter says as much in his coming-out speech to Dorian:

as I worked at it [i.e., the portrait], every flake and film of colour seemed to me to reveal my secret. I grew afraid that others would know of my idolatry. I felt, Dorian, that I had told too much, that I had put too much of myself into it. (114–15)

Basil's painting is a narcissistic reflection of his own desire. Yet at the same time that it obliterates the object (the "sitter"), it telegraphs its desire *for* the object. For Dorian and for fin-de-siècle psycho-analysis, narcissism is self-enclosure; for Basil Hallward, narcissism is self-*dis*closure, but a self whose place on the axis of regression/progression is impossible to determine.

In a way, Basil's narcissism works both sides of the street: on one side, this painting records a surface Dorian that is really a metonymic reflection of Basil, his desires, his self. The two-dimensional surface of the painting is a ruse, a Symbolist circumlocution getting at the *real* point of the painting, the vertical axis by which Basil looks into his own soul. But on the other side, Basil's own representation of this optic is multivalent and complex:

I worshipped you. I grew jealous of every one to whom you spoke. I wanted to have you all to myself.... You had leant over the still pool of some Greek woodland, and seen in the water's silent silver the marvel of your own face. And it had all been what art should be, unconscious, ideal, and remote. (114)

Basil's focus on his "soul" — which I take to mean the strength and coloration of his desire — is knowable not (only) through the ver-tical optic of introspection but (also) through the horizontal one of the desiring, erotic look, a look whose object is both narcissistic and "unconscious, ideal, and remote." Like the optic we saw faintly con-figured in Polidori's *The Vampyre*, narcissism here puts the desiring subject at the center and removes him completely. This decentering — what inspires Basil's "jealousy" — was anticipated by Dorian's own reaction to his portrait, which I noted earlier: Dorian had become jealous of the portrait because it would be forever young, forever a reflection of Dorian's current beauty. The "Dorian" who looks on jealously is and is not the "Dorian" replicated in the portrait, and the portrait-as-surface is and is not the mirror-window of Dorian's soul. By knowing depth only through surface, by scoring the self only by scoring off the other, narcissism is always and never about the narcissist.

Nor is narcissistic art ever really about its object of desire, as Basil has just explained. Except, of course, that the status of Narcissus as an object of his own desire is precisely the "problem" that Western culture has not tired of denouncing. Narcissus's focus on surface beauty has rendered him object when he "should" know himself as subject. For Ed Cohen, this split can be theoretically explained as the difference between a presymbolic imaginary and a symbolic structuring of that imaginary. Basil's painting, he argues, is a visual register of Dorian's beauty and Basil's desire for him; but such desire is sublimated into the nonverbal, and its status as "extralinguistic" renders the painting easily codeable as ideal, remote, Platonic (1987, 78). Lord Henry's narcissistic projection, conversely, is symbolical and discursive, so that Henry moves Dorian from the imaginary plenitude of bodily reality into the "symbolic order of desire," a desire that, forecasting Rank, both constitutes Dorian's sexual self and leads him to ruin. Now, leaving aside the assumption that Dorian has not been inducted into the symbolic order until his first meeting with the painting, I would emphasize another of Cohen's contentions, that "Lord Henry first becomes interested in Dorian through the story of Basil's passion" (78). This mediation of homoerotic desire through the desire of another man not only characterizes Henry's somewhat superficial desire for Dorian; it is also at the heart of the surface of the painting (oxymoron intentional). As Lori MacDonald, one of my students, has argued in a seminar presentation, Basil's "deep desire" for Dorian is shot through with Henry's desire for Dorian: the painting captures Dorian in a particularly fetching way *because* of the cruisy dialogue with which Henry bastes the youth on the final day of the painting. Basil is recording on the surface of the painting not only his desire for Dorian but his recognition of Henry's desire as well; he is recording, in other words, his desire for Henry's desire. What gets called narcissism here is really a tête-à-tête that is itself a tête-à-tête-à-tête, a ménage à trois whose replications are beginning to appear endless. In Gide's terms, narcissism is a *mise en abyme,* by which Gide means "a device from heraldry that involves putting a second representation of the original shield 'en abyme' within it" (quoted in Dällenbach 1989, 7).[16] Through such *mise en abyme* (a "narcissistic" reflection of Gide?) Wilde demonstrates how narcissism is always inflected by the desire for the other and by the desire of the other, wrenching it from the degenerate regression where Nordau's proto-psychoanalysis places it and moving it relentlessly back and forth along the axis of solipsism and sociality, reflexivity and creativity. Basil's surface painting gestures both to the regression toward a psychically enclosed self and to the progression toward an erotically cathected self-other dyad, a dyad that, in the queer aesthetics of narcissism, is always triangular.

Basil's sometimes quaint, sometimes richly allusive definition of aesthetic creativity is shared by René, the artistic pianist in *Teleny* . . . and with a more audaciously articulated eros. Just as a horny Camille sees the image of Teleny in his own looking glass, so does Teleny-as-artist look for an erotic other in his own creative productions. René looks for a "sympathetic listener": "someone who feels, while listening, exactly as I do whilst I am playing, who sees perhaps the same visions as I do — ," someone, in short, like Camille (34–35). So good an audience member is Camille, in fact, that he punctuates his first exposure to Teleny's piano-playing by ejaculating in his trousers. This moment, of course, contrasts Camille as ideal listener to the vulgar, bourgeois public in a way that places *Teleny* in the tradition of decadent Symbolism. In this novel, as in Wilde's comedies, the bourgeois public is incapable of appreciating art. At the concert hall Teleny bemoans, "The young men are obliging the ladies, these are scrutinizing each other's toilette; the fathers, who are bored, are either thinking of the rise and fall of the stocks, or else counting the number of gas-lights, and reckoning how much the illumination will cost" (34). But more to the point, the scene seems to want to rewrite Teleny's familiar artistic petulance from infantile "degeneracy" to a form of narcissism whereby the audience member sees the world through the lens of the artist. Like Basil Hallward, for whom all art was a creation of the artist rather than the object represented or the audience who appreciated it, art here is a form of eroticism in which sympathetic individuals — narcissists all — see each other's world by having each other see their own.[17] And contrary to the lamentable sexuality that arises in Gide's Adam — the desire that is produced by inescapable narcissism — this novel revels in narcissism as a sexual trope, one whose *jouissance* is clear. In effect, art returns us to the narcissistic unity that constitutes sexual relations between men in the novel.

That Is All

I want to conclude my discussion of these two novels by positing one more bifurcation in their deployment of Narcissus: Wildean erotic nov-

els situate the queer artist within the burgeoning sexological discourse
of narcissism in a way that should remind critics (like me, like Gregory
Bredbeck, like Earl Jackson) that they were written prior to Freud and
Rank and within a surface-based materialism where we all want depth
to be. These tragic novels, in other words, *de*psychologize the very
psychologies that use them as their test cases. While one might accept
Otto Rank's thesis that Dorian Gray's death is the inevitable product
of his (homosexual) narcissism, what is one to do with Basil Hallward's death? Basil dies, we remember, not because some regressive,
infantilizing fixation drives him to suicide; nor does his doppelgänger,
his monstrously projected other, rise up to destroy him. Rather, he
is repeatedly stabbed in the back of the head by the man with whom
he is in love yet from whom he is different in every conceivable way.
Narcissism plays no discernible part in his death. Teleny and Camille
are perhaps a more conventional test case for psychoanalytic study,
but the dangerous doppelgänger that disturbs the narcissistic bliss is
troubled by the scene I quoted earlier, where the suicidal Camille is
pulled from the river by "My own image. A man exactly like myself —
my *Doppelgänger,* in fact" (183). Now, presumably, René Teleny was
his doppelgänger — unless doppelgängers come in triads — yet the
emergence of another double actually saves Camille's life; it ensures
his presence not only as the retrospective narrator of the novel but
also as a subject whose erotic interests do not die with Teleny. By
this logic the novel replicates the narcissistic paradigm in order to
triangulate it and to destroy the dyadic insularity of narcissism at the
same time that it makes possible further narcissistic dyads.

Moreover, if the novel at points adopts the doppelgänger motif in
order to unravel it, it utterly rejects it in the end. The spectral fear
that interrupts the lovers' relationship is not the product of some psychological maladjustment, as Otto Rank would have it; nor is it the
logical extension of the narcissistic infatuation, as seems to be suggested by the eponymous Dorian Gray. Rather, Teleny's fear, the ghost
that haunts him, is a fear of a specifically external, extrapsychic social
force. Camille's mother, we find out, has become Teleny's lover, and
it is she whom he is trying to hide from Camille. Teleny has amassed
great debts, which Camille's mother has paid off, and her resulting blackmail scheme is the reason for Teleny's infidelity to Camille.
She becomes a kind of panther with whom Teleny has to dine, a
Mrs. Chevely to Teleny's Robert Chiltern. If Teleny had reneged on
his sexual favors to the mother, she would have destroyed him. This
plot twist, thrown in at the end of the novel, not only is a convenient
and sensational way to end (and isn't the ability to end the generic

problem that pornography faces?) but also makes an important point about queer love in the novel. While the imagery figuring same-sex desire has suggested a kind of narcissistic self-love whose uses, I have tried to show, are multivalent and revisionist, the novel ultimately suggests that narcissism has nothing whatever to do with the lovers' tragedy; rather, it is money and the regulatory powers of compulsory heterosexuality, the very material earnestness that Nordau extolled, that kill Teleny and homosexual desire. The double here represents not narcissistic guilt but rather the impossible attainment of desire in a world where the homosexual is vulnerable and blackmailable. Doubleness interrupts the otherwise blissful narcissistic union by inserting into the love relationship a crass, bourgeois power struggle over money. In *Teleny*, the real impediment to same-sex relations is material rather than psychological. Oppression comes from the outside and forces the homosexual man away from sameness and into the tyranny of the other.[18]

At the same time, however, these texts utilize the premises of psychoanalysis to resist, perhaps naively, the antihumanism that psychoanalysis will expound. As Freud's oeuvre makes clear, the doubling optic of Narcissus is a staple in theories of the other, the imago, desire, melancholia, and panic. Moreover, it is the radical brilliance of psychoanalytic critique that it wrested the "self" from a humanist premise of unity and stability to show a self divided against itself, always at war with itself (could one imagine a more narcissistic condition than "where id is, there ego will be also," where both *Es* and *Ich* are part of the "I"?). Thus is Modernism born. But for Wilde, self-representation and self-doubling have the same potential efficacy that we saw in Coleridge's *Opus Maximum*, in that they can be deployed to constitute a certain kind of self. Henry Wotton, the only narcissist to survive in *Dorian Gray*, bequeaths the following principle that has, for Oscar Wilde (as for another great Modernist queer, Virginia Woolf), the ring of truth:

> Is insincerity such a terrible thing? I think not. It is merely the method by which we can multiply our personalities.
>
> Such, at any rate, was Dorian Gray's opinion. He used to wonder at the shallow psychology of those who conceive the Ego in man as a thing simple, permanent, reliable, and of one essence. To him, man was a being with myriad lives and myriad sensations, a complex multiform creature that bore within itself strange legacies of thought and passion. (142–43)

The multiplicity of self is, of course, the heart of the antiessentialist demoralizing that Dollimore sees in Wilde's corruption of Gide. And while Dollimore locates the erotic component of this corruption in the famous Algiers incident, we can also see its fictional counterpart in *Teleny*. One of the most curious parts of the novel is Camille's repeated out-of-body experiences:

> In the cab, that night, my mind was so intently fixed upon Teleny that my inward self seemed to disintegrate itself from my body and to follow like his own shadow the man I loved. I unconsciously threw myself into a kind of trance and I had a most vivid hallucination, which, strange as it might appear, coincided with all that my friend did and felt. (73)

The narcissistic paradigm that I have been tracing as a queer aesthetic should need no elaboration here. And of course, the "disintegration" that desire brings to Camille's sense of self is fully realized when they first have sex:

> I was melting away, but he never stopped till he had quite drained me of the last drop of life-giving fluid there was in me. My eyes were swimming in their sockets. I felt my heavy lids half close themselves; an unbearable voluptuousness of mingled pain and pleasure, shattered my body and blasted my very soul; then everything waned in me. He clasped me in his arms, and I swooned away. (126–27)

Like the shattered self that Leo Bersani posits is the only one open to desire or the inter-irrupted self that Jackson finds in contemporary gay pornographic film, the Wildean lover employs narcissism to double, to replicate, and to undo the stability of a homoerotic self that psychoanalysis will insist is regressing to stability, unity, and imaginary wholeness.

Wilde's indulgence in surface as a strategic gesture to the "depth" of desires may strike us as dangerous business, first because it tacitly acknowledges the discursive assumptions of psychoanalysis at the same time that it rejects them.[19] Moreover, to posit multiple personalities as a way of shattering the self and thus of creating new pleasures (a legacy reflected in Foucault's advocacy of SM and Bersani's advocacy against SM) may strike us as a utopian wish. After all, one hears the corrective echoes of Judith Butler reminding us that such performances of utopianism are always bounded by the mechanics of performativity, that the laws that authenticate self-dissolution continually hold, phantasmatically, a self to be dissolved. The disintegrated self, in other words, is never a free-floating, transhistorical thing, immune to other related cultural imperatives (like the wish that gay men would die or disappear, their selves disintegrating in literal ways). Perhaps the best we can hope for here is a kind of queer aesthetic whose agency is never guaranteed, can never be known in advance, but that enables us continually to rethink the erotic possibilities of narcissistic replication. In a homage to the first "gay" text, Oscar Wilde's *Ballad of Reading Gaol,* Wayne Koestenbaum considers the contemporary queer disdain for the clone — his sameness, his aping of hegemonic masculinity — and argues that "To consider replication degrading is, literally, homophobic: *afraid of the same.* If the patriarchal pen is, figuratively, a fertilizing penis, let us enjoy the fact that the gay male instrument of textual dissemination may well be a xerox machine" (1990, 182–83). And perhaps such textual narcissism allows us new — or renewed — purchase on the critique of compulsory heterosexuality as being itself a form of narcissism. On this point, Oscar Wilde's double articulation is as trenchant as usual: "The nineteenth century dislike of Realism is the rage of Caliban seeing his own face in a glass. The nineteenth century dislike of Romanticism is the rage of Caliban not seeing his own face in a glass" (1987, xxiii).

Chapter 3

SONS AND LOVERS,
BIRDS AND JOHNS

Sons

Mamma's boys: we've met a lot of them so far. Coleridge's speaker in
"The Picture" is captivated by Isabel's maternal, domestic drawing of
a small boy at a cottage. Byron's Arnold seeks his transformation into
Achilles because his mother rejected him: she threw him out of the
house because he was ugly, and much of the first act of *The Deformed
Transformed* reads like a fulfillment of the son's wish to become the
beautiful child his mother wants. Wilde and company's Camille Des
Grieux not only lives with his mother well into adulthood but finds
himself in an erotic triangle with her, competing against her for the affections of his lover, Teleny. Richard Ellmann relates a scene in which
Wilde goads the virginal André Gide about his relation to his mother
(1988, 337–38). Nor does this list of maternal presences in queer
male desire appear accidental. Narcissus himself, some might argue,
is actually seeking his mother as a love-object: Liriope, we remember,
was a "wave-blue water nymph" whom Cephisus raped to produce
Narcissus (Ovid 1986, 61). For Julia Kristeva, "The mythical Narcissus would heroically lean over that emptiness [of his own subjectivity]
to seek in the maternal watery element the possibility of representing
the self or the other — someone to love" (1987, 42).[1] From the outset,
it seems, Narcissus is never monologic but dyadic, never dyadic but
triangulated. Wedged between himself and his own image, injected
into his desire for his lover/himself, is the figure of the mother, sometimes subdued, sometimes spectral, but always, apparently, necessary
in constituting his eros.

However, let us admit the anachronism immediately. If the mother
seems overdetermined in relation to Coleridge, Byron, Wilde, and
Narcissus, it is because the Freudian enterprise has told us that she
must be. When Freud wrested the male invert from medical models
of pathology and laid him out on the psychoanalytic couch, he placed
the mother there too. As an object of the homosexual man's desire,

as a subject who herself desires men, as an imago whose desire the homosexual male will incorporate, the mother and her eros come to hold a place in the twentieth-century construction of sexuality that would have been impossible before the turn of the century. And the shelf life has been long: can we really watch Harvey Fierstein's Arnold in *Torch Song Trilogy* and not get the emphasis on the role of the mother? Would a men's toilet stall be complete without the ubiquitous graffiti, "My mother made me a homosexual," followed by the response, "Gee, if I got her the wool, would she make me one too?" And isn't it significant that the heads of the drag houses in *Paris Is Burning* are all "mothers"? Indeed, one of the most loaded and volatile questions one can ask a young man emerging from the closet is the same one ABBA asked in 1979: "Does your mother know that you're out?" (Anderson, Ulvaeus, and Anderson 1979). If the nineteenth century imagined a Narcissus who saw his sister, his feminine soul, his beloved lady when he looked into the pool, the twentieth century's Narcissus sees his mother, who seems to serve all the same functions.

While Freud never stopped returning to the question of the psychogenesis of male homosexuality, he encapsulated his position succinctly in the 1921 "Group Psychology and the Analysis of the Ego":

> The genesis of male homosexuality in a large class of cases is as follows. A young man has been unusually long and intensely fixated upon his mother in the sense of the Oedipus complex. But at last, after the end of puberty, the time comes for exchanging his mother for some other sexual object. Things take a sudden turn: the young man does not abandon his mother, but identifies himself with her; he transforms himself into her, and now looks about for objects which can replace his ego for him, and on which he can bestow such love and care as he has experienced from his mother. (1921, 108)

In the Freudian narrative, homosexual desire is every bit as triangulated as it was in Coleridge and Byron, but whereas the Romantic Narcissus identified with another man's heterosexual desire (an identification that, in Coleridge, threatened to slip into desire), Freud's Narcissus places a woman at the center of his identificatory scheme. Indeed, Freud's Narcissus plots his desire in two stages. First, the mother triangulates and inflects desire by providing the model that the male homosexual imitates; he "identifies himself with her" and "transforms himself into her," taking her object of desire (the phallus) as his own. Second, and causally, this maternal identification enjoins the narcissistic homosexual to find in other males an image of the whole that he should have had (through identifying with the father) but does not, having sacrificed his male ego to the passive, objective attitude of the feminine maternal. Thus does he enact a narcissistic replication of his own undeveloped, even fictional, ego and seek in the other male a mirror that, by replicating the self, will reflect an ego in the place of his own absent one.

We may find such a thesis quaint — depending as it does on a bourgeois family romance statically universalized to all subjects — or downright ludicrous in its assumption that a male child will always and only read maternal desire as one thing and that, in his (mandatory, compulsory) identification with the mother, his desire will be stable and monologic as well; in other words, that everyone's desire can only be understood to have one obvious and erotic object. But Freud's proffered equation of homosexuality with narcissism, like all of his ideas, has a history of shifts and revisions, changes of position and contradictions. The equation begins with the 1910 footnote to "Three Essays on the Theory of Sexuality" (1905), moves through the 1910 essay on Leonardo da Vinci, to the 1914 "On Narcissism: An Introduction," and only then on to the work of the early 1920s that I quoted above. What interests me here are two related issues that will underlie my discussion in this chapter. The first is what I, and other critics, take to be Freud's contradictory and imprecise treatment of anaclitic versus narcissistic libidinal investments (the subtending narrative of heterosexual versus homosexual object-choice). The second is the relation of this slippery treatment to the function of sublimation and, in particular, sublimation of eros into art. The history of narcissism's reliance on the maternal begins in the realm of the artist — Freud gives birth to it in the essay on da Vinci — but he does not seem to return to the problem of art in his later considerations. I find this curious not only because Narcissus himself was a work of art created by Ovid, his predecessors and his descendants, but also because Narcissus is himself an artist, according to the Neoplatonic and Romantic tradition. How might such issues converge, then? How might the supposedly stable relation between homosexuality and the maternal be troubled by the figure of Narcissus, the artist whose own fleeting image refuses to be pinned down?

Lovers

In the 1914 essay "On Narcissism: An Introduction," Freud catalogs the range of psychic motivations for choosing a love object. The catalog is remarkable for the number of bases it covers:

A person may love: —

(1) According to the narcissistic type:

    (*a*) what he himself is (i.e. himself),

    (*b*) what he himself was,

    (*c*) what he himself would like to be,

    (*d*) someone who was once part of himself.

(2) According to the anaclitic (attachment) type:

    (*a*) the woman who feeds him,

    (*b*) the man who protects him,

and the succession of substitutes who take their place.

(1914, 90)

Freud's designation of the narcissistic versus the anaclitic is the founding narrative of homosexual versus heterosexual object-choice. However, as the work of Michael Warner and Gregory Bredbeck has emphasized, Freud offers no stable reason why heterosexual object-choice should be any less narcissistic than homosexual object-choice is (Warner 1990, 198), nor why homosexuality is not itself a cathexis on an other, anaclitic object (Bredbeck 1994, 64). Freud himself refuses to conclude that "human beings are divided into two sharply differentiated groups, according as their object-choice conforms to the anaclitic or to the narcissistic type; we assume rather that both kinds of object-choice are open to each individual, though he may show a preference for one or the other" (1914, 88). This is all very queer as far as it goes: Freud seems to set up an infinite range of possible desires that include the narcissistically heterosexual (the child who loves someone who was once part of himself) and the anaclitically homosexual (the male child who loves the man who protects him or more significantly the succession of substitutes who take the father's place). But Freud does not allow the free play of objects for too long; immediately after the catalog he writes that "[t]he significance of narcissistic object-choice for homosexuality in men must be considered in another connection," the connection he laid out four years earlier in the essay on da Vinci. By doubling back (narcissistically? anaclitically?) on his own work, Freud posits a homosexual difference within a theory that explicitly denies it and creates a category that "On Narcissism" has already explained away.

By returning to the 1910 essay on da Vinci, Freud can submit homosexuality to the laws of narrative that Gregory Bredbeck sees in late-nineteenth-century sexology (61). Freud's narrative of Leonardo looks back through three stages in the artist's psychic career. The latest and most manifest stage is Leonardo's production of art, which Freud reads as a *sublimation,* a culturally valued diversion from a sexual aim that is socially forbidden. That buried sexual aim Freud designates as homosexual, evidence for which he reads in both Leonardo's biography and his art. And at the heart of that homosexuality, says Freud, is Leonardo's relation to his mother. For Freud, this mother origin is crucial: by prioritizing the male child's emotional bond with the mother, he can claim to locate an origin for same-sex perversion, and at the same time he can mute the possibilities of anaclitic homosexuality (the father and his substitutes as objects for the male child) that he later opens up in "On Narcissism." The Leonardo essay provides what will become the capsule theory from "Group Psychology" that I quoted above and provides the privileged narrative of maternal cathexis from which "On Narcissism" seems to be a temporary aberration. Freud says:

> In all our male homosexual cases the subjects had had a very intense erotic attachment to a female person, as a rule their mother, during the first period of childhood, which is afterwards forgotten; this attachment was evoked or encouraged by too much tenderness on the part of the mother herself, and further reinforced by the small part played by the father during their childhood. (1910, 99)

Always already an anaclitic relationship dependent upon the presence of the mother, this primary bond then undergoes a transformation in the nascent homosexual male, a transformation "whose mechanism is known to us but whose motive forces we do not yet understand" (99–100):

> The child's love for his mother cannot continue to develop consciously any further; it succumbs to repression. The boy represses his love for his mother: he puts himself in her place, identifies himself with her, and takes his own person as a model in whose likeness he chooses the new objects of his love. In this way he has become a homosexual. (100)

What marks off this process of identification/desire from the heterosexual one where the boy identifies with the father and takes the mother (substitute) as desired object is precisely that, for Freud, it is not a *process* but a *recess,* a regression to autoerotism. The male child, he postulates, loves other males in the way his mother loved him and "finds the objects of his love along the path of *narcissism,* as we say; for Narcissus, according to the Greek legend, was a youth who preferred his own reflection to everything else" (100). A strange narcissism this, shot through with multiple anaclitic investments; yet it has provided the model for the twentieth-century gay male.

Among the curiosities in Freud's treatment of male narcissism is his claim not to understand the "motive forces" that effect the transformation from primary narcissism to identification with the mother and the replication of her desires. We know *what* happens, says Freud, but we don't know *why*. I find this claim curious because Freud seems to have spent much of the Leonardo essay prior to this moment explaining exactly why such a transformation should occur. Earlier in the essay, Freud runs up against the signifier of Leonardo's homosexual desire: the artist's "memory" of the vulture that put its tail into the infant Leonardo's mouth and repeatedly beat against his lips. Freud reads this fantasy of fellatio as "merely a reminiscence of sucking — or being suckled — at his mother's breast" (87). He chooses here to defer discussion of this equation until later in the essay — until the material in chapter 3 that I quoted above — in favor of discussing the mythological and psychological connection between the mother and the vulture.[2] But what is remarkable about the discussion of the myth is not how it postpones the discussion of homosexuality but rather how it answers the question Freud will later claim to be stymied by. Look at what Freud has to say about the mythological mother:

> Now this vulture-headed mother goddess was usually represented by the Egyptians with a phallus; her body was female, as the breasts indicated, but it also had a male organ in a state of erection.
>
> In the goddess Mut, then, we find the same combination of maternal and masculine characteristics as in Leonardo's phantasy of the vulture.... Mythology may then offer the explanation that the addition of a phallus to the female body is intended to denote the primal creative force of nature, and that all these hermaphrodite divinities [Mut, Isis, and Hathor in Egyptian mythology, Dionysus and Aphrodite in Greek] are expressions of the idea that only a combination of male and female elements can give a worthy representation of divine perfection. (94)

In the mythological framework, creativity in males does not depend on *sublimating* the desire for the phallus of another, as it does in Freud's discussion of Leonardo; rather, it makes phallic desire as crucial to creativity as is the desire for the mother. In other words, the male child's desire for another's phallus is not *secondary* to his identificatory/desiring processes but is actually *constitutive* of them.[3]

In his discussion of the Egyptian mother-vulture, Freud anaclitically relies on myth to deconstruct the centrality of the maternal nipple in the psychogenesis of male desire. He then makes his discussion more narcissistic, attaching it to his own theories of infantile sexuality. And what he finds through this attachment is itself a theory of homosexual narcissism. Alluding to his 1908 essay "The Sexual Theories of Children," Freud argues the following:

> When a male child first turns his curiosity to the riddles of sexual life, he is dominated by his interest in his own genital. He finds that part of his body too valuable and too important for him to be able to believe that it could be missing in other people whom he feels he resembles so much. As he cannot guess that there exists another type of genital structure of equal worth, he is forced to make the assumption that all human beings, women as well as men, possess a penis like his own. (95)

While this statement is perhaps Freud's most famous and lucid declaration of a phallocentric economy, he also uses it to open another kind of phallocentrism that has implications beyond the reign of masculine primacy and power. For Freud, this phallocentrism heralds the desire that makes men *seek* the phallus at the same time that they *possess* it:

> Before the child comes under the dominance of the castration-complex — at a time when he still holds women at full value [?] — he begins to display an intense desire to look, as an erotic instinctual activity. He wants to see other people's genitals, at first in all probability to compare them with his own. The erotic attraction that comes from his mother soon culminates in *a longing for her genital organ, which he takes to be a penis.* (96; emphasis added)

A metamorphosis: whereas Freud earlier postulated a phallic mother that could abstractly represent creativity, here he posits a mother's phallus that is at the heart of every male child's fantasy. And that phallus moreover is not an *anaclitic* attachment, a Freudian strap-on; rather, it is a *narcissistic* phantasmatic projection of the child's own penis. By this logic, then, male homosexuality is not a symptom for what is "really" a cathexis on the mother; rather, the cathexis on the mother and on her breast is, in Freud's treatment, secondary to the narcissistic investment in one's own penis. If the mother in fantasy is always a phallic mother, then that phallus can never be separated from the fantasies of returning to her — indeed, that phallus seems to predicate the desire to return to her. Thus does Freud provide a narrative trajectory that contradicts the other, major one structuring the essay: narcissistic homosexuality comes to occupy an original or at least coterminous place with the anaclitic and heteronormative; as in an allegedly sexless Neoplatonism that puts the erotic Narcissus squarely into the field of desire, narcissistic homosexuality in Freud is as much a progressive beginning as a regressive end.

But it is the mother-cathexis story, of course, that gets Leonardo to art: in Freud's analysis, the Mona Lisa and her famous smile become the perfect embodiment of the painter's fixation on his mother. Quoting Walter Pater's discussion of da Vinci from *Studies in the History of the Renaissance,* Freud notes that the maternal smile "plays over all Leonardo's work" (110; see also Pater 1873, 117). But if the Mona Lisa del Giocondo is merely an aesthetic translation of Caterina, Leonardo's mother, why then do we need the seemingly gratuitous narrative of homosexuality in Freud's analysis of Leonardo? What is served by homosexuality's being an intermediate point between mother and Mona Lisa? To extend the questions further: What effect does the primacy of an imaginary phallus/mother have on Freud's theory of sublimation? How does Narcissus's insistence that he love another man inform the Freudian etiology of artistic production? Perhaps no more than to lay bare some of the contradictions in the Freudian corpus on narcissism and its supposed connection to art (a connection, we have seen, that goes back at least as far as Plotinus). And those contradictions might include the following:

1. Narcissistic male homosexuality, as I've already argued, is supposed to be rooted in maternal cathexis, yet maternal cathexis itself appears to be predicated on a kind of homosexual male narcissism.

2. Sublimation of this homosexual desire renders Leonardo at some points completely free of neurosis-producing repressions (80) while at other points sublimation is evidence of neurotic repressions (131). Thus, sublimation is diagnosed on the assumption that its aim is "not sexual" (80), yet nothing in sublimation can guarantee the absence of a sexual content.

3. While Freud bases his entire theory of sublimation on Leonardo's rerouting of homosexual desire, he also opines that the original repression that produced sublimation was desire for the mother, suggesting that the homosexual desire itself was not that strong; thus, homosexuality comes to occupy the contradictory place of being a cause and an almost insignificant effect.

4. Freud treats the thesis of maternal investment with his characteristic tentativeness — "What is for practical reasons called homosexuality may arise from a whole variety of psychosexual inhibitory processes" (101) — yet this thesis ossifies into his standard account. It becomes the master narrative.

5. And, finally, homosexuality (with its narcissistic component) may have many "causes," but each is considered to be an "inhibitory process." This inhibitory process seems to produce only homosexuality, a claim the rest of the Leonardo essay attacks.

Indeed, it seems that the inhibiting of homosexuality itself comes to constitute sublimation, but not as a tertiary mechanism for protecting heterosexuality; rather, homosexual inhibition comes to constitute the sublime normalcy of heterosexuality itself.

Such a rich and contradictory terrain provides the space within which later authors can think about artistic production. Two such authors, whose debts to Freud's essay on Leonardo I hope to make clear, are Hermann Hesse and Tennessee Williams. Now it may seem ludicrous to talk about these two men in the same breath: a heterosexual German novelist whose works explore the philosophical intersections between Eastern Buddhism and Western Christianity, and an American playwright, separated from Hesse by decades, whose plays and short stories document the collapse of southern gentility with almost hopeless gloominess. However, both Hesse and Williams found psychoanalysis useful for uncovering unconscious impulses that they could then inscribe in their work; both underwent psychoanalysis after the deaths of their fathers; both ultimately rejected the therapy as limited and distorting; and most important, both explore the complex and slippery relation between the mother, the son, and the creative process. In this exploration I will want to suggest that both Hesse and Williams foreground the problem of sublimation in the creative process; both deploy queer narcissistic masculinity to highlight the problems of the Freudian narrative; and both interrogate the elusive connections between art, mothers, and homosexual desire.

Birds

A narcissist:

> *It seems that I was always destined to be so deeply concerned with vultures; for I recall as one of my very earliest memories that while I was in my cradle a vulture came down to me, and opened my mouth with its tail, and struck me many times with its tail against my lips.*
> — LEONARDO AS QUOTED IN FREUD, "Leonardo da Vinci"

An echo:

> *One day I saw [Demian] standing there, notebook in hand, sketching. He was drawing the old coat-of-arms with the bird above our front entrance....*
>
> *That night I dreamed of Demian and the coat-of-arms. It kept changing. Demian held it in his hands; sometimes it was small and grey, sometimes large and multicoloured, but he explained to me that it was always the same bird. Finally, however, he ordered me to eat*

the coat-of-arms. When I had swallowed it, I realized in a terrible panic that the heraldic bird I had swallowed was inside me, swelling out and was beginning to devour me from within. Full of a deadly fear, I awoke with a start. — HESSE, *Demian*

Mother always told me never to put dirty things in my mouth, and it is perhaps the force of this injunction in the lives of nascent gay boys that explains the two quotations above and my fascination with them. Both deal with birds, a signifier whose connotations range from the female (in British slang) to the phallic (in Freud's explication of the fantasy).[4] Both deal with orality (eating and a fantasy of flying are two of my great fixations). And both, quite predictably, deal with queerness. In Freud's analysis of Leonardo's childhood memory, the bird's tail is a screen for the mother's breast, a breast upon which the child cathected for too long, and which then transforms itself into the penis that the homosexual Leonardo will desire, even if he doesn't act on that desire. And while the case of Emil Sinclair in Hesse's *Demian* (1969) is, as I will demonstrate, a lot less clear, the bird he associates with Max Demian conflates homoerotic desire, figurations of the mother, and the production of art. Like Freud, of whom Hesse was a great fan, the novelist sees in psychoanalysis the possibility of liberating and exploring all desires, no matter how socially forbidden.

Demian's debt to Freud, though, is not simply its celebration of uncovering the hidden; *Demian* explicitly employs Freud's exploration of the relation of the artist to the mother from "Leonardo." Like "Leonardo," *Demian* is a narrative of the maternal; it locates the elusive, abjected, yet omnipresent mother at the heart of artistic creativity. In "Leonardo," that mother is the too-attentive yet soon-to-be-banished Caterina who inaugurated in the infant a desire for the breast that he spends his artistic life trying to recover; and Freud's analysis "confirms" his "suspicion that the smile of Mona Lisa del Giocondo had awakened in [Leonardo] as a grown man the memory of the mother of his earliest childhood" (1910, 114). Prior to del Giocondo herself, prior to the homosexual desire that Freud says da Vinci felt without enacting, is a mother whose presence generates art. As she does in Hesse's Sinclair. Sinclair's narrative, like Leonardo's, is a coming-of-age story in which the boy searches for the symbol of individual wholeness, completion, self-sufficiency. This Sinclair finds in the figure of Frau Eva, Demian's mother: "Whatever might happen to me, I was blessed in my knowledge that this woman was in the world, that I could drink in her voice and breathe her presence. If she could only become a mother to me, a lover, a goddess" (132). This goddess, this "universal mother" (135), pacifies the fear generated by the coat-of-arms dream, the fear that the bird may tear him to pieces. As Sinclair enters her house for the first time, he notices a sketch of the bird that he had made and sent to Demian, "a bird of prey with a narrow and cruel sparrow-hawk head" (84), fighting to get out of its eggshell. This bird, clearly, is Eva: "With eyes moistened with tears I gazed at my painting, absorbed in my reflections. Then my glance dropped. Under the picture of the bird in the opened door stood a tall woman in a dark dress. It was she.... Her gaze was fulfilment, her greeting a homecoming" (131).

This sense of closure and fulfillment as represented by the mother is germane to Hesse's project in a number of novels. The mother-bird is "cruel" and hawk-like because she is meant to suggest the worldly, the sensual, the carnal.[5] In this sense, she is the necessary counterpoint, the Jungian anima, to balance Hesse's overly thoughtful, abstract, intellectual males: Sinclair, Haller in *Steppenwolf* (1990), Goldmund in *Narziss and Goldmund* (1971). Thus, Hesse's novels read a bit like Nathaniel Hawthorne's: they employ curiously realistic figures and settings to enact what often feels like allegory. This allegory (often tiresomely repeated in each novel) usually follows a Jungian paradigm and is ultimately about the unification of the fragmented self. Frau Eva, a variant of Mother Earth, spans the register from sexual knowledge to world war, but her range of significances is merely a convenient backdrop for the artist's exploration of self:

> My love for Eva seemed to me to fill my whole life. But every day she looked different. On many occasions I believed that it was not really just her as a person, whom I yearned for with all my being, but that she existed as an outward symbol of my inner self and her sole purpose was to lead me more deeply into myself. Things she said often sounded like replies from my unconscious mind to burning questions which tormented me. (1969, 141)

If Coleridge's transcendental Romanticism felt trapped by narcissism, Hesse's Jungian[6] psychomachia dines out on it. And this use of the mother to heal fragmentation — this use of the mother as narcissistic reflection — strikes a biographical chord in Hesse too suggestive to be ignored. Five weeks after a young Hesse wrote to his father from school to tell him that he had ruined the young scholar's life,[7] Hesse had this to say to his mother: "Poor Mother, forgive me, forgive your fallen son; forgive me, if you love me, if you believe there's a divine spark in me yet.... I'm just a miserable being who rails against man and fate and cannot and will not ever love himself" (1991, 12). Cannot and will not love himself, unless he returns to mother:

Walking along the great, flowing Rhine, I have often imagined how wonderful it would be to perish in these dear, familiar waves. My life and my sins would vanish into oblivion. But best of mothers, I can still find some respite, a haven, in your heart. If anybody understands me, it is you. You are the only person who knows that I, too, am capable of love. (1991, 13)

Here Narcissus, who psychoanalysts like Otto Rank are sure is wracked by self-loathing, is compelled to by-pass his own reflection in the waters and seek Liriope, for it is only she who can hold him together, affirm his worth, offer him love.

But such a mother may be too easily vacuated of her actual psychological importance; like the figure of Narcissus in Neoplatonism, Hesse's Jungian "mother" can readily become a Symbol, a mother who is not one, a metonym encompassing eros, carnality, and death, instead of a metaphor for the actual mother in the artist's life. Such an implicit triumph of Jungian archetypalism over Freudian psychodynamic conflict cannot be sustained by Hesse's later writing. For while *Demian* is the product of a useful psychoanalysis with Jung's student Josef Lang, Hesse was always ambivalent about Jung's approach: "I have always respected Jung," he once wrote, "nevertheless have never been as impressed by his writings as by Freud's" (quoted in Mileck 1978, 104). This resistance to the Jungian archetype suggests that the Freudian "real" mother should be more important than the symbolic one, a suggestion that frames Goldmund's experience in the 1930 *Narziss and Goldmund.* Having come to the monastery at Mariabronn as a child, Goldmund has forgotten his mother, who died when he was very young. The novel turns on Narziss's command to Goldmund that he remember her and that he live the full, sensual life that he was meant to live, a life symbolized by her. Thus, as in *Demian,* the mother comes to symbolize carnality, desire, and gusto, as well as the abstract principle of wholeness and unity. After much indulgence in the pleasures of the flesh, Goldmund becomes an artist, a sculptor, and longs to carve "the face of a mother" that haunts him (Hesse 1971, 158). Significantly, though, "[i]t was no longer his own dead mother that he saw, since her colouring and features, by degrees, were lost in an impersonal mother-image, a vision of Eve the mother of all mankind" (158). However, when poverty and illness reduce Goldmund to a stark confrontation with his own soul, the mother is not so symbolic or abstract: as he cries out "mother! Oh mother!" "[a]n image answered this magic name as he said it, her shape, from the secrecy of his heart. Not the mother he had longed to carve in wood, the Eve of his craftsman's thoughts and dreams, but the very mother he remembered, clearer and more living than he had seen her since the dream he had had of her in Mariabronn" (245–46).[8] Here Hesse moves out (comes out?) of the Jungian analysis and replaces the archetypal with the biological — though intensely metaphorical — mother. Like Freud's Leonardo, Hesse's hero is intensely cathected on a corporeally embodied, desiring maternal figure.

I have dwelt on the embodiment of the mother here not merely to stake out my position on the long-standing debate in Hesse criticism about the primacy of Freud or Jung in his work, but to suggest that we can return to Freud's essay on Leonardo — his text on mother-lovers cum artists — to understand more fully what is going on in the male-male relations in Hesse's novels. As I argued earlier in this chapter, the concept of sublimation provides a rich field for thinking about the Freudian artist and his libidinal investments. So too is it rich for Hesse, for artistic production in *Demian* is a sublimation of erotic desire. As Demian leads Sinclair to an awareness of his own "heterosexual" erotic impulses, Sinclair meets a young woman whom he calls "Beatrice." Modeled less on the virginal inspiration of Dante's vision (Emil tells us he's never read Dante) and more on Rossetti's voluptuous painting, Beatrice nevertheless becomes an "ideal" (Hesse 1969, 75) for Sinclair, an "honoured image" (75):

> once more I lived for the sole aim of getting rid of the darkness and evil within me and regaining the world of light, on my knees before God. . . . The sexuality which was a torment from which I was continually in flight was now transfigured into spirituality and devotion in this holy fire. There would be no more darkness, nothing hateful, no more tortured nights, no excitement in front of lascivious pictures, no eavesdropping at forbidden doors, no lewdness. In place of all of this I raised my altar to Beatrice. . . . My goal became purity, not pleasure; happiness was replaced by beauty and spirituality. (76)

And beauty and spirituality seek appropriate expression: "Of all the new practices in which I sought to express my new mood, one had become all-important. I began to paint" (76). From a Jungian perspective, anima and animus come together in a wholeness and harmony that produces creative expression. Desire gets displaced into idealism, and the whole thing is then sublimated into art. However, the clearly narcissistic focus of this relationship raises other questions about gender and desire. Freudians, start your engines.

While Freud's analysis of Leonardo suggests that art was for the master a sublimation of homosexual desire (a desire Freud paradoxically suggests Leonardo was not all that enflamed by), he also makes clear the degree to which that desire, rooted in the mother, manifests itself in art: the outlines of the vulture that Oskar Pfister discovered in the *St. Anne with Two Others* portrait in the Louvre marks for Freud the degree to which Leonardo equated mothers with vultures (see the footnote added in 1919 to the "Leonardo" essay, 115–16). But given that the portrait is already about mothering, should we be so shocked by the connection to the mother? Moreover, given that, in the earlier part of the essay, Freud discussed the imaginary vulture as a maternal figure with an enormous phallus, does this not make the portrait at least partially about the homoeros that seems to have blended into Leonardo's psychic configurations? Analysts of Emil Sinclair certainly might think so. When Sinclair finally produces his portrait, he realizes: "It was not the face of the girl; it had long ceased to be that but something quite different, unreal, yet it meant just as much to me. It looked more like a boy's head than a girl's" (Hesse 1969, 77). Now, this should not surprise Emil: one of the first things he noticed about Beatrice was that she had "a boyish face, . . . a touch of exuberant boyishness in her face which made a particular appeal to me" (75). Nor does it surprise the reader to learn a few pages later that, while the portrait "looked so fantastically familiar" to Emil and indeed "appeared to know me as a mother" (78), it is actually Demian's face (79). If Sinclair, like Leonardo, has sublimated his desires into art, then what Emil's art, like Leonardo's, betrays is a primacy of the homoerotic that sublimation has both repudiated and fortified. And Hesse makes this logic clear as Sinclair continues to stare at the portrait. In an echo of Dorian Gray, Sinclair tells us: "gradually a feeling came over me that it was neither Beatrice nor Demian but myself. Not that the picture was like me — I did not feel it should be — but the face somehow expressed my life, it was my inner self, my fate or my daimon" (79). My daimon? My Demian? The logic of justification is fascinating here. Sinclair was never painting the ostensible object of his desires (Beatrice); Leonardo, conversely, was never painting anything but the object of his desires (his mother). But if Leonardo's desires took a wrong turn through homosexuality to get back to the mother, Sinclair detours through heterosexuality only to get back to a narcissistic reflection that is a reflection not of himself — "the picture was [not] like me" — but of his erotic object, Max Demian. The face is Sinclair's only to the degree that it is his lover's, and the scene comes to read more like *Teleny*'s queer pornography than like a spiritual meditation. The erotic male may have been a way station on Leonardo's libidinal highway, but in Sinclair's it is the endpoint.

In Freud's analysis of Leonardo, we can plot a chronology backward from art through homoerotic desire to the maternal; Leonardo's images document this layering, as the vulture = the penis = the maternal breast. This definition of homosexual narcissism ultimately reifies the heterosexual model of object cathexis (son-mother) in what purports to explain same-sex narcissistic object-choice, a reification that Michael Warner and Gregory Bredbeck read elsewhere in Freud. Hesse's treatment of the problem takes the complications one step further. In one way, the Hessean hero's quest, as I have already noted, is to return to the mother as the ultimate site of object-relations and the appropriate marker of heterosexed desire: Sinclair passionately longs to take Frau Eva as his lover. This, I have been arguing, is the Freudian psychomachia: I love me in her — I love her — I love those like her. But in another way, the "mother" to whom the hero wants to return is emptied out into a philosophically abstract symbol whose erotic content is more medieval than Freudian and that makes the quest more narcissistic than anaclitic. This is the Jungian influence: I love her — I love her in me — I love what is most fully realized and complete in me. What Hesse does in effect is to render undecidable whether the anaclitic or the narcissistic is to be privileged in the psychogenesis of subjectivity. The narcissistic can be deployed in service to the anaclitic (as Bredbeck says happens in Freud), but the anaclitic and its supposed normative proprieties can as easily be marshaled to service the narcissistic. If there is in the end an ethical or normative content to anaclitic and narcissistic libidinal investments, Hesse refuses to adhere to it.

Which is not to say that the Hessean artist cannot learn to love in any satisfactory or "healthy" way. Quite the contrary. If narcissistic desire is fundamentally same-sexed, and if anaclitic object-investments (even investments in the "other" gender) are ultimately inaugurated to fulfill the narcissistic, then male homosexuality comes to occupy a privileged position in Hesse's philosophical program. What Freud sublimates Hesse celebrates in the character of Max Demian. Sinclair first finds Demian noteworthy because of his *differences:* as the new boy in school, Demian "did not attract me; I was conscious, on the contrary, of a certain antipathy between us; he was too self-possessed and cool" (27). However, after Demian rescues Sinclair from the school bully, Emil begins to feel an attraction for him, one that he fears may surpass his love of his parents and to which Emil responds with a defensive regression: "I retreated to my mother's lap and the security of a pious and hedged-in childhood, without so much as a glance at the world outside. I made myself into someone younger, more dependent and childish than I was. . . . If I had not followed this course, I would have had to stick to Demian and confide in him" (44–45). Hesse's intervention into the psychoanalytic narrative here is devastating: whereas Freud and company would consider homosexuality as a regression to the maternal as a way of avoiding relations with the other, Hesse makes homoerotic desire — desire for another male — that from which the narcissist retreats. Mother is not the cause of queerness in Emil; she is the temporary refuge from it.

And the refuge *is* temporary. Only a few pages later, Emil and Demian come upon a dying horse in the street:

> As I turned away with a feeling of nausea, I noticed Demian's expression. . . . His glance seemed directed at the horse's head, and again it showed that deep, quiet, almost fanatical yet passionate absorption. I could not help staring at him for some moments and it was then that I felt aware of a very uncanny sensation in my remote consciousness. I saw Demian's face and remarked that it was not a boy's face but a man's and then I saw, or rather became aware, that it was not really the face of a man either; it had something different about it, almost a feminine element. And for the time being his face seemed neither masculine nor childish, neither old nor young but a hundred years old, almost timeless and bearing the mark of other periods of history than our own. . . . Perhaps he was handsome, perhaps I found him attractive, perhaps he repelled me too, I could not even be sure of that. All I saw was that he was different from the rest of us, that he was like an animal, a spirit or an image. (49)

A scene worthy of D. H. Lawrence at his most phallo-philic, this moment utilizes the masculine horse to frame an anaclitic moment that is also tremendously homoerotic; from this moment, Demian will be at the heart of Sinclair's desirous identifications throughout the novel. Demian becomes a constant insertion, a median in Sinclair's heterosexual investments: his is the face upon which Sinclair models his attraction for Beatrice, and he is the force of desire that leads Sinclair to the ostensibly heterosexual longing for Frau Eva at the end. (Indeed, at one point Sinclair notes dispassionately that Demian "was suspected of being his mother's lover" [50].) If the Freudian trajectory ultimately gets us beyond the narcissistic-homoerotic to the anaclitic mother, the Hessean narrative gets us beyond the narcissistic-anaclitic mother to the narcissistic-anaclitic male lover. *Demian* ends with a Walt Whitmanesque scene in a battle camp and a wounded Sinclair being visited by a (visionary?) Demian. With "lips . . . quite close to mine," Demian brings Sinclair a message from the maternal:

> "Frau Eva said that if things ever went badly with you, I was to pass on a kiss from her which she gave me. . . . Close your eyes, Sinclair."

> I closed my eyes in obedience. I felt the brush of a kiss on my lips on which there was a bead of blood that never seemed to diminish. Then I fell asleep. (155)

What began in Freud with a vulture beating the lips ends in Hesse with a light, teasing, yet passionate kiss. And what gets pathologized in Freud as a narcissism that must be sublimated in the m/other is, in Hesse, the triumph of narcissistic homosexuality. The novel closes with these words:

> when on the many such occasions I find the key and look deep down into myself where the images of destiny lie slumbering in the dark mirror, I only need to bend my head over the black mirror to see my own image which now wholly resembles him, my friend and leader. (155)

Heterosex in this novel is homo in the way Coleridge may have feared and Wilde suspected, but the homosexed is hetero in a way that perhaps neither could have imagined.

Johns

In 1918, one year before the publication of *Demian*, Hermann Hesse jubilantly declared that he had read Freud, Jung, and others

> with the liveliest sympathy and found in general that their conception of psychic events confirmed almost all my own surmises based on the poets and on my own observations. I saw explicitly formulated what already in part belonged to me as unconscious knowledge derived from presentiment and fleeting insight. (1974, 47)

For the young writer psychoanalysis could do three things: (1) it could legitimate fantasy and fiction, rescuing them from the demands of bourgeois practicality; (2) it could offer the artist a deeper insight into what has been buried in his own unconscious; and (3) it could help to liberate the truth of existence, thus fulfilling an ethical imperative of liberation (48–49). However, by 1928, two years before *Narziss and Goldmund,* his enthusiasm had waned. He wrote to Theodore Schnittkin on 3 June:

> Psychoanalysis is quite problematic. In theory, the method — that is, the simplified categories which Freud uses to depict psychic mechanisms and also the Jungian mythology and typological classifications — ought to help identify psychic phenomena. But in practice the situation is very different. Of the half dozen psychoanalysts I have known, not one would, for example, be capable of noticing any positive or worthwhile qualities in a person such as myself or, let's say, a poet like Rilke, if we hadn't received any public recognition! (1991, 145)

As we saw earlier, Hesse always preferred Freud to Jung, but here he is ready to jettison them both. Indeed, as he writes in the same letter, "the shallow and absolutely bourgeois-modern attitude of psychoanalysis (including Freud's) precludes any understanding or assessment of creativity. That is why the voluminous psychoanalytic literature about artists hasn't yielded anything worthwhile" (145).

Hesse's dismissal of the Freudian enterprise has the slight odor of bad faith, given that the relation of the artist to the mother is such a strong theme in both Hesse and Freud. But it is an odor we could have smelled earlier: in *Demian,* Sinclair temporarily befriends an organist named Pistorius, who is actually a stand-in for Hesse's Jungian analyst, Josef Lang. At first, Sinclair's relation to Pistorius is quite fruitful: he finds in the organist's music "a peculiar and extremely individual expressiveness of will and determination" (Hesse 1969, 93), and he learns to accept his own penchant for the "irrational forms in nature" that "produce[] in us a sense of the harmony of our inner being" (99). (Many years later, he tells us significantly, "I found this view recorded in a book by Leonardo da Vinci" [99].) Pistorius's views, Sinclair says, "helped to shape me, to peel off my layers of skin, break the egg-shells, and as I emerged from each stage I raised my head a little higher with a greater feeling of freedom until my yellow bird pushed his handsome predatory head out of the shattered shell of the terrestrial globe" (101). However, their discussions are not completely candid; Sinclair has one recurrent dream that "I could never bring myself to recount...to my friend":

> I was always dreaming that I was entering our old house under the heraldic bird; I advanced to embrace my mother but she would turn out to be the large, half-male, half-maternal woman who filled me with awe and for whom I felt the most violent attraction. (104)

Presumably, there is something in the nature of the dream that keeps Sinclair from sharing it; or, conversely, there is something in the Jungian system that Sinclair sees as being hostile to the dream. It is the purpose of the rest of the scene to figure out what that something is.

Sinclair eventually separates from Pistorius, ostensibly because "I found too much didacticism in his words; I felt that he only fully understood one part of me" (116). Pistorius operates in the realm of the abstract, the antiquarian, the mythic, whereas Sinclair is interested in the personal, the individual (and remember how the later Goldmund will abandon the search for the Universal Mother in preference for his own biological mother). Finally, says Sinclair, "I felt a repugnance against the whole business, this cult of mythologies" (117).

Jungian symbolism is thrown over here for Freudian particularity. But there is more going on here than a mere statement of ideological preferences. Pistorius gradually comes to meld with Demian in Sinclair's imagination: Emil can no longer remember whether certain wisdoms came originally from the organist or from Max, and he gradually finds both Pistorius and Demian at his spiritual core. This masculine replication is of course essential to Hesse's program: the analyst, like the Jungian shadow Demian, comes to represent the element of one's own personality that one must accept and heed; both figures are part of his "enhanced version of myself" (115). But in another way, this replication gestures to the play with homosexuality that I have been tracing in Hesse. The mental picture of Pistorius that Sinclair develops, which is also the picture of Demian, soon turns into "the painted picture, the half male, half female fantasy of my daimon" (114). And if Demian is as much queer lover (the phallus of the phallic mother) as he is symbolic counterpart, then we see what is involved in the giving up of Pistorius/Lang. As A. W. Brink argues in an article on *Steppenwolf,* "Jungian mythological archetypalism allows Hesse to avoid the aetiological issue to which Freud's understanding of latent homosexuality gave at least some guidance" (1974, 75). Pistorius/ Lang is rejected not because Sinclair has a reluctant sexual attraction to him but because the analyst's philosophical views refuse to address seriously or intelligently the significance of that desire. For Jung, the shadow or imago (Demian) is the image of an ideal self to be pursued, whereas for Freud such ego idealism can actually result in homosexual identity formation (Freud 1914, 93–94). For Hesse, homosexuality is as crucial to the development of the artist's whole personality as is the disembodied abstractness of ideas and the heteronormative search for the mother.[9]

Thus a kind of compulsory (homo)sexuality drives Hesse's representation not only of the "whole" and "harmonious" humanist subject but also of the very concept of sublimation as German psychologism thought it related to art. In other words, Hesse relies on homosexual desire as *the* great "forbidden" to pit Freud and Jung against each other and to fashion his own theory of sublimation. According to Jung, Freud's theory of sublimation is nothing more than "the alchemist's trick of turning the base into the noble, the bad into the good, the useless into the useful" (1966, 37), and the work of art in Freudian thought is nothing more than a catalog of the artist's neuroses (100). This much Hesse agreed with: as he told Jung in a letter of September 1934, Freudian psychoanalysis is "difficult and dangerous" for artists, and "Those who take it seriously might easily have to refrain from all artistic creativity for the rest of their lives" (1991, 187). But Hesse found Jung's view of artistic creativity hardly more palatable than Freud's, and precisely because it negated the concept of sublimation. For Jung,

> The essence of a work of art is not to be found in the idiosyncrasies that creep into it — indeed, the more there are of them, the less it is a work of art — but in rising above the personal and speaking from the mind and heart of the artist to the mind and heart of mankind. The personal aspect of art is a limitation and even a vice, . . . [and the artist] is neither autoerotic, nor heteroerotic, nor erotic in any sense. He is in the highest degree objective, impersonal, and even inhuman. . . . The artist is not a person endowed with free will who seeks his own ends, but one who allows art to realize its purpose through him. (101)

Neither autoerotic (Freud's narcissistic homosexual) nor heteroerotic (Freud's anaclitic straight man), the Jungian artist is a conduit for the *collective* unconscious, the universalizing system of archetypes that has nothing to do with sublimating the personal. And it is this universalizing with which Hesse takes issue in the now-famous interchange with Jung. In his 1934 review of Jung, he claimed an important place for sublimation in the production of art, and in the same letter to Jung I quoted above, he argued that great art is the product of "expression and discipline, in which the entire groups and even generations of masters have — for the most part completely unwittingly — transferred their drives to an arena that, by virtue of those genuine sacrifices, achieves a degree of perfection" (1991, 186). Artists, he says, "practice a genuine form of *sublimatio,* not out of assertiveness and ambition, but in a purely graceful way" (187). Not only a "victim" of his psyche but also its "servant" (187), the artist's sublimation appears less as a vulture than as a dove, a divine expression of personal energies.

It is precisely the degree to which those sublimated/sublime energies are homoerotic that is the subject of Hesse's 1930 novel, *Narziss and Goldmund,* a novel whose queer longings it would take a heart of stone to read without noticing. The story (yet again) of two men who are opposite in temperament yet whose very opposition keeps them spiritually bonded, the novel charts the gradual recognition in both the main characters that the other is a necessary complement to the self each is searching for. Goldmund, whose carnal experiences and erotic desires dominate the novel, needs to return at the end to the monastery at Mariabronn (a combination of Maulbronn, Hesse's first boarding school, and Maria, the name of his mother) and to the ascetic Narziss, whose idealism and discipline provide for Goldmund the harmonizing structure for his libidinal urges: and, as I shall discuss momentarily, it is through Narziss that Goldmund comes to "sublimate" his desires into art. Narziss, conversely, is the intellectual monk who sees in Goldmund the carnal sensuality that he, Narziss, does not enact (shades of Leonardo?). But contrary to critical commonplaces about Narziss, he *feels* this attraction intensely. His religious devotion is not a sublimation of homosexual desire; it is instead founded upon it. He tells Goldmund:

> Men of dreams, the lovers and the poets, are better in most things than the men of my sort; the men of intellect. You take your being from your mothers. You live to the full: it is given to you to love with your whole strength, to know and taste the whole of life. We thinkers, though often we seem to rule you, cannot live with half your joy and full reality.... Your home is the earth, ours the idea of it. Your danger is to be drowned in the world of sense, ours to gasp for breath in airless space. You are a poet, I a thinker. You sleep on your mother's breast, I watch in the wilderness.... Your dreams are all of girls, mine of boys — . (46)

In Narziss, Hesse portrays with startling candor what may have been allegorically abstracted in *Demian:* the primacy of the homoerotic in the complete soul. And if the ostensibly (indeed ostentatiously) "straight" hero in Hesse needs to find his ascetic male half, then the ascetic hero in Hesse needs to desire the erotic, carnal male as *his* other half; he must not only identify with male desire but also desire it and desire the person who embodies it. About such homosexuality Hesse was clear. He wrote of the novel:

> That these friendships, because they exist between men, are completely free of eroticism is an error. I am sexually "normal" and have never had physical sexual relations with men, but to consider friendship on that account to be completely unerotic seems to me absolutely false. (Quoted in G. W. Field 1970, 115)

Thus Narziss — the figure of Narcissus — performs an intellectual devotion that *sublimates,* but does so knowingly, non-neurotically, "gracefully," to use Hesse's word. Moreover, he does so in a way that has nothing to do with mothers: Narziss neither has a mother nor wants one. This homosexual is *not* seeking the mirror replication of his mother's desire for him; rather, he has a "strange hankering after differences" (42), differences that constitute in Narziss/Narcissus an anaclitic desire for (the desire of) another man.

And what of Goldmund, the character who vacillates between rampant sexuality and ponderous artistic creation? Can he be said to sublimate anything? Doesn't he consciously indulge all desires as a way of tasting life fully? Or is his obsessive heterosexuality itself a sublimation of the homoeroticism that seems to structure all sexual desire? After all, Goldmund's early and intense friendship with Narziss became subject to public disapproval and policing, as the "evil-tongued" of the monastery, "those who had themselves loved one of the friends, slandered it as a vice against nature" (35). But in Goldmund, Hesse is less interested in exploring an "unconscious" wish that we can smugly diagnose than he is in exploring the *aesthetic* implications of the heterosexual's omnipresent phallic desire: throughout his travels, Goldmund is visited by the image of Narziss, the figure who gets equated with the mother in Goldmund's imaginary (113) and in his dreams (117). Indeed, Goldmund never forgets that it was Narziss who first inspired him to seek his mother; as he tells his friend, "you raised her up, and gave her back to me" (299). In Goldmund, Hesse brings to completion the phenomenon I traced in Freud: Narziss is the homoerotic phallus that complements the mother; he is, if not the origin, then at least the co-genesis of both erotism and creativity in the novel. As Hesse tells us, Goldmund's diligence as an artist

> had all been nothing save the deep longing to satisfy Narziss, whose esteem, he felt, was only to be gained by grateful industry. Then he would toil for days and hours together to earn one smile of recognition, and this, when it came, had been ample recompense. (155)

Nor does Goldmund repress/sublimate such knowledge. As he tells Narziss at the end of the novel, "Now I see that I was really as I thought, and indeed I know that you love me. I have always loved you, Narziss. Half my life has been a striving to gain your love" (296). But more than just a queer lover, Goldmund is Hesse's attack on a psychoanalytic enterprise unable to think about sublimation in terms that Hesse can stomach: he is the humanistic refusal of Freud's two assumptions: (1) that (queer) art evolves from potentially neurotic anxiety, and (2) that libido gets hydraulically redirected from boys into art — and of Jung's notion that art should not be erotic at all. Goldmund celebrates homoeros by affirming Hessean "sublimation" for artistic deployment.

And with this refashioning of sublimation, Hesse brings into the twentieth century the kind of dynamics we saw operating in nineteenth-century Neoplatonism; like Coleridge, Gide, and Wilde, Hesse meditates on the function of the image and uses it to construct a queer aesthetic. As we remember, Freud argued that sexuality is born of the child's "intense desire to look" (1910, 96); the image of the present/absent phallus is that which drives him into relations (sexual or verbal/artistic) with the other. In *Narziss and Goldmund,* the image holds a similarly overdetermined status. As a developing artist, Goldmund seeks "[t]hat first, quiet, happy gentle love with which, rejoicing in his discipleship, he had given his whole being to Narziss, [and which] returned to him again, with Narziss' image" (160). This image Goldmund carves as the face of John the beloved disciple, his first major artistic accomplishment — a John whom Christ loved and who lay on Christ's bosom (see John 13:23); a John whom Christopher Marlowe declared the bedfellow of Christ and who has functioned in queer iconography as a heroic figure; a John who, in late medieval German sculpture, was set off with Christ from the rest of the disciples, suggesting dyadic completion and complementarity as well as privacy (Dynes 1990, 125); a John whose name surely conjures that of Hesse's own estranged and desired father, Johannes. And this queer John has the same intersubjective, homoerotic resonances we saw in Byron's poems to Edleston, for at the end of the novel Narziss tells Goldmund that he took the name of John when he was consecrated (250), a nomenclature that Goldmund connects to his own artistic/ narcissistic creation of Narziss (253). This dizzying vortex of Johns, this liquid exchange of image with eros and art, is simultaneously the register of subjective completion and of personal fragmentation; the image is what is split off from the self at the same time that it guarantees completion (as Buddhist humanism meets Jacques Lacan's mirror stage); the image is an extension of one's own self, one's energies and talents, as well as the signifier of the other, the erotic object, the homosexual counterpart. In his redeployment of image, then, Hesse combines two different definitions of sublimation: one is a *process,* a transformation or submission to difference, and the other is a distillation, an expression of perfection and completion. *Narziss and Goldmund* is queer not because men go to bed (although Narziss clearly wants to) but because it enacts a definition of image that is at the same time narcissistic and anaclitically homoerotic.

As Hesse reclaims from Freud and Jung the idea that sublimation can bring out the best in an artist, he uses psychoanalysis against itself to affirm an optimistic, humanistic definition of the artist. Moreover, he shares this artistic optimism with Tennessee Williams. In 1958, Williams said:

> If . . . writing is honest it cannot be separated from the man who wrote it. It isn't so much his mirror as it is the distillation, the essence, of what is strongest and purest in his nature, whether that be gentleness or anger,

serenity or torment, light or dark. This makes it deeper than the surface likeness of a mirror and that much more truthful. (1978, 100)

And the Hessean echoes do not end there: in 1958, the same year that Williams produced this alchemical definition of art, he also produced *Suddenly Last Summer* (1958b), a story, like Hesse's, about the relation of an artist to his powerful mother, a story of homoeroticism, a story of self-knowledge. But whereas the Hessean artist painfully breaks through the shell of his consciousness to emerge into a harmonious being, the Williams artist is painfully broken, killed and dismembered on a foreign beach, absent before the play even opens. In what sense, then, can we read *Suddenly Last Summer* as a "distillation," as the expression of the "strongest and purist" in the artist's nature? What kind of sublimation does Sebastian Venable, that mother's queer son, that artist, draw out in the play? What kind of psychic terrain is depicted in the pages of the play?

Birds and Johns

A narcissist:

> *It seems that I was always destined to be so deeply concerned with vultures; for I recall as one of my very earliest memories that while I was in my cradle a vulture came down to me, and opened my mouth with its tail, and struck me many times with its tail against my lips.*
> — LEONARDO AS QUOTED IN FREUD, "Leonardo da Vinci"

An echo:

> *To escape the flesh-eating birds that made the sky almost as black as the beach!... And the sand all alive, all alive, as the hatched sea-turtles made their dash for the sea, while the birds hovered and swooped to attack and hovered and — swooped to attack! They were diving down on the hatched sea-turtles, turning them over to expose their soft undersides, tearing the undersides open and rending and eating their flesh.*
> — TENNESSEE WILLIAMS, *Suddenly Last Summer*

In Freud's analysis of Leonardo da Vinci, the vulture is an over-determined signifier: it represents the phallus in homosexual fantasy; it represents the maternal nipple in archaic primary narcissism; and its mythological resonances suggest an even more primal fantasy of wholeness, the healing of gender division. Thanks to these multiple resonances, Freud can use the predatory vulture in a distinctly salvational way. By placing homosexuality as the middle point in a tripartite movement from the maternal nipple to artistic production,

Freud can simultaneously read *backward* from homosexuality (the vulture's tail as phallus) to the heterosexual cathexis on the maternal nipple and *forward* to sublimation, the socially valued production of art. For Freud, the vulture's overdetermination allows it to be inscribed in two socially palatable narratives, two that become one to the degree that they write out/write off homosexual desire. And in a curious way, Hesse does much the same thing. The multiple significance of his bird of prey (mother, male lover, sex, war, death, . . . self) provides the elements necessary for his humanist pluralism: only because the elements are initially discordant can they be brought together, harmonized, subjected to the totality of Hesse's magnificent "soul." As in Freud, Hesse's narcissism both depends upon anaclitic investments in otherness and then leads to other anaclitic investments: in Hesse's case, the philosophy of the total self.

But what if we reclaim Narcissus from the compulsory and compulsively anaclitic? What kind of reading does the vulture give us if Narcissus sees in it nothing but his own reflection? For Tennessee Williams's Sebastian Venable, the vulture may provide another "salvational" chain of associations. In my second epigraph above, the vultures constitute a narcissistically self-condemning trope for Sebastian's — and Williams's own — practice of buying sex on foreign beaches. Like Williams himself, Sebastian "talked about people, as if they were — items on a menu" (39), articles for oral consumption.[10] According to Williams's biographer Ronald Hayman, the sea turtle/vulture trope

> was the most ferocious theatrical image Tennessee had yet found to express the guilt he felt at eating luxuriously in cities where the natives were starving, and at paying boys to make love when they were too poverty-stricken to say no. He writes as if his own predatory homosexuality had come to nauseate him. (Hayman 1993, 174)

As if to take to completion this alleged guilt over "predatory homosexuality," Williams then sounds a second chord in the sea turtles and vultures: Sebastian himself becomes the vulnerable victim with the soft underside, while the ravenous boys of the town of Cabeza de Lobo swoop down on him and "*devour*[] parts of him" (1958b, 92). With a punishment due to the selfish, narcissistic queer, The Empire Bites Back. And finally, this image of predatory consumption expands to consume the entire universe: it becomes a metaphor for God himself and for a cosmic order where, as Williams put it, "egos eat egos, personalities eat personalities, and the human being is a cannibal in the worst way" (quoted in Hirsch 1979, 54–55). Whereas Hermann

Hesse could imagine birds eating him as a figure for the destructive-regenerative principle of rebirth and self-awareness, Williams seems to imagine it as the ultimate product of self-awareness, the inexorable fate of the homosexual who falls outside the dictates of bourgeois acceptability. Sebastian can do nothing but "complete[] — a sort of! — *image!* — he had of himself as a sort of! — *sacrifice*" (64);[11] Narcissus can do nothing but plunge into the pond and kill himself. And just as Freud and (to a degree) Hesse can "save" the homosexual by making him into something else, Williams can save him(self) by sacrificing his narcissistic desire to a brutal, divine justice.[12]

Or so the play reads at first blush. However, the violent self-loathing that critics like Ronald Hayman assume underlies the play depends upon a far-too-limited definition of the "vulture" signifier. Williams's predatory metaphor may represent the homosexual narcissist, his oral pleasures[13] and his atonement for those pleasures, but it also carries with it some other tropic equivalencies that are less comfortable for psychoanalytic diagnosis. Whereas the Freudian fantasy metonymically associates the vulture with the mother (the vulture's tail as part-object represents the mother's nipple as part-object), Williams's play metaphorically *equates* Violet with the vultures: surely Sebastian's sex with young men is no more reprehensible than Violet's insistence that Catharine be lobotomized, that she be ripped open with a surgeon's knife and part of her brain be cut out so that she will stop telling the story of what "really" happened to Sebastian last summer. Nor are Violet and Sebastian, that narcissistic mother and son, the only vultures we see. Good intentions aside, the surgeon, Doctor Cukrowicz, is in the business of boring into people's skulls and entering their brains. Mrs. Holly and George, Catharine's mother and brother, have authorized the psychosurgery so that they can get their hands on Sebastian's trust fund, which Violet has tied up in probate until Catharine can be silenced (a fund that Cukrowicz too wants to get his hands on as a way of funding his hospital and his career). And finally, there is Catharine herself, who is certainly more preyed upon than preying, but who gives voice to the overarching predatory ethic in the play: "we all use each other," she tells Cukrowicz, "and that's what we think of as love, and not being able to use each other is what's — *hate*" (63). Although much less deadly than the other exploiters in the play, Catharine used Sebastian as comfort, as protection from a hostile world, as a companion — she used him as somebody to love: "He liked me and so I loved him . . . [in the] only way he'd accept: — a sort of motherly way" (63). If the homosexual is narcissistic in this play, his narcissism is mere synecdoche for the social, "normal" world against which he is defined. Predatory vulturism is rendered morally reprehensible here, but it is divested of its supposedly homosexual psychic configurations. It is simply "a true story of our time and the world we live in," as Catharine says (47). Birds in Williams, then, do not inspire a simple, straightforward chronology of transformations and sublimations, as they do in Freud. Rather, as in Hesse, they signal multiple affiliations, associations, signifieds that obfuscate — or perhaps focus — the ethical and psychological center of the play and destroy its salvational possibilities.

If I appear to be emphasizing a dismissal of the "salvational" here, it is not only because I want to resist the ethical imperatives of homosexual silencing in Freud's discussion of Leonardo. Rather, I want to follow Leo Bersani's critique of "the *redemptive reinvention of sex*" (1988, 215) to consider how Williams's treatment of Sebastian may give us new purchase on the alleged cultural equation of mothers and queer sons through narcissism. For Bersani, the "pastoralizing project" we can detect in recent theories of gender and sexuality (221), most notably in the porn/antiporn debates within feminism (215), attempts ultimately to reinscribe an "ideal self" that is a chimerical but politically potent agent of "normal" and humanitarian ideas about sexuality. Regardless of which side of an issue one takes, that process of idealization is brutal, Bersani argues, because it carves out the "healthy" from the "unhealthy," the "ethical" from the "dangerous," and works in the end to resituate the very definition of phallic, masculine wholeness that it has been feminism's and queer theory's project to deconstruct. What Bersani advocates instead is a celebration of sexuality's "very potential for death," a death to be understood metaphorically, a death of the fictitious, whole, phallic self. As I briefly noted in my discussion of *Teleny*, Bersani argues that only a "radical disintegration and humiliation of the self" can open the subject to desire, to a form of powerlessness in which sexuality can be enjoyed qua sexuality (1988, 217). He concludes "Is the Rectum a Grave?" (1988) with the following:

> Gay men's "obsession" with sex, far from being denied, should be celebrated — not because of its communal virtues, not because of its subversive potential for parodies of machismo, not because it offers a model for genuine pluralism to a society that at once celebrates and punishes pluralism, but rather because it never stops re-presenting the internalized phallic male as an infinitely loved object of sacrifice. Male homosexuality advertises the risk of the sexual itself as the risk of self-dismissal, of *losing sight* of the self, and in so doing it proposes and dangerously represents *jouissance* as a mode of ascesis. (222)

To the degree that *Suddenly Last Summer* is about a gay man's obsession with sex, to the degree that Sebastian Venable is wealthy, controlling, and thus a "phallic male" who is also "an infinitely loved object of sacrifice," and to the degree that Williams may have written the play as his own act of "self-dismissal" — indeed, to the degree that the play *refuses* a salvational or redemptive reading of sex — it opens up a wide field (a pan-optic) of meanings about homosexual narcissism and its representations. And like Coleridge's "The Picture" or Wilde's *Dorian Gray* or *Teleny,* the play engages Narcissus as a figure of simultaneous repudiation and desire. By charting three major refusals that underlie the play — refusals of the Law of the Mother, the Law of the Psychoanalyst, and the Law of the Signifier — I want to suggest that in *Suddenly Last Summer* Tennessee Williams heralds the arrival of a poststructuralist queer subject and his sexual/textual possibilities.

First, the Law of the Mother. In Freud's analysis of Leonardo, the mother occupies the contradictory positions of homosexuality's *cause* and *cure:* Caterina's place in the infant's libidinal economy both established the possibility of homosexual desire (he could identify with her) and rendered that desire heterosexual in its phantasmatic return to the maternal nipple. Violet Venable's place in Sebastian's economy is not dissimilar. On the one hand, she is the Freudian phallic mother par excellence whose proximity to Sebastian resonates with psychic dangers: "We were a famous couple. People didn't speak of Sebastian and his mother or Mrs. Venable and her son, they said 'Sebastian and Violet, Violet and Sebastian.' . . . I was actually the only one in his life that satisfied the demands he made of people" (25). But, on the other hand, she also rescues him from an excessive introspection symptomatic of narcissism:

> We had an agreement between us, a sort of contract or covenant between us which he broke last summer when he broke away from me and took her with him, not me! When he was frightened and I knew when and what of, because his hands would shake and his eyes looked in, not out, I'd reach across a table and touch his hands and say not a word, just look, and touch his hands with my hand until his hands stopped shaking and his eyes looked out, not in, and in the morning, the poem would be continued. (76)

In Sebastian's infantile life, mamma clearly knows best. However, while Freud suggests that homosexuality is a means to the maternal end, Williams disrupts the normalizing script by reversing it. Catharine, that other, "substitute" mother, explains the real role mothers play for Sebastian: "I was PROCURING for him! . . . *She* [Violet] used to do it, too" (81). In this play, boys are not used to get to mothers (as they are in Freud and often in Hesse); rather, mothers are used to get boys: Violet and Catharine attract the attentions of desirable young men so that Sebastian can then seduce them. And the joke here may be as much on Freud as it is on Violet: if the mother can encourage the son to "look out, not in," if she can lure him away from the narcissistic and into the anaclitic, then the other whom he anaclitically desires can as easily be male as it can be maternal. Sebastian's self-dismissal, his return from the depths of narcissism to the object-world, is not, as Freud would have it, a move from the homosexual to the heteronormative; rather, Williams collapses the binary of homosexual narcissism and anaclitic object-desire so that they become the same thing.[14]

Williams's interruption of the narrative that sees homosexuality as the arrested and regressive rerouting of maternal cathexis has clear implications for his career as an artist and for the process of sublimation that supposedly informs that career. In Violet's understanding of Sebastian as artist, she is his sole inspiration, his support and encouragement through the creative process; because of her, he would leave his paralyzing introspection and finish his annual "Poem of Summer." Moreover, she is the only person to read the poems, as Sebastian had refused to have them circulate while he was still alive. Thus, in one way, artistic creativity in the Venable household is a narcissistic wonderland, proceeding from the mother and returning to her in a bond of erotic circularity — a bond that offers further "evidence" for the psychogenesis of the poet's homosexuality while maintaining that Sebastian was "chaste," that he had no sexuality prior to last summer.[15] Indeed, criticism on *Suddenly Last Summer* adopts wholesale Violet's self-proclaimed status as W. H. to Sebastian's Shakespeare. Here is the play:

> DOCTOR: He wrote one poem a year?
>
> MRS. VENABLE: One for each summer that we traveled together. The other nine months of the year were really only a preparation.
>
> DOCTOR: Nine months?
>
> MRS. VENABLE: The length of a pregnancy, yes...
>
> DOCTOR: The poem was hard to deliver?
>
> MRS. VENABLE: Yes, even with me. *Without* me, *impossible*, Doctor! (14)

Here is Andrew Sofer: "Sebastian's writings nourish him no more than the little white pills he ingests instead of food. His poetry, thin and costive, is not a poetry of the body, but rather represents a denial of the body's propagative function. Sebastian's art is still-born, engendered through a poisonous combination of incest and narcissism" (1995, 342). (This is an interesting bit of textual criticism, given that we never see the "Poems of Summer.") And here is Robert F. Gross, the play's most sophisticated critic:

> The maternal image presented here is one of a phallic, impregnating Mother who provides the will necessary for artistic creation to take place. Through Violet's description, Williams represents Sebastian's creation of his poetry as a maternal process. The poem gestates for nine months, "the length of a pregnancy"...and is brought forth each summer, the season in which the vegetative goddesses' powers are strongest. This account is one of maturation rather than struggle. Violet is presented as the agent of Sebastian's creativity. It is with Sebastian's separation from Violet that his inability to write begins. Catharine admits that she was completely incapable of helping Sebastian write his final *Poem of Summer*. Clearly, Sebastian's existence as an artist depends completely on his mother. (1995, 241)

In their readings of the play, Sofer and Gross seem to adopt the assumption that underlies Freud's theory of sublimation in the "Leonardo" essay, a theory Hesse made his life's work to attack: one either fucks or produces art, but one cannot do both. Thus Gross can claim that Catharine's world is one of "the physical body with its sexuality, aging, and violent death," whereas Violet's is of poetry and the "human spirit" (241), and that the play documents Sebastian's move "from Violet's world to Catharine's" (244), a world where Sebastian writes no poem.

But what then are we to do with Catharine's claim that "I was PROCURING for him!" and that "*She* [Violet] used to do it, too.... We both did the same thing for him, made contacts for him, but she did it in nice places and in decent ways" (81)? To say that there was sex last summer when there was no poem is not the same as saying there was no sex every other summer when there were poems. Violet and Sebastian's world of "*grandeur*" (25), of masked balls and Renaissance costumes (22), of "little entourage[s] of the beautiful and the talented and the young" (22), is not necessarily a sexless world; indeed, it is counterintuitive to assume that Sebastian was not sexual before last summer and that his mother was not somehow complicit in his cruising.[16] Rather, if Sebastian wrote no poem last summer, I suspect it was because "he wasn't young anymore" (77). Tortured by Williams's great bogey — old age — Sebastian "suddenly switched from the evenings to the beach" (77) where sex is bought, not acquired genteely or "decently." Sebastian's inability to write last summer may have been caused less by his inability to sublimate his desire for the now-absent mother than by his inability to seduce boys of his class and breeding. As any gay man in the 1950s would know, especially if he were familiar with the story of Oscar Wilde or had read a novel like *Teleny,* buying gay sex presented numerous possibilities for persecution and blackmail, which we could reasonably assume might shake one's concentration for writing poetry. And while our postcolonial sensibilities may not like the idea of such "exploitation," Williams's point here seems to be to wrest the homosexual from a paralyzing — because sanitizing — diagnosis that makes the gay man captive to his mother. Homosexuality, Williams insists, is much more a social structure than a psychodynamic inevitability, and the writing of poetry, likewise, need not depend upon the presence of the mother.

Williams's critique of psychoanalysis through a rejection of the mother is by no means tangential to his career as a playwright. In 1957, following the death of his father and the critical failure of *Orpheus Descending* (1958a), Williams had begun to suffer acute paranoia and depression. To combat this, he entered into Freudian psychoanalysis with Dr. Lawrence Kubie, a New York psychoanalyst to the stars and theorist of the relation of neurosis to creativity. Williams's ambivalence about the experience echoes Hesse's. In the beginning, the analysis was extremely useful: in a letter to Maria St. Just on 27 August 1957, Williams wrote, "The 'good doctor' has shown me many things about me which I hope will make me less self-centered, gradually, in the future. I can be a better friend some day than I've been up till now" (1990, 150). While we do not have the records of the analysis, it is safe to assume that Kubie "showed" Tennessee something about himself as an artist and the function of art in his neurosis. For Kubie, according to his book *Neurotic Distortion of the Creative Process* (published 1958, the year *Suddenly Last Summer* was first performed), neurosis could not be sublimated into valid art; it could only mar the creative process (1961, 6). Thus, Kubie's analysis focused on the "hate, anger and envy" he detected in Williams's work (Williams 1975b, 5) and resulted in the production of *Suddenly Last Summer,* a play that gets past sublimation to the "truth," the truth not only about what really happened to Sebastian last summer but also about a "human weakness" and "guilt" that are "universal" (1975b, 6). If Williams could write to Donald Windham on 3 January 1958 that "analysis has helped me" (1976–77, 294), it is presumably because analysis gave him a language to analyze his own relationship with his mother, his absent father, his homosexuality, and the cultural context in which that sexuality got lived out.[17] Hence, the therapeutic value of *Suddenly Last Summer.*

However, if psychoanalysis was revealing for Williams, as it was for Hesse, it was also dangerous and limiting, as it was for Hesse. For not only did Kubie believe that neurosis-producing anxiety could destroy art rather than create it;[18] he also believed that creativity could itself become neurosis when the artist repeatedly and automatically returned to his private obsessions, when he narcissistically indulged his own murky and tedious psyche. (And self-indulgent repetition, of course, was one of the grounds on which critics condemned *Orpheus Descending.*)[19] In the case of Williams, these private obsessions were twofold. First, there was the sexual. As Williams wrote, caustically, to Maria St. Just, "Of course he is attacking my sex life and has succeeded in destroying my interest in all except the Horse [Frank Merlo], and perhaps the Horse will go next" (1990, 150). In his *Memoirs* he talks about "the mistake of strict Freudian analysis" with Kubie, who "taught me much about my true nature but he offered me no solutions except to break with Merlo, a thing that was quite obviously untenable as a consideration, my life being built around him" (173).[20] Indeed, Kubie suggested that Williams try having sex with women for a while. The second obsession, according to Kubie, was writing, which the analyst suggested Williams also give up, at least temporarily (Spoto 1985, 215; Hayman 1993, 170). Writing, Kubie apparently reasoned, not only was a direct source of anguish for a playwright who was falling out of favor with the critics but actually exacerbated the patient's problems by inviting him to dwell on them in his texts. Indulging himself in what has come to be called his "punishment plays" (Sofer 1995, 336), Williams could only make himself more neurotic; and as Kubie argues in *Neurotic Distortion,* "the influence of [neurosis] can be observed in the stereotyped repetitiousness of form and content in the works of the musician, of the artist, of the writer, and of the scientist" (140). Williams's response to this dual prescription is itself twofold: first, "I got restless and started hopping back and forth between the analyst's couch and some Caribbean beaches" (1975b, 6); and, second, he wrote *Suddenly Last Summer* in a white heat. If sex and text are narcissisms, then Williams immerses himself fully in both, rejecting the very demand to sublimate that Kubie had elsewhere decried.

In Kubie's double prescription that Williams give up gay sex and writing, we can detect a Law of the Signifier, a slick and comfortable equation of sex and text that coalesce under the sign of neurosis. Moreover, this equation suggests a mutual *causality:* writing about the self promotes a narcissism that desperately and futilely seeks gay sex to satisfy it; gay sex indulges a libidinal sameness that inspires no other narrative than a narcissistic one. By refusing to get outside a homosexual economy, the artist has nothing to write about but sameness. Which brings us back to the "Poems of Summer," the apparitional writing of our apparitional homosexual. If the poems were "written" in response to a "quite obviously untenable" suggestion that the playwright stop writing and fucking; if they exist from and for Violet (as she vehemently, violently asserts), yet were composed and consumed within a sexual arena that Violet could not recognize; if they were printed in the French Quarter, where Catharine (and presumably Sebastian before her) had "come out" long before doing so in the Garden District, the former being an area that is famous in New Orleans geography for its sexual accessibility;[21] in other words, if these poems metonymically gesture to the plenitude of gay sex rather than to its (Freudian) sublimation/displacement, then we are compelled to wonder what exactly the "Poems of Summer" are about. What precisely does Violet read when she reads them? Does she read what Sebastian wrote? Does she read the same thing I would read if I were given the Blue Jay notebooks in which they were composed? Or is Williams throwing into question the very notion of a "same text" that is produced by a writer and read by a reader or multiple readers? Need we assume that Sebastian's poetic corpus is any more legible than his physical one? Or can we claim that a sublimating maternal reader may find spiritual chastity in a text that a queer reader interprets as erotic? Perhaps this is the undecidability that Williams really wants us to get to: by forging a text — *Suddenly Last Summer,* with its embedded yet spectral "Poems" — that registers both spiritual purity and homosexual pleasure (the "chaste" and the "chased" [24]), Williams creates what Linda Hutcheon (1980) calls the "narcissistic narrative," a text in which the reader is forced to project his/her own imaginative processes and preoccupations onto the page's mirrored surface. If the "Poems of Summer" are queerly erotic, it is because I have made them so, but if I have made them so, it is because Williams has seduced me, cruised me, invited me to bring my own eros, which is also, at least partially, his own.

Such a reflexive handling of the poems, such a subcultural exchange of signifiers between readers presumed to know, marks in Williams what feels distinctly like a poststructuralist attack on signifying laws, one that he repeatedly places in queer contexts. Indeed, Williams uses the ambiguous perversions (literally, the turnings-away) of the signifier to figure the queer relation between language and the self. For

Williams, the word *is* flesh, the signifier is the material manifestation of desire. In a letter to Donald Windham, he wrote: "There are only two times in this world when I am happy and selfless and pure. One is when I jack off on paper and the other is when I empty the fretfulness of desire on a young male body" (1976–77, 105).[22] In *Moise and the World of Reason* (1975a), Charles makes the same point after having sex with the poet LaLanga: "I saw LaLanga as a living poem which I know that he is and I also know that what he put in my body was a poem, too!" (146). Sex is "the living poem of poets" (1975a, 160), and the living poem *is* sex. But language is also that which displaces the self and puts it outside of experience. Freud had noted in Leonardo's notebooks the artist's curious tendency to speak to himself in matters pertaining to other masters (102). After Catharine is raped at her debut, she writes in her journal in the third person as a way of controlling, manipulating, and understanding her "self." And in *Moise and the World of Reason*, Moise charges the narrator-poet with using language to falsify the real: "you writers, you people of the literary persuasion, you substitute words and phrases, slogans, shibboleths and so forth for the simplicities of true feeling. Put a few words in what you think is a clever arrangement, and you feel absolved of all authentic emotion" (160–61). While this charge may endorse the image of the superficial, conventionally narcissistic homosexual, it also indicates how the moment of writing and sexuality — the moment of writing sexuality — is also the moment of selflessness. Writing effects what Bersani calls a "radical disintegration and humiliation of the self" at the moment when the self is rendered textually present (1988, 217).[23] "I am happy and selfless and pure," said Williams, when he writes and when he has sex. Happy *and* selfless? Perhaps the very contradiction moves us far enough away from Freud's neurosis, far enough from his sublimation, to posit a queer *sublime,* a *jouissance* that provides the subject with intense joy at the same time that it displaces that subject, "kills it," in Bersani's terms. The "Poems of Summer," by their refusal to be inscribed and thus to be "authentic," enact a simultaneous inscription and displacement of the self that is narcissistically structured and that allows the homoerotic to circulate freely.[24]

And it is Narcissus, I have wanted to argue, that stands at the center of the gay man's erotic identity/identification in narratives that claim to place the mother there instead. It is Narcissus, moreover, who provides the model for textual creativity, as the gap that exists between his desiring gaze and the state of being gazed at *is* the paradoxical space marked out by the play. And it is precisely because of Narcissus's cathexis upon *image* that he can be deployed as a queer trope. In Hesse, we remember, the narcissistic circulation of eros is most profoundly achieved through a meditation on image: Goldmund's statue of St. John the Beloved promiscuously intermingles with Narziss's religious identity, with queer iconography, with erotic German sculptural practice. Williams deploys a similar strategy, using the theatrical stage to visualize for the play as a whole the narcissistic splitting that underlies the "Poems of Summer." He does this through Doctor Cukrowicz, who stands as the play's erotic center at the same time that he displaces it. As Robert F. Gross has argued, Cukrowicz is "a spectral echo of the late Sebastian Venable" (237). He wears the same white suit that Sebastian had worn, he issues orders for Catharine to stand and speak, he draws her out of herself (as Sebastian had done for her, as Violet had done for Sebastian). But what is most important for Gross in this figuration is its therapeutic possibilities, the degree to which it saves Catharine from madness. Cukrowicz, he says, "elicits Catharine's sexual desire as her cousin had done before him" (237). The doctor's blondness *metonymically* suggests Sebastian's desire, since he was heading for northern blonds after Cabeza de Lobo, and so Cukrowicz comes to figure as a visual representation of Sebastian's desire, a desire with which Catharine can identify as a way of salvaging some erotic connection with her dead cousin: "if she cannot have *him*," Gross argues, "she can at least have *his desire* by imitating it. As a result, [Cukrowicz] becomes a compelling sexual object for Catharine, since he both summons up her desire for Sebastian and Sebastian's desire for men" (237). By implication, then, Cukrowicz functions as the psychoanalyst (as opposed to the psychosurgeon) onto whom Catharine transfers her desires and through whom she can reorient herself to the outside world, the world of other people, the world beyond the paralyzing secret that even she cannot always reach. And once again the homosexual narcissist is safely deployed in the service of another, more palatable end.

But what if we insist, one more time, that narcissism is *about* homosexuality and that Narcissus's loved image is the image of another man? For Gross, the dressing of Cukrowicz in Sebastian's attire (both sartorially and erotically) inflects the "threatening advances" Catharine makes to the doctor and "erase[s] any difference between gay and straight *eros;* a seemingly heterosexual action is permeated with gay desire" (240). I agree completely, but I also see in this play the figuration of gay desire that is *not* filtered through women's eros: Cukrowicz's is a queerly charged body not only because it is *identified* with Sebastian's body but also because it is the kind of body

Sebastian would have *desired* — Cukrowicz, as the stage directions
tell us, is "very, very good-looking," and he has an "icy charm" (10).
Violet explicates: "You would have liked my son, he would have been
charmed by you. . . . He was a snob about personal charm in people,
he insisted upon good looks in people around him" (22). The doctor's
blondness is not only a metonymic suggestion of Sebastian's eros, it
is the object of it. Thus Cukrowicz (first name "John," according
to the film version) is both the desiring Sebastian and the object of
Sebastian's desire, a theatrical embodiment of the queerly split subject. What gets carved into the face of Goldmund's narcissistic statue,
what gets textually figured in the "Poems of Summer," is erotically
visualized in the spectacle of Cukrowicz (whose embodiment, or displacement, in the film by the seductive Montgomery Clift was lost on
few queer moviegoers). He enacts the narcissistic bifurcation and its
homoerotic desire that underlies Ovid's myth: Sebastian's eros, like
that of Narcissus, refuses to be inscribed in a linear trajectory that
begins and ends in mothers; rather, "Sebastian" as a signifier circles
around the gay male who engages other men, enters them, and has
them enter him in a ludic shuttle of theatrical images that belies (or
completes) the drama of mothers. Like the narcissistic image-play of
Hesse's Johns, Sebastian (himself a john) is queer not only in genital
practice but in specular signification.

Chapter 4

QUEER QUEER VLADIMIR

When you speak of the great difference between us I always feel that it lies in nothing, save in your own strange hankering to find differences.
— HESSE, *Narziss and Goldmund*

[T]here is no resemblance at all....Resemblances are the shadows of differences.
— NABOKOV, *Pale Fire*

Thanks to Freud, mothers inaugurate a legitimation crisis. On the one hand, "mother" emerges as that loved and lovable icon who, from her eighteenth-century roots, has been responsible for defining the moral tone of a culture; she stands along with her apple pie as signifiers of the good and the true (in America at any rate); and psychoanalytically she is the lever who pries the male child off his narcissistic fixation and lures him into the anaclitic, that otherness that will found his heterosexuality. Remember Hesse's Frau Eva. But, on the other hand, her adored status as moral and sentimental goddess, her figuration with the national symbolic as She Who Must Be Worshiped, her function as conveyer of the anaclitic, threaten her boys with fixation. They not only may want to protect, adore, and idolize her but also may want to be like her, to *be* her, to replicate her desires rather than admire them from afar. Remember Williams's Violet Venable. As the ideal for male self-definition, Mother is the original Narcissus. According to Philip Wylie (whose 1955 *Generation of Vipers* claims to have "put the word 'momism' indelibly in our language" [194]),

> Mom steals from the generation of women behind her (which she has, as a still further defense, also sterilized of integrity and courage) that part of the boy's personality which should have become the love of a female contemporary. Mom transmutes it into sentimentality for herself....Her policy of protection, from the beginning, was not love of her boy but of herself, and as she found returns coming in from the disoriented young boy in smiles, pats, presents, praise, kisses, and all manner of childish representations of the real business, she moved on to possession. (208–9)

The logical conclusion to the Freudian premise, Mother not only induces narcissism in the potentially homosexual boy but provides the model of narcissism that he will imitate. He adores (himself) as she adores (herself); homo is where the heart is.

According to Michael Rogin, the mother-son narcissism denounced by Wylie's diatribe characterizes a broader social anxiety in Cold War America. While the mother of the 1940s and 1950s ruled the domestic sphere and thus protected it for the interests of American bourgeois ideology, her role as moral guardian functioned by *influence*, by the ability (the imperative) to invade the boundary of the individual. Hers was to *socialize* and *democratize* under the guise of shoring up the private and the individual (1984, 5). These contradictory imperatives — to be or not to be a mother's son — reinforced the troubled logic of the inside and the outside, since to pay allegiance to the American value of mother-love was also to risk betraying that one had been invaded by mother-love, that one was as much a product of another's influence as one was a self-contained individual. Thus, mother became a problem in the Cold War not merely because she could seduce her son into weakness, effeminacy, and potential homosexuality, but because the son, the self, *could be seduced*. Like Dorian Gray, susceptible to Lord Henry Wotton's toxic and homosexualizing influence, sons of mothers in 1950s America were understood to be vulnerable to a narcissism that, paradoxically and perfidiously, was not "naturally" their own. In a curious twist of Freudian logic, the anaclitic bond between mother and son was to be policed and regulated; perverse narcissism may be the disease, but normative anaclisis was the virus that spread it.

While a raft of psychological studies undertaken during the Cold War lined up with Wylie in blaming the overattentive mother for homosexuality, projects such as *Homosexuality: A Psychoanalytic Study* (Bieber et al. 1962) make clear that the sheer range of sexual types and performances within homosexuality makes diagnostic practice often very difficult. And this diagnostic problem is a political one as well. Lee Edelman and David Savran, among others, document the way straight America during the Cold War was plagued by the feeling that homosexuals were everywhere in culture and politics yet were impossible to detect. Like communists, their very invisibility led them to be "seen" everywhere; indeed, in 1951 Jack Lait and Lee Mortimer argued in *Washington Confidential* that there were no fewer than six thousand fairies in government offices, yet they could go easily unperceived: "some are deceptive to the uninitiated" (quoted in Katz 1976, 101).[1] For Edelman, this troubling (in)visibility engenders what he calls "homographesis," the attempt to posit

homosexuality as a legible phenomenon while simultaneously acknowledg-
ing the frequency with which it manages to escape detection[;] it constructs
male homosexuality in terms of what the "public eye" can recognize even
as it situates it in an ontological shuttle between perceptual sameness and
difference. (1994, 154)

In Edelman's analysis, what "the 'public eye' can recognize" is effeminacy, which becomes the diagnostic homographic designation that
absorbs the different (the gay man) into a familiar sameness, the rec-
ognizably feminine. As he says of the 1960s, "Male homosexuality
...must be conceptualized in terms of femaleness not only because
the governing heterosexual mythology interprets gay men as defini-
tionally wanting to *be,* or to be *like* women" — a phenomenon so
vividly displayed in Freud's analysis of Leonardo and in the inversion
theories — "but also because the heterosexual must insist that the gay
man *is,* in fact, like a woman to the extent that his 'difference' can
be discerned on his body, subjecting him to discrimination in more
ways than one" (155). The metonymically totalizing diagnosis of effeminacy, then, could collapse the more ominous effects of momism
with the perfidies of communistic treason. Effeminacy guaranteed the
presence of a far-too-influential mother and a far-too-influenced son.
Effeminacy was the guarantor of difference.

However, as both *Washington Confidential* and Edelman's work
indicate, the visible difference inscribed on the effeminate male body
is a deceptive signifier; the homosexual male is as much "the same"
as he is different. The phallus, that irrefutable marker of sexual difference and ticket of admission to the privileges of the masculine
economy, refuses to perform its function in the gay male: it bespeaks
a masculinity that we must rely on maternally induced effeminacy to
belie; it makes difference into sameness by equalizing the straight and
gay body; it makes legibility illegible. In this sense, it puts another
spin on the rich textual problems of narcissism I have been exploring
throughout this book. America in the 1950s was plagued by the concept of the equalizer — not only the equalizing phallus that refuses to
separate the straight from the not-ostentatiously-effeminate gay man
but also the affiliations that such queerness had in the political arena,
the affiliation with communism, itself a horribly equalizing ideology.
America in the 1950s desired social sameness yet feared it; it pro-
moted individual difference yet loathed it. In this chapter I want to
draw out some of the ways in which narcissism was made to negotiate
the problem of sameness and difference within the sexualized politics
of the Cold War. For the narcissist's difference is defined not only
by his cathexis on mother (which makes him no different from any

red-blooded American male) but by his orientation to sameness — the sameness of object-choice, the sameness of disparate elements in the object-world as they are drawn together through the narcissistic lens. Yet this orientation to sameness, like that of the communist, renders him dangerously different.

Freud's Fairy Tales: Take Two

This confusing mixture of sameness and difference, its critical leverage in the problem of politics, and the purchase it affords art for making interventions into Narcissus are nowhere more obvious than in the novels of Vladimir Nabokov. One of Nabokov's earliest novels, *Otchaianie* (written in 1932 and translated from Russian into the English *Despair* in 1966) sets up a paradigm that the novelist will use repeatedly throughout his career. The central character, a madman named Hermann, meets and befriends a vagabond called Felix, who, in Hermann's imagination, looks exactly like him (although we learn later that there is no resemblance): "He appeared to my eyes as a double, that is, as a creature bodily identical with me. It was this absolute sameness that gave me so piercing a thrill" (1966a, 23). In fact, shaking hands with the recumbent Felix "provided me with the curious sensation of Narcissus fooling Nemesis by helping his image out of the brook" (23). So easily fooled is Nemesis that the narcissistic Hermann can use him to execute the perfect crime: he will dress the seemingly identical Felix in his own clothes and then murder him to collect his own insurance money. Hermann covers his tracks, he assumes, by giving his wife, Lydia, the alibi: Felix is really Hermann's long-lost younger brother with whom, in earlier days, he shared an "indescribable oneness, for we resembled each other so closely that our nearest relatives used to mistake us" (148). This younger brother wants to die, he says, both to atone for a murder he had committed and to make his treasured Hermann rich. Thus does Hermann believe his crime to be flawless, rendered perfect by the existence of his narcissistic double. The only problem: the vagabond Felix looks nothing like him, and so his wearing Hermann's clothes and carrying his identification become the evidence that implicates the murderer.

Despair (1966a) is most interesting for the texture of delusional consciousness it presents. Hermann ascribes his own penchant for hallucinating similarity both to this fictional brother — "Felix" supposedly saw Hermann as "his adored double, ... the optimal edition of his own personality" (148) — and to the real Felix: "Note: it was he and not I who first perceived the masonic bond in our resemblance . . . as if I were the mimic and he the model" (22). (Note: Felix sees no resemblance at all!) Moreover, Hermann's narrative of the fictional brother ascribes to him a perversely erotic charge, one that Nabokov added to the 1966 English edition:

> At first we shared a bed with a pillow at each end until it was discovered he could not go to sleep without sucking my big toe, whereupon I was expelled to a mattress in the lumber room, but since he insisted on changing places with me in the middle of the night, we never quite knew, nor did dear mama, who was sleeping where. (147–48)

Now, while Hermann does warn the reader not to "discern mirages of sodomy in my partiality for a vagabond" (169), the construction of sameness that he then projects onto the fictional Felix marks a narcissism that permeates his own erotic practices. Of Lydia he tells us, "I loved her because she loved me" (35), and during sex he "dissociates," that is, projects himself outside of his own corporeality so that he can watch his own eroticized body in the act of lovemaking: "From my magical point of vantage I watched the ripples running and plunging along my muscular back" (37).[2] Moments after this observation, Hermann describes Lydia's fascination with the contours of his face, but then the prose moves seamlessly into Hermann's fascination with Felix's face; Hermann takes the place of Lydia admiring the image of Narcissus in the pool. Thus at the heart of this delusion is a homoerotic projection, a narcissism in which one repeatedly finds self where other is supposed to be.

This homoerotic, narcissistic projection makes of Nabokovian madmen like Hermann an echo of another homosexual narcissist, the Daniel Paul Schreber who is presented to us in Freud's "Psychoanalytic Notes on an Autobiographical Account of a Case of Paranoia (Dementia Paranoides)." Written in 1910, the same year as "Leonardo," "A Case of Paranoia" undertakes to interpret the memoirs of a Saxony court judge who suffers delusions of persecution and eventually fantasizes himself as the wife of God, submitting to the pleasurable penetrations of divine rays of light. Like Hermann, who saw Felix as an exact replica, a mirror double of himself different only by the lines of care that poverty had etched on his face, Schreber saw himself as other. He hallucinated himself "in a second, inferior shape, and in this second shape he one day quietly passed away" (1911, 68). Like Hermann, whose assumptions of complete similarity to Felix completely contradict external evidence, Schreber withdrew his libido entirely from the external world and directed it onto his own ego (1911, 70). And like Hermann, who treats Felix, Lydia, and her cousin Ardalion with murderous hostility or paranoid suspicion, Schreber suffered under the apprehension that he would be castrated by his physician, Fleschig. In what has become the seminal study of the connections between homosexuality and paranoia, Freud lays out the ways in which an internal crisis is projected onto the object-world. This crisis, Freud argues, proceeds from a fixation at the narcissistic stage. The argument is worth quoting at length:

> There comes a time in the development of the individual at which he uni-fies his sexual instincts (which have hitherto been engaged in auto-erotic activities) in order to obtain a love-object; and he begins by taking himself, his own body, as his love-object, and only subsequently proceeds from this to the choice of some person other than himself as his object. This half-way phase between auto-erotism and object-love may perhaps be indispensable normally; but it appears that many people linger unusually long in this condition, and that many of its features are carried over by them into the later stages of their development. What is of chief importance in the subject's self thus chosen as a love-object may already be the genitals. The line of development then leads on to the choice of an external object with similar genitals — that is, to homosexual object-choice — and thence to heterosexuality. People who are manifest homosexuals in later life have, it may be presumed, never emancipated themselves from the binding condition that the object of their choice must possess genitals like their own. (1911, 60–61)

One could not imagine a more succinct analysis of Nabokov's Hermann: his misperception of Felix is a projection of his own fixation in homosexual narcissism, and this narcissism returns to inflect and infect the possibility of healthy heterosexual desire for Lydia. What psychoanalysis has joined together, Nabokov does not put asunder.

Moreover, such homosexual narcissism will come to define the "political" in both the Schreber analysis and *Despair*. Freud continues his line of argument thus:

> After the stage of heterosexual object-choice has been reached, the homo-sexual tendencies are not, as might be supposed, done away with or brought to a stop; they are merely deflected from their sexual aim and applied to fresh uses. They now combine with portions of the ego-instincts and, as "attached" components, help to constitute the social instincts, thus contributing an erotic factor to friendship and comradeship, to *esprit de corps* and to the love of mankind in general. (1911, 61)

Such esprit de corps, such erotically charged comradeship, appears in *Despair* as the proffered equation between homosexuals and communists (an equation that takes us back to Edelman's point about the homographic legibility crisis in Cold War America). Nabokov has Hermann theorize his propensity to see doubleness as follows:

"This remarkable physical likeness probably appealed to me (sub-consciously!) as the promise of that ideal sameness which is to unite all people in the classless society of the future" (168). Hermann has "such faith in the impending sameness of us all" that "Communism shall indeed create a beautifully square world of identical brawny fellows, broad-shouldered and microcephalous" (30). And Nabokov's satire is searing; Hermann continues:

> Felix and I belonged to different, sharply defined classes, the fusion of which none can hope to achieve single-handed, especially nowadays, when the conflict of classes has reached a stage where compromise is out of the question. . . . In fancy, I visualize a new world, where all men will resemble one another as Hermann and Felix did, . . . a world where the worker fallen dead at the feet of his machine will be at once replaced by his perfect double smiling the serene smile of perfect socialism. (169)

The Leninist regime — the one political ideology Nabokov never ceased denouncing — becomes eroticized in Hermann's narcissistic projection. It metamorphoses the homoerotic into a politicized dissolution of difference and individuality, a dissolution that was especially threatening to the 1950s, where fairies and communists — narcissists all — lurked in every closet.[3] It's both predictable and ironic, then, that when the BBC asked Nabokov in 1968 what authors had influenced him most, he responded, "I'd much prefer to speak of the modern books I hate on first sight: the earnest case histories of minority groups, the sorrows of homosexuals, the anti-American Sovietnam sermon" (1973c, 116). With a flourish of generalizing that he had scathingly condemned in Hermann, Nabokov groups together, equates, levels the triad of Cold War villains: minorities, homosexuals, and communists.

But if Freud is useful for psychically linking communism with homosexual narcissism as a love of sameness, and if the paranoid delusions of Schreber can be made to align richly with the political tendency to project, replicate, and equalize, then it might be useful to unpack further Freud's own mechanisms of argument to see how he gets to where he wants to go. Leaving aside the extensive debate over whether Freud was "right" in his diagnosis of Schreber's repressed homosexuality for his physician, Fleschig,[4] or whether Freud accurately and responsibly represents Schreber's points in the *Memoirs of My Nervous Illness* (1955), let's look again at this politicized narcissism. The argument in "A Case of Paranoia" is significant for the pains it takes to drop out the mother. In "Leonardo," we remember, the mother provided a useful salvational intervention in the child/

artist's homosexual life history: to the degree that the vulture's phallic tail was really a signifier of the maternal nipple, it (re)instated normative heterosexuality where homo-narcissism was seen to operate, thus offering the clinician a forward-looking promise of the "return" to a primary heterosexuality. (That such heterosexuality was homo-narcissistically structured, I argued in chapter 3, was a problem that Freud did not take up.) However, in "A Case of Paranoia" the mother is never mentioned. The patient loves "his own body," "himself," "an external object with similar genitals." Schreber's history with his mother is never mentioned; rather, Schreber (like Hermann's fictional brother) is reportedly much more cathected on his dead brother and father than on his mother. That Freud should ignore the mother in a case history written the same year as "Leonardo" may simply mark a homophobic taxonomy within male narcissism: to the degree that the maternal nipple is at the heart of male narcissism, it authorizes the socially productive act of sublimation that, in Leonardo da Vinci, produced art; to the degree that another male and another male's phallus are at the heart of homosexual narcissism, it authorizes pathology, delusion, schizophrenic paranoia. Thus, the centrality of male narcissism ultimately engenders the Gothic terrorism that we have seen operating in men as different from one another as Coleridge, Williams, and Dorian Gray.

However, as Freud moves toward reinstating the homoeros of the narcissistic paradigm by removing the compulsorily heterosexualized figure of the mother, he invites us to consider a same-sex economy that uses narcissism to structure normative social relations. Friendship, comradeship, and esprit de corps may translate in Nabokov's *Despair* into detestable socialism or communism, but in Freud they become the "active share" that manifest homosexuals take in "the general interests of humanity" (1911, 61). Freud expands this theory in the 1922 essay "Some Neurotic Mechanisms in Jealousy, Paranoia, and Homosexuality." Here he again recounts the theory that male homosexuality is caused by an unduly long cathexis on the mother (the male wanting to be or to be like women), but then he changes course to suggest another, very different psychogenesis. In this new account, early childhood jealousy of older brothers or other rivals for attention paid to the child produces an "exceedingly hostile and aggressive attitude toward these brothers" (1922, 231) and even a wish for their deaths. However, "[u]nder the influences of upbringing — and certainly not uninfluenced by their own continuing powerlessness — these impulses yielded to repression and underwent a transformation, so that the rivals of an earlier period became the first homosexual love-objects" (231). This repression and transformation, Freud contends, are homologous with "the social feelings of identification" that, like homosexuality, "arise as reactive formations against the repressed aggressive impulses" (232). In this account, homosexuality and social relations proceed from the same dynamic: a kind of Rousseauistic social contract with erotic overlay, in which we cathect on others as a way of circumventing anger and hostility. But by the end of the essay, Freudian coexistence has (as so often happens) become equivalence; the social and homosexual are no longer related but are the same thing. Freud cites the "well known" idea that "a good number of homosexuals are characterized by a special development of their social instinctual impulses and by their devotion to the interests of the community" (a lesson many conservatives and Republicans must have slept through) and concludes that "in the light of psychoanalysis we are accustomed to regard social feeling as a sublimation of homosexual attitudes toward objects" (232). Narcissistic homosexuality is not the product of social relations; it is their genesis. Thus, what purports to be a theory explaining how gay men collapse otherness into the self comes to explain how the self — and the self's relation to itself as erotic other — establishes all relations with all others. Freud's Homo-Narcissus makes possible the political field.

Pale Fire, Faggotry, and the 1950s

The tension I see in Freud's analysis of homosexual delusion and paranoia: the self is narcissistically projected onto the other while the self's narcissism is necessary to constitute the existence of the other. This tension, its slippages and vicissitudes, becomes the subject of Nabokov's most sustained meditation on narcissism, homosexuality, and politics, his 1962 novel, *Pale Fire*. While *Despair* engages a narcissism whose homoerotics are emphatically denied, *Pale Fire* places a self-identified homosexual at the center of the text. And like Hermann, Schreber, and Narcissus, Charles Kinbote is a study in delusional projection. For some weeks, he had been feeding the local poet laureate, John Shade, the story of the land of Zembla, a prerevolutionary utopia over which Charles the Beloved (Kinbote in earlier days) presided as king. After a revolution instigated by the Shadows, Charles flees to New Wye, Appalachia, where he suspects that he is hunted by the revolutionary assassin Jacob Gradus, thus signaling the paranoia that Freud claims is endemic to narcissistic projection. In Kinbote's version of the story, Gradus attempts to murder him but shoots Shade instead. (Actually, Shade is shot by Jack

Grey, an ex-con who mistakes the poet for Kinbote's landlord, Judge Goldsworth, who had sent Grey to prison.) Upon Shade's death, Kinbote finds the poem on which Shade had been working, but it contains nothing of the history he had been giving Shade over the past weeks. Kinbote complains:

> Where was Zembla the Fair? Where her spine of mountains? Where her long thrill through the mist? And my lovely flower boys, and the spectrum of the stained windows,...and the whole marvelous tale? None of it was there! (296)

As Shade lies dead, Kinbote bewails the lack of *his* life-story in the poem and then writes that story through paranoid and intrusive endnotes. For Kinbote, the poem becomes a carefully crafted account of the commentator's life, of "the underside of the weave that entrances the beholder and only begetter, whose own past intercoils there with the fate of the innocent author" (17). Like the mythical Narcissus, this "beholder and only begetter" is unable to distinguish self from other. Indeed, "without my notes," Kinbote proclaims in the foreword, "Shade's text simply has no human reality" (28). Thus does Kinbote expose himself to his critics as an "incurable pederast and lunatic," a "narcissist and madman" whose "invulnerable egotism and megalomania" (Haegert 1984, 405, 415) characterize "a boringly tenacious pedant with homosexual urgencies" (Galef 1985, 427). His "rampant homosexuality,...mad egocentricity...[and] preposterous unreliability" (Boyd 1991, 426) and his "colossal self-conceit and self-obsession and his undisguised homosexuality" (Boyd 1991, 434) refract and distort Shade's poem and give his readers license to volley diatribes against the purported apposition between Kinbote's homosexuality and his madness, an apposition conveniently coalescing in the term "narcissist."

Kinbote's megalomaniacal appropriation of Shade's life and work carries the personal into the political in ways that Freud has made familiar to us. Kinbote's narcissistically cathected body becomes so overdetermined that it eradicates all sense of difference in external objects. As Kinbote explains, his (fictional, projected) land of Zembla is a land where all people look like him: "all bearded Zemblans resembled one another — and...in fact, the name Zembla is a corruption not of the Russian *zemlya,* but of Semblerland, a land of reflections, of 'resemblers' " (265).[5] Indeed, this instinctual investment is figured in a scene that literally appropriates the Narcissus myth: having escaped revolutionary Zembla, Charles traverses the countryside in a red sweater. His supporters stymie the Shadows by donning red sweaters as well, so that the real king cannot be detected in the context of widespread public masquerade. (One thinks here of the king of Norway who, along with his subjects, wore Stars of David to confuse the Nazis.) However, there is some suggestion that the villainous Gradus too may be wearing a red sweater, and so the enemy and the hero have become indistinguishable. During the escape, Charles comes to a pond and, looking into it, sees reflected there a "counterfeit king"; this king, he then realizes, is actually standing on the ledge above him. Either enemy or supporter or self, the mirror image soon gives way to "a genuine reflection, much larger and clearer than the one that had deceived him" (143), one that consoles and focuses the desperate fugitive. This narcissistic moment moves Charles from the anxiety of personal threat and fragmentation to an affirmation of self, whole and strong. Like Hermann, Kinbote uses external objects — other people, Shade's poem — as a way of negotiating an ego in a world that is hostile to it. In this sense, Nabokov places Kinbote firmly in a post-Freudian world of object-relations, where narcissism comes to be seen as an adaptive strategy for constructing and maintaining a self rather than as a regression or malformation of the self.[6] In Jacques Lacan's less optimistic version of this phenomenon, the response to external rupture and fragmentation is to gather the different pieces of one's self into a seeming whole, one that produces a "self" (1977, 2). Such constructions of similarity or doubleness narcissistically attempt to display a unified self. But it is only an attempt. As Nabokov has said, "there are no real doubles in my novels" — only people's obsession with seeing similarity where none exists (quoted in Proffer 1968, 263).

Thus, Kinbote's purported psychosis seems to replicate Freud's argument that the paranoid hallucination is merely the external projection of an internal perception, a narcissistic crisis centering on the erotic investments in one's own body. Jacob Gradus is the persecuting other in Kinbote's delusion, but he is also indistinguishable from other Zemblans, from those signifiers of national pride and nostalgia that Kinbote idolizes. But, significantly, Kinbote "resembles" not only King Charles but also Gradus, the revolutionary murderer with whom he shares a birthday, a homeland, and a physiognomy (all Zemblans look alike). The king's bedroom mirror, the very signifier of his identity, was made by Sudarg of Bokay, "Jacob Gradus" spelled backward (111). The word "kinbote," we are told, is Zemblan for "regicide" (267). And, in a way, Kinbote's distortion of Shade's poem kills the author as Jack Grey kills the man. As Freud might suggest were he to lay Kinbote out on his couch, Gradus is the evil double who proceeds from Kinbote's own ego ideal, the libido he has invested erotically in the projection of his own body. And that he should do so in 1962 places him within the legibility crisis that Edelman argued earlier: in his similarity to the communist revolutionary, Kinbote signifies the very orientation to appropriate and transform the other into sameness. Kinbote emblematizes the impossibility of distinguishing persecuted citizen from persecuting communist, thus unearthing in the homosexual psyche a penchant for communism that Cold War America was sure was there. Like Hermann in *Despair,* Kinbote deploys narcissism to conjoin the "earnest case histories of . . . homosexuals" with the "anti-American Sovietnam sermon."

But what are we to make of the ethical implications of Kinbote's distortions when he is defended by John Shade, the voice in *Pale Fire* that is clearly closest to Nabokov's own? For Shade, the "lunatic" is that familiar Nabokovian artist "who deliberately peels off a drab and unhappy past and replaces it with a brilliant invention" (238). And in this sense, he echoes Freud's own assertion that the narcissistic paranoid not only destroys the world but "builds it up by the work of his delusions. *The delusional formation, which we take to be a pathological product, is in reality an attempt at recovery, a process of reconstruction*" (1911, 71). Moreover, what are we to make of Kinbote's distortions when they flow from the pen of an author who, like Kinbote, was, "as far back as I can remember, . . . subject to mild hallucinations" (Nabokov 1966b, 33)?[7] Or of the creation of an author who used to imagine, "in bedtime reveries, what it would be like to become an exile who longed for a remote, sad, and . . . unquenchable Russia" (Nabokov 1973c, 178) and who pictures himself "a passportless spy standing on the blue-white road in his New England snowboots" (1966b, 99–100)? What are we to make of a seeming homophobic narrative that uses the homosexual to ventriloquize Nabokov's own nostalgia for the lost glory of Russia? Kinbote writes, "When I was a child, Russia enjoyed quite a vogue at the court of Zembla but that was a different Russia — a Russia that hated tyrants and Philistines, injustice and cruelty, the Russia of ladies and gentlemen and liberal aspirations" (245). Indeed, how do we read a seeming homophobic narrative that proceeds from a man firmly self-identified as "queer"? The term itself, signaling vitriol rather than joyful transgression in the 1960s context, becomes a recurrent referent in *Speak, Memory* (1966b), as Nabokov describes his career as a butterfly collector. And while I am not suggesting that every man who collects butterflies is gay, what are we to make of lepidopterological descriptions like the following?

> In the summer of 1929, every time I walked through a village in the Eastern
> Pyrenees, and happened to look back, I would see in my wake the villagers
> frozen in the various attitudes my passage had caught them in, as if I were
> Sodom and they were Lot's wife. (Nabokov 1966b, 131)[8]

While Nabokov may gesture to a rather simple homophobia in his dismissal of homosexual narratives, his self-proclaimed queerness, and his love of creating new worlds through fictional reverie suggest that there may be more to the "lunatic" Kinbote than the homophobic lens can encompass.

Indeed, to place Kinbote in a psychoanalytic paradigm that equates homosexuality with paranoid delusion is not merely to simplify Freud; it is to read Nabokov straight by placing his characters in standard, flat, taxonomizing psychoanalytic paradigms. But as any reader of Nabokov will know, the use of psychoanalysis to locate a sexual politics is slippery. Nabokov invokes "the Viennese quack," as he repeatedly calls Freud, only to contradict him.[9] While the homosexual story that Charles inserts into the commentary is meant in some ways to signify madness and paranoia, it also contains elements of *real* persecution: early in the foreword, Charles is called before his department head to hear a student complaint, which he and we are sure will involve his attractions to his male students. Moreover, King Charles has emigrated from a land of gay freedom where, based on Greek models, "male homosexuality seems almost the norm, and 'manlier' than love between men and women" (Boyd 1991, 428); he has come to the America of the 1950s where, conversely, his "fancy pansy" desires are constantly derided (268). He is told: "Your majesty will have to be quite careful here" (248), a warning that echoes that of his department head. Kinbote's enforced closetedness reflects the intense homophobia that characterizes America after the war, homophobia that saw gay men as by definition subversive.[10] And this *real* persecution aligns Kinbote sympathetically with Daniel Paul Schreber. As Roy Porter argues, Freud read Schreber's fear of castration as proof of the universality of the oedipal complex. But Schreber's fear of castration was neither paranoid nor necessarily oedipal: his physician, Fleschig, was well known for using castration as therapeutic treatment. Schreber would have known this, even though Freud did not (Porter 1987, 156). A diagnosis of paranoid delusion may have its analytic uses — for both Freud's reading of Schreber and our reading of Kinbote — but it cannot, must not, negate the abuses of practice. (As Nabokov has Humbert Humbert say, the difference between "therapist" and "the rapist" is "a matter of nice spacing in the way of distinction" [1970, 152].) Rather, what gets called paranoia in the diagnosis of Kinbote may have an extremely practical purpose. Kinbote's narcissistic appropriations of Shade's poem provide a safe closet in which to express a censored sexuality: "despite the control exercised upon my poet by a domestic censor [Shade's wife Sybil], . . . he has given the royal fugitive a refuge in the vaults of the variants he has preserved" (81).

But beyond the elements of physical threat is an all-out attack on the Freudian construction of narcissism (or perhaps, more accurately, the way Freudian thought has been taken up in clinical practice). Whereas Freud defined homosexual perversion as narcissistic projection — the appropriating of another's identity to subsume it within one's ego, to destroy identity by rendering it "the same" — Nabokov mirrors this theory to show us its reverse. The source of this reversal may be Havelock Ellis, whom Nabokov read in his father's library and preferred to Freud. While Ellis too saw the homosexual as a narcissist, desiring himself in the love object, he also argued the opposite:

> It remains true, however, that there may be usually traced what it is possible to call a pseudo-sexual attraction, by which I mean a tendency for the invert to be attracted towards persons unlike himself, so that in his sexual relationships there is a certain semblance of sexual opposition. Inverts are not usually attracted to one another. (1897, 118)

One such invert is King Charles: he desires *difference* — difference in class, in age, in look. He can enjoy the high-born dauphin Oleg, whose blond Nordic features contrast with his own, or he can desire the revolutionary guards watching over him in prison. There is a similar orientation toward difference in the way Kinbote transgressively desires his students, who are clearly in asymmetrical power relations to him; indeed, his erotic attraction to "two charming identical twins and another boy, another boy" (23), signals both thematically and syntactically an orientation toward similarity while at the same time evoking a spectrum of differences (the identical twins are remarkable for a similarity that is juxtaposed with a world that looks different from them, a world both synecdochically embodied in and grammatically suggested by the phrase "another boy, another boy"). As a professor, Kinbote reminds us of the Greek models of desire discussed by Foucault (1985) and Halperin, models whose erotic charge magnetizes around fundamental *differences* in age and status. And it was these differences, we remember, that constituted for Jerome Christensen a sexuality in Byron that was nothing more than imperialistic exploitation. What Charles's transgression points to is that, for all the vaunted desire for difference, contemporary surveillance still constructs very strict limitations on that difference, in that only certain differences are appropriate to introduce to the arena of male eros. The gay man must be somewhat narcissistic but not too much, somewhat other-invested, but not too much.

Moreover, if Kinbote seems to embody Nabokov's sympathies at the same time that he parodies them, this is because Kinbote is as prone to seeing differences as he is to constructing false similarities. If narcissism means projecting oneself onto another and collapsing all others into one, Kinbote's perceptions are hardly narcissistic: his disposition to see the world through his own interest does not contract the possibilities for object-relations in that world but rather expands them. He fragments the murderous Jack Grey into Jacob Gradus, Jack Degree, Jacques de Grey, James de Gray, Vinogradus, and, most important, Leningradus. He sees his colleague Gerald Emerald as both faculty member and the Shadow Izumrudov. The verbose and tedious Professor Gordon of the music department is also "a slender but strong-looking lad of fourteen or fifteen dyed a nectarine hue by the sun" and wearing only "a leopard-spotted loincloth" (199), a Gordon who is also called "Narcissus" (202). And Kinbote himself is both academic and exiled king, two selves operating in independent narratives, yet who gradually get revealed as the same person.[11] His bedroom mirror in Zembla, whose significance I shall discuss in a moment, is a triptych in which the self is reflected not once but thousands of times in infinite arcs. If the homosexual in this novel is narcissistic, his is a narcissism that *multiplies* personalities rather than collapsing them into one.[12] Such difference is most forcefully and queerly inscribed in Kinbote's gloss on Shade's syllogism, *"other men die; but I / Am not another; therefore, I'll not die"* (lines 213–14); Kinbote responds, "This may please a boy. Later in life we learn that we *are* those 'others' " (164).[13] And it is precisely that fragmentation of the self into the spectrum of political differences — from Kinbote to Leningradus, from Emerald to Izumrudov — that unites Nabokov's resistance to Freud with his dismissal of the Cold War politics of narcissism, a politics that dangerously aligns the communist and the homosexual by collapsing their differences into "identity."

That resistance is most obviously conveyed in Nabokov's representation of Kinbote/King Charles as the gay man. Unlike the later *Despair*, translated and amended at a point in the 1960s when the anti-American Sovietnam sermon and homosexual case histories were proliferating (much to Nabokov's disgust), *Pale Fire* casts the aristocratic king and not the communistic Gradus as the gay man. In this novel, Nabokov bifurcates the equation between the queer and the communist that he would easily inscribe in Hermann — and that Cold War America homographically inscribed on the gay male body — and returns us to a perhaps premodern notion of the aristocrat as sodomite. Indeed, in *Pale Fire,* homoerotic bliss is *pitted against* Bolshevist-style revolution and sameness to mark a difference that could easily be identified and persecuted. Nor is this the first time Nabokov has represented the aristocrat as homosexual. Jane Grayson points out that

> in a prefatory note to the English translation of *Solus Rex* [Nabokov] speaks of the "restoration of a scene that had been marked in the *Sovremennyya Zapiski* by suspension point." This turns out to be a graphic description of the Prince's homosexual practices: "With fat fingers, the prince undid Ondrik's fly, extracted the entire pink mass of his private parts, selected the chief one, and started to rub regularly its glossy shaft." (1977, 78–79)[14]

Like the additions that Nabokov made to the 1966 English publication of *Despair,* this moment indicates his growing fascination with the representation of queer sexuality and his alignment of it with the aristocratic world for which he had some nostalgia. Nabokov may have found homosexual case histories tiresome, but he also found them representative of victimization, and precisely for their metonymic links to the aristocracy. To that end, he found useful the queer narcissist's alleged tendency toward sameness because in it Nabokov could figure its opposite — the inexorability of difference and individualism, the hallmark of his aesthetics.

Perhaps one of the richest schisms in the novel, then, is Nabokov's use of Kinbote not only as a psychoanalytic "type" — whose diagnosis his critics brutally offered above — but also as the refusal of the psychoanalytic tendency to type, to generalize the homosexual into a constellation of easily identifiable traits, to see, obsessively, a similarity where none exists. Indeed, Nabokov has suggested that it is not narcissism but psychoanalysis that breeds fascism: "what a great mistake on the part of dictators to ignore psychoanalysis," he writes in *Speak, Memory,* "a whole generation might so easily be corrupted that way" (1966b, 300–301).[15] And in *Pale Fire,* we find that condemnation exactly where we would expect it: the Nabokovian John Shade lists in his poem the things he loathes, including "Freud, Marx, / Fake thinkers, puffed-up poets, frauds and sharks" (67, lines 929–30).[16] But we also see it where we might least expect it, in Kinbote himself, who is as resistant to Freud and Marx as Shade is. In a discussion of pedagogy, Kinbote remembers, "The respective impacts and penetrations of Marxism and Freudism being talked of, I said: 'The worst of two false doctrines is always that which is harder to eradicate' " (155–56). And it is those "false doctrines," that tendency to generalize, that earns Jacob Gradus both Kinbote's and Nabokov's condemnation:

> He worshipped general ideas and did so with pedantic aplomb. The generality was godly, the specific diabolical. If one person was poor and the other wealthy it did not matter what precisely had ruined one or made the other rich; the difference itself was unfair, and the poor man who did not denounce it was as wicked as the rich one who ignored it. People who knew too much, scientists, writers, mathematicians, crystalographers and so forth, were no better than kings or priests: they all held an unfair share of power of which others were cheated. A plain decent fellow should constantly be on the watch for some piece of clever knavery on the part of nature or neighbor. (152)

And compare this to Nabokov's evaluation of Lenin in *Speak, Memory:*

> All cultured and discriminating Russians know that this astute politician had about as much taste and interest in aesthetic matters as an ordinary Russian bourgeois of the Flaubertian *épicier* sort.... [T]he more radical a Russian was in politics, the more conservative he was on the artistic side. (263)[17]

Communism, psychoanalysis, their generalizing politics: all destroy the discriminating, distinctive, aesthetic mind, and all come under fire by the character supposed to be the most interested in, most representational of, the libidinal investments in sameness.

That Nabokov should figure in the homosexual his vitriolic hatred of psychoanalysis and communism resonates with his own troubled relationship to his brother, Sergey. "For various reasons I find it inordinately hard to speak about my ... brother. ... [H]is boyhood and mine seldom mingled. He is a mere shadow in the background of my richest and most detailed recollections" (1966b, 257). Sergey was homosexual, and his very designation as "a mere shadow" in Nabokov's memory registers *Pale Fire*'s prismatic shimmers of Shade and Shadow, of Kinbote and Gradus, of sameness and difference. In 1932, Nabokov visited Sergey and his lover in the Luxembourg Gardens of Paris. Nabokov later wrote, with the happy incredulity of a tolerant liberal, "The husband, I must admit, is very pleasant, quiet, not at all the pederast type, attractive face and manner" (quoted in Boyd 1990, 396).[18] Nabokov's admission that "the husband" was likable betrays the epistemology of a closet that is both homophobic and queer, one that sees the gay man as a "type" yet that ostentatiously dissociates him from typology. Like John Shade of *Pale Fire*, who generously allows Kinbote to visit him in his bathtub — "Let him in, Sybil, he won't rape me" (264) — the straight Vladimir registers both the assumptions surrounding gay male behavior (pederasty, seduction, male rape) and the liberal distance from such assumptions.

But what is more urgent in Nabokov's troubled reflection (and in the text of *Pale Fire*) is the way gayness slips from the psychological condition of narcissism into political victimization. Years after the Luxembourg visit, Sergey was imprisoned by the Nazis for his homosexuality. He was later released, but his proclamations against the Nazi regime returned him to prison under suspicion as a British spy, and he died in a concentration camp from complications stemming from malnutrition. Moreover, Sergey's persecutions did not come solely from the Nazi — and more than Nazi — equation of homosexuality and political subversion. Vladimir himself was guilty of persecution. When the two were still young boys, he snooped through Sergey's diary and discovered the secret of his brother's desires. Vladimir immediately conveyed this information to their tutor, who told their father — a father who had been a tireless advocate against the persecution of homosexual men in turn-of-the-century Russia. However, despite his liberal juridical and political stances, Vladimir Dmitrievich was not sympathetic: Sergey was promptly withdrawn from the school he had been attending, and where he had had some romances, and was placed in another.[19] For biographer Brian Boyd, this moment of invasion engendered a guilt that expressed itself in Nabokov's later work: "Perhaps Vladimir's self-reproach for that glance at the diary and his unthinking impulse to pass on the information may account in part for his fierce opposition in later years to any infringement of personal privacy" (1990, 106).[20] If Nabokov hated homosexuality, that hatred was self-contested: the notoriously homosexual condition of loving sameness gets eradicated by a political and domestic regime seeking *real* sameness in a pure society of like-minded, like-blooded (narcissistic?) individuals. Types like the Shadows, Kinbote tells us,

> have been known to go berserk at the thought that their elusive victim whose very testicles they crave to twist and tear with their talons, is sitting at a pergola feast on a sunny island or fondling some pretty young creature between his knees in serene security — and laughing at them! One supposes that no hell can be worse than the helpless rage they experience as the awareness of that implacable sweet mirth reaches them and suffuses them, slowly destroying their brutish brains. (149–50)

As Eve Kosofsky Sedgwick has pointed out, what we think of as homophobia is often really *heterophobia,* the fear of difference (see especially chapter 10 of *Between Men* [1985]). And this fear united the homosexual with the communist as common targets of persecution. Nabokov's intervention into queer narcissism here is not that dissimilar to Michael Warner's, which I summarized in this book's introduction: narcissism as a diagnosis is crucial not just to cordon off and debilitate gay men but to provide the very definition of heterosexuality that will be used (narcissistically) to legitimate the normative. Narcissism is as much a national expression of homophobia as it is a sexual psychodynamic.

"A Bothersome Defocalization"

As Sergey returns as "a mere shadow" to haunt the pages of *Speak, Memory* (figuring as he does a love of sameness that is persecuted for its difference), he personifies Nabokovian *memory,* the faculty that seeks to incorporate the past into the construction of the current self. In *Pale Fire* (1962), Nabokov meditates on the texture and flavor of this memory, and on the way its curiously murky quality fashions a sense of history. Not surprisingly, he captures the strange presence/absence, the paradoxical there/not there quality of history through a narcissistic image, that of the mirror. King Charles's bedroom mirror, we remember, is a triptych, multiplying images. When Fleur, Charles's spurned lover, steps into it, its reflectivity takes on a significance that connects the narcissist's multiple identity (the prototypical Lacanian mirror ego) to national history:

> She turned about before it: a secret device of reflection gathered an infinite number of nudes in its depths, garlands of girls in graceful and sorrowful groups, diminishing the limpid distance, or breaking into individual nymphs, some of whom, she murmured, must resemble her ancestors when they were young. (111–12)

Here Echo is not only the rejected lover of Narcissus but a Narcissus herself. In a *mise en abyme,*[21] Fleur replicates herself into other, erotically posed women who are both sexual and historical figures. Like the red-sweatered king moving through Zembla and staring at the pond, Fleur sees herself many times over and in so doing suggests affinities with the people in her past, people she resembles but has never known. The ancestry of the nation, it would seem, is visible only through our own optics, through the narcissistic moment of beholding a self that both includes us and is other than us, the self that is isolated synchronically in history but stretches diachronically through history in selves we do not know. Such a resonance is even built into the myth's history: as Louise Vinge tells us, what Ovid's Narcissus "sees in the water and mistakes for another person is called both *imago* and *umbra,*" reflection *and shadow,* the two words being for a long time interchangeable and connoting "the 'shadows' of the dead" (12). Furthermore, the coding of history in Charles's mirror is replayed in Hesse's *Demian,* in an even more homoerotic register. During the scene of the dying horse, which I discussed at length in chapter 3, Emil Sinclair is struck by the multiple images of Max Demian's face: "And for the time being his face seemed neither masculine nor childish, neither old nor young but a hundred years old, almost timeless and bearing the mark of other periods of history than our own" (49). Emil's daimon, his other, his lover, his self is the figure by which he places himself within history, a history predicated on narcissistic homoeros.

If the almost indiscriminate interweaving of self through other defines the relation between memory and history — if memory and history are ultimately narcissistic — Nabokov makes such an interweaving compulsory for his definition of the artist. The description of memory in *Speak, Memory,* differs little from what gets condemned in Kinbote as narcissistic "hallucination." For John Burt Foster Jr., memory in Nabokov's oeuvre is modeled on Proust's "willed recovery of lost time," a pondering and probing of the mnemonic image that "restores [the subject's] self-esteem along with bringing back forgotten aspects of his life-story, and much later even helps him achieve his long-postponed artistic aims" (17). As Foster makes clear, this attraction to Proust frames a Modernism that celebrates the individual, the specific, that which belongs to the particular artist (and this is of course what Hermann Hesse thought psychoanalysis could fruitfully dredge up from the depths of the psyche). However, we must also see it in a queer history and homoerotic influence. Foster reminds us that *Lolita*'s Humbert Humbert, who may also have a homosexual past, considers "calling part 2 of his confession *Dolorès disparue,* thereby placing his beloved Lolita in the role of Proust's Albertine" (Foster 1993, 220). This homoerotic influence is most clearly registered in Nabokov's Uncle Ruka, the avuncular homosexual whose ostentatiously queer performances embarrassed the young Vladimir, yet whose death made the boy a millionaire until the money was lost in the revolution. As Foster says, Ruka is clearly remembered in chapter 3 of *Speak, Memory,* for his affinities with Proust: his "*belle époque* affluence, his poor health, and his homosexuality" — indeed, "in the Russian version of the autobiography, Nabokov even states that his uncle looks like him. . . . Ruka is also the one poet in the family, and when he writes, he does so in French, driven by what is called a 'Proustian excoriation of the senses' " (Foster 1993, 204–5). Nabokov remembers most vividly Ruka's and his own reading of the children's books of Madame de Ségur, and as the older Vladimir rereads the books, he connects to his queer uncle in significantly Proustian ways: "I not only go through the same agony and delight that my uncle did, but have to cope with an additional burden — the recollection I have of him, reliving his childhood with the help of those very books" (1966b, 76). No anxiety of influence or homosexual panic, this passage demonstrates an aesthetic transmission whose queer resonances are multivalent. Nabokov does not relive his own childhood here, with his uncle placed in it — he relives his *uncle's* childhood, identifying with him and his pleasures and agonies, inhabiting his subjective space. Nor is Vladimir the only person in this queerly overdetermined space. Along with the reference to Proust, Nabokov remembers that "the only person who memorized the music and all the words [to Ruka's composed romance] was my brother Sergey, whom he hardly ever noticed, who also stammered, and who is also dead" (1966b, 74). And, significant for its omission, who was also homosexual. Here artistic production centers in the homosexual who both hypostatizes queer subjectivity and incorporates that subjectivity into a history of influence and depersonalized aestheticism. By this definition, history and memory do not merely record the queer — history and memory *are* queer to the degree that they are structured in Nabokov on male replications, affiliations, and homoerotic identifications.

This queer memory, achieved through and against Uncle Ruka, achieved through and against Kinbote, becomes central to Nabokov's definition of the artist in *Speak, Memory.* In writing about his tutors, he turns "the queer dissonances they introduced into my young life" into "the essential stability and completeness of that life" (1966b, 170). Thus, "the pulsation of my thought mingles with that of the leaf shadows and turns Ordo into Max and Max into Lenski and Lenski into the schoolmaster and the whole array of trembling transformations is repeated" (171). Indeed, Nabokov has said that Kinbote merely "retwists" his own experiences, rather than opposing them (1973c, 77). And what is even more striking here is the way the dialectic of self and otherness is gendered. In the specifically heterosexual memories of *Speak, Memory,* women are either isolated and presented for their particular, individuating characteristics (see for example the disjointed catalog of nurses and governesses on page 86), or they all collapse synecdochically into the idea of one: "all would merge to form somebody I did not know but was bound to know soon" (213). These aspects of narcissistic remembering, what Nabokov ultimately calls "a bothersome defocalization" (240), which we might as easily attribute to Ovid's Narcissus, *either* isolate *or* erase female subjectivity altogether, whereas the passage describing male tutors moves in and out of male subjective space. Moreover, these scenes replicate and eroticize the male self in ways reminiscent of *Despair*'s Hermann: "In looking at it from my present tower I see myself as a hundred different young men at once, all pursuing one changeful girl in a series of simultaneous or overlapping love affairs" (1966b, 240). We have in this heterosexual field, then, a sexualized aesthetic of memory whose primary prophet is narcissistically homosexual: an erotic subject whose self is continually split, bifurcated, and defocalized yet always kept fully in view. The males of one's past blend and intermingle with the "male" of one's present as a queer history constitutes and places a current self. As Nabokov states in an interview in *Strong Opinions,* it is through "the combination and juxtaposition of remembered details" that one probes "not only one's personal past but the past of one's family in search of affinities with oneself, previews of oneself, faint allusions to one's vivid and vigorous Now" (1973c, 187). That isolated, private self, those affinities with others displaced into history, are all made possible only by an aesthetic of queer, homoerotic narcissism.

The Politics of Feigned Remoteness

It is that "vivid and vigorous Now" that can bring us back to *Pale Fire,* to the immediacy of John Shade's poem, and to its inscription within a sexual and political America. For just as Nabokov weaves the "artist" out of his own queer take on Narcissus, so does John Shade. Shade opens the poem "Pale Fire" by stating, "I was the shadow of the waxwing slain / By the false azure in the windowpane" (lines 1–2). The subject of the poem is the self as it exists within an artistic reflection and yet is obliterated by it. The death of the author occurs by an act of artistic similarity, a "feigned remoteness" (line 132) that replicates him at the same time that it displaces him from his image in the window and from his "self" as the subject of the poem. This displacement has clearly narcissistic overtones in that Shade describes how, Narcissus-like, "I'd duplicate / Myself" (lines 5–6), constructing in a false, chimerical reflection an object into which one can never enter, a mirror division that leads, in classical literary and psychoanalytic accounts, to death. Only the darkness of night "unites the viewer and the view" (line 18), in that it simultaneously increases the intensity of the image reflected in the window and foreshadows how such reflection metaphorically suggests death and everlasting darkness. If Kinbote's narcissism is a symptom of madness that is conveniently associated with gayness, then Shade too is narcissistically engulfed, infatuated by the creative possibilities of gazing at his own reflected image. Shade is not only his own Shadow (the Modernist source of his own narcissistic death) but also his own inspiration, the other whose reflection he desires to have and to become (shades here of Coleridge in "The Picture"). Both authors, by this standard, are queer.

Shade's narcissism, moreover, reflects Kinbote's in its tendency to see the object-world through the lens of its own desires. In Canto II, Shade looks at his fingers and constructs a "dazzling synthesis" of "certain flinching likenesses" between his digits and his neighbors: "the thumb, / Our grocer's son; the index, lean and glum / College astronomer Starover Blue" (lines 184–89). After he has a near-death vision of a white fountain and reads of another person who had the same vision, he seeks in this similarity a theory of the afterlife; he hopes to use another's experience to validate his own. However, it is in this supposedly shared experience of an afterlife that Shade halts the intersubjective mingling and replication that we saw in Kinbote and in *Speak, Memory*. Despite his narcissistic desire to affirm himself, Shade also hopes to avoid in the woman any "fond / Affinity, a sacramental bond, / Uniting mystically her and me" (lines 791–92). And he is in luck: the woman has seen a *mountain*, not a fountain; the article that had recounted the woman's near-death experience had misprinted the word. "Life Everlasting — based on a misprint!" Shade harumphs (line 803) and decides that the meaning of life is that there is no pattern of order or connection but rather "topsy-turvical coincidence" (line 809), "accidents and possibilities" (line 829) whose interconnectedness is mere wishful thinking.[22] Shade's fountain (the fountain of Narcissus?) remains his and his alone, thus countering Kinbote's affirmation of similarity and connection. In an echo of the conventional critical understanding of Nabokov, Shade proclaims "there is no resemblance at all. Resemblances are the shadows of differences. Different people see different similarities and similar differences" (265). And this individualism has political consequences for the kind of culture that Lee Edelman has described, the kind of culture that insists on turning sameness into difference. Shade's narcissism does not celebrate the possibilities of a social fabric so much as it avoids them in favor of an individualizing difference. Whereas Kinbote's narcissism constructs differences in order to meld them into a one that is at the same time erotically communal and politically anticommunist, Shade's narcissism attempts to cut the self off from participation in society and from acts that could be said to construct a history. It engulfs the self in a protective individualism that the Cold War culture of the 1950s and 1960s tried so desperately to construct.

But Narcissus, as I have been suggesting along the course of this study, is an agitator, an agent provocateur. He is the instigator of a cultural critique by situating Shade's protective individualism, and its 1950s correlative of anticommunist sentiment, within a Romanticism whose homoeros we have been tracing throughout this book. The novel is set in New Wye, which, if it suggests New York, must also suggest a new Wye valley, the site of Wordsworth's musings on Romantic memory in "Tintern Abbey." It is the New England of Herman Melville, for whom "the story of Narcissus . . . is the image of the ungraspable phantom of life, and this is the key to all" (26). According to Robert K. Martin (1986) and Eve Sedgwick (1990), the "key" that Narcissus holds is the troubled homosociality whose inflections through narcissism (it takes one to know one) become volatile and murderous. As they do in Edgar Allan Poe's "William Wilson," where the fleeting, desired image of one's double/opposite might match, point for point, Kinbote and Gradus, Hermann and Felix, Humbert and Quilty (in *Lolita*), V. and Sebastian (in *The Real Life of Sebastian Knight*). But perhaps most importantly, it is the New England of Walt Whitman, whose influence Kinbote may lovingly invoke when he calls Shade a "bad gray poet" (74), punning as strongly the good gray poet as he does Jacob Gradus/Jack Grey. For Whitman's dialectic of communalism and individualism is not all that different from Nabokov's and is just as narcissistic. As Whitman stares into the waters of the East River in "Crossing Brooklyn Ferry," he sees the "fine centrifugal spokes of light" that angelically encircle his head (1990, line 33) — thus proclaiming his own greatness, the uniqueness of his perception. Yet he also knows that this light proceeds "from the shape of my head, or any one's head, in the sunlit water!" (line 116). All people on the ferry have this vision, but each can only see his or her own halo; each can only see the self through a different similarity. And it is that Romantic dialectic of perception that underwrites Whitman's homoeroticism in particular, making the love of "comrades" in "Calamus" little different from the love of similarly different men in King Charles's Zembla. To the degree that America is built on what Leslie Fiedler called a "delicate homosexuality" (1960, 330), indeed, to the degree that "comradeship," "friendship," and the social have in Freud a homoerotic foundation, the social and literary fabric may be as much a mirror reflection of Zembla as its mirror opposite. Shade's world is queer not because he or most of the people in it are homosexual but because the aesthetic that creates and describes its culture makes inescapable the eroticized relations between men, the men of the past, the men of the present, the men in one's "self."

It is that reflection in opposition, that fundamental (narcissistic) similarity within difference, that twists John Shade and American anticommunist individualism into the crowning irony of the novel. For in the end, it is not the communist subversive that enters New Wye and kills the American citizen; rather, America's social woes come from inside America itself. Shade's murderer is not Leningradus but Jack Grey, who escapes from "the Institute for the Criminal Insane, *ici*" (295), here, among us. Grey mistakes Shade for Judge Goldsworth, who sent him to prison: perhaps all Americans look alike as well? And while Nabokov would come to hate the suggestion that America was "just as oppressive" as Russia — that detestable "anti-American, Sovietnam sermon"[23] — he does represent in Jack Grey both an antiauthoritarian regicide existing in the American public as well as in the Soviet and the possibility that this common man was unlawfully imprisoned. In fact, Nabokov once included in a list of tyrants not only the predictable Leninist gang but also "the lean American lyncher, the man with the bad teeth who squirts antiminority stories in the bar or the lavatory" (1966b, 264). Given Nabokov's inclusion of America within the list of possible tyrants, Shade's assertion that he is "slain / By feigned remoteness" is more accurate than he intends: if "remoteness" means an inoculated safety from the social context in which he lives; if "remoteness" assumes disconnection from the political forces of American culture, then such remoteness is indeed revealed to be "feigned." While the States in the 1950s loved to see the Soviet Union as its antagonistic opposite, its political and military other, *Pale Fire* identifies postrevolutionary Russia as America's narcissistically reflected self, an image repeated, albeit reversed, in a mirror. Through the trope of queer narcissism, Nabokov homographically turns the male-male bond by which American democracy is figured — a trope that both reveals and hides the homosexual — into the terrifying obliteration of difference whose implications cut across both gender and national boundaries. And like *Lolita* (1970), *Pale Fire* takes upon itself "the task of inventing America" (1970, 314). Homosexual narcissism not only is detested by American Cold War purity but also is omnipresent to it. While used ostensibly to engender postrevolutionary Russia, narcissism turns its triptych mirror and engenders America as well.

"Come Here, Come Herrr . . . "

Nothing I have said here is true.

In his definition of a queer cultural politics, Lee Edelman coins the term "homographesis" to refer to a "double operation: one serving the ideological purposes of a conservative social order intent on codifying identities in its labor of disciplinary inscription, and the other resistant to that categorization, intent on *de*-scribing the identities that order has so oppressively *in*scribed" (1994, 10). It is that double operation that I have tried to trace here. On the one hand, *Pale Fire* inscribes a character whose alleged lunacy slickly and metonymically links to his homosexuality in an equation that authorizes his critics to flay him, critics whose academic voice is reflected when "a certain ferocious lady" attacks Kinbote: "You are a remarkably disagreeable person. . . . What's more, you are insane" (25). But, on the other hand, Nabokov bifurcates Kinbote into shades of Shade, echoes of himself, mirrored fragments of a decentered "identity" that opens up the space for Nabokov's own aesthetic credo, his need for the magnetism of sameness in order to posit difference within it. And, of course, Kinbote and Shade, not to mention the communists, criminals, and homophobes who circle around them, do not exist: they are, according to Nabokov's diary, the fantasy projections of one Veselav Botkin, a disaffected scholar in the Russian department of Goldsmith University (Boyd 1991, 443; see Nabokov 1962, 155). As an "American scholar of Russian descent" (Nabokov 1962, 306), Botkin both mirrors Nabokov and displaces him, signaling an authorial identity that Nabokov then deconstructs. Thus does the novel mark through homosexuality — its penchant for sameness/difference, its homographic dialectic — the affirmation and destruction of authorial, sexual, political identity. Kinbote concludes his commentary:

> I shall continue to exist. I may assume other disguises, other forms, but I shall try to exist. I may turn up yet, on another campus, as an old, happy, healthy, heterosexual Russian, a writer in exile, sans fame, sans future, sans audience, sans anything but his art. . . . I may pander to the simple tastes of theatrical critics and cook up a stage play, an old-fashioned melodrama with three principles: a lunatic who intends to kill an imaginary king, another lunatic who imagines himself to be that king, and a distinguished old poet who stumbles by chance into the line of fire, and perishes in the clash between the two figments. (300–301)

To the degree that "identity" authorizes the oppressive categories of sexual, political, and aesthetic normalcy, Nabokov places them all within mirrored triptychs to *de*-scribe, intermix, mutually constitute, and mutually destroy any central identity or veracity in the novel.

Thus, nothing I have said here is true.

And if the novel seeks to dramatize the multiplication and decon-struction of identity through homo-narcissistic mirror play, it does so most graphically through its emphasis on *words,* on written words, as signifiers performing the very phenomenon Nabokov is espousing. If "kinbote" is an anagram of "botkin," the "original" author, then John Shade, the "distinguished old poet who ... perishes in the clash between the two figments," is a "kinbote," a "botkin," which is "a person closely wedged between two other persons" (Boyd 1991, 444). Moreover, he is another kind of botkin — according to the *OED,* a botkin is an awl-like tool used in printing to correct set-up type by picking out unwanted letters. "Kinbote" itself is supposedly the Zem-blan word for "regicide" — and "a king who sinks his identity in the mirror of exile is in a sense just that" (267), as he projects and destroys himself by adopting another signifying name. As a word, "Shade" too playfully denotes the poet, the murderous revolutionary Shadows, the shades and shadows of memory that construct history in Shade's "Pale Fire," in Kinbote's commentary to "Pale Fire," in Nabokov's *Pale Fire* and autobiography. It denotes too Shade's daughter Hazel, that other (dead) poet who also "twisted words: pot, top, / Spider, redips. And 'powder' was 'red wop' " in the mirror of her signifying conscious-ness (lines 347–48). Finally, Gradus is not only a shade, a shadow; he is also a character who is ultimately written by Shade (78, 136); and Shade is written by Kinbote, without whom there is "no human reality" (28); and Kinbote's own self is equated with his notes (300), notes written by someone else, some other Russian exile. A queer *mise en abyme* is not only Fleur's in this novel; it defines the book's entire authorial structure. *Pale Fire* in total seems to be one long exercise in a homographesis that, as Edelman says, puts into writing "and there-fore into the realm of *différance* — ... the sameness, the similitude, or the essentializing metaphors of identity ... that homographesis, in its first sense, is intended to secure" (12).

For Edelman, that submission of writing to a homographic *dif-férance* is itself a queer enterprise. Homographesis, he says,

> exposes the metonymic slippage ... [and] articulates a difference from the
> binary differentiation of sameness and difference, presence and absence:
> those couples wedded to each other in order to determine identity as same-
> ness or presence to oneself. In this sense, homographesis, in a gesture that
> conserves what it contests, defines as central to "homosexuality" a refusal
> of the specifications of identity (including sexual identity) performed by the

cultural practice of a regulatory homographesis that marks out the very
space within which to think "homosexuality" itself. Like writing, that is,
it de-scribes itself in the very moment of its inscription. (14)

The project of analyzing homographesis has political purchase for
Edelman because it can

> locate the critical force of homosexuality at the very point of discrimina-
> tion between sameness and difference as cognitive landmarks governing the
> discursive field of social symbolic relations. Not only the logic of sexual
> identity, but the logic informing the tropology through which identity and
> difference themselves are constructed, registered, and enforced by the nat-
> uralized operation of the Law thereby becomes susceptible to gay critical
> analysis. (20)

That *Pale Fire* should place at its center Charles Kinbote, a narcissistic homosexual writer, foregrounds these queer slippages within
language itself, a language we always rely on to convey identity (identity in language, the identity we construct for ourselves, that culture
constructs for us, the identities of homo and hetero), and makes the
regulatory regimes of those identities impossible to sustain. *Pale Fire*
enacts at the level of the signifier the same homographic imperative
and impossibility that Cold War America installed in its obsessively
failing diagnosis of the communist-homosexual.

And all of this because Narcissus himself speaks "the tongue of
the mirror" (Nabokov 1962, 242). As the death of John Shade, performed by his own poem, immortalizes him in a university building
formally known as "Parthenocissus Hall" (22), we sense the Nabokovian blending of the gods and Narcissus, a blending half-celebrated and
half-parodied, a blending that signals Narcissus's own homographic
relation to another signifying image that simultaneously identifies
(with) him and inaugurates his desire. Curiously, that tongue of the
Narcissan mirror, that watery *mise en abyme* that gives us "something
more than mirrorplay or mirage shimmer" (Nabokov 1962, 135), is
the mutually dependent, mutually exclusive seduction into identity
("Come here" [line 68]) and into the erotic bond with another man
("come herrr" [line 68]) that Shade hears in a mockingbird's song (another bird for another john?). It is a queer discourse that engages male
selves by shattering them, that unites signifiers by differentiating them
and by sounding "the repetition of that long-drawn note" where "the
assonance between its second word and the rhyme gives the ear a kind
of languorous pleasure as would the echo of some half remembered
sorrowful song whose strain is more meaningful that its words" (135).

Chapter 5

THE GOTHIC IN A CULTURE OF NARCISSISM

And so, by the late twentieth century, Narcissus had become political. Not that he hadn't always been; this book has attempted to trace the imbrications of Narcissus in the politics of various periods and classes, not to mention the specific political concerns in which an author was invested. But at least since the 1950s, Narcissus came to be associated with large *p* politics: communism, socialism, nationalism, a partisan affiliation that is made self-consciously and purposefully. Yet, in his very status as queer, Narcissus could also disrupt the alleged coherence of any of those political positions. Inflecting them with same-sex eros, or even demonstrating the degree to which national politics is so often constituted around same-sex eros, Narcissus could sometimes partake in the hegemonic power structure of masculine desire and could other times transgress it, making his transgression just as obvious, just as jubilant, just as self-conscious as was his inclusion in the reigning class. As Vladimir Nabokov's *Pale Fire* or Tennessee Williams's *Suddenly Last Summer* makes clear, Narcissus effects a political legibility crisis: he produces and is produced by a literary language that makes him both visible and invisible. He is invented by diagnostic discourses that he at the same time escapes. This paradox of de-scription Lee Edelman has termed "homographesis": Narcissus is subversive because he undermines the authority of the very discourses that produce him.

This diagnostic (in)stability is not confined to Narcissus's role in the theater of national politics; it is also produced by the language of sexual politics in the late twentieth century. Of course sexual politics, like nationalist ones, have been nascent in Western thought at least since the ancient Greeks, but with the development of second-wave feminism in the 1960s they took on a new lexicon, a different intellectual arsenal, and constituted a radically new discursive project. With this proliferation of feminist theories of masculine economy, coupled with "out" gay self-representations after Stonewall, Narcissus underwent his, if not final, then at least most damaging series of bifurcations: feminists (following Freud) could begin to deplore him as the prototype of misogyny while gay filmmakers like Derek Jarman could see in him a trope of homosexual desire and identity, a usage that Earl Jackson has thoroughly described. As the late twentieth century seeks to sort out Narcissus's overdeterminations and, if possible, to privilege one over the other, we are witnessing the culmination of a self-consciousness in Narcissus that it has been the project of this book to explore. Since at least the eighteenth century, Narcissus has been not simply a case history for normalizing or transgressing politically invested discourses; he has been the *metalanguage* for those discourses, the underlying figure for how they are produced. How, we might ask, does this complexly allusive figure inflect the metalanguage of contemporary gender theory? How does Narcissus de-scribe the postmodern moment?

These questions are obviously too huge for one chapter, so to localize my discussion I want to consider some post-Freudian theorists as they converge with a popular novel, Peter Straub's 1979 *Ghost Story*. I choose this "minor classic" for a number of reasons. First, it recapitulates the kind of Gothic homosexual panic that Eve Sedgwick so deftly theorized within the late-eighteenth-century Gothic, and so dramatizes a number of the subplots playing throughout this study: male-male transmutability, maternal cathexis, hallucination and projection, the über-language of psychoanalysis. Second, the novel's myriad characters and discrete plots seem to encode different, although fully articulated, recent theories of narcissism. This chapter will bring together Straub's various narratives with thinkers such as Christopher Lasch, Luce Irigaray, Jacques Lacan, Julia Kristeva, and Roland Barthes, all of whom join Straub in trying to articulate the narcissism of the 1970s, a culture that was thought to have degenerated into the self-indulgence and masculine self-congratulation of the disco decade, the "me generation."[1] Third, by falling under the vague rubric of "the popular," the novel offers us some insight into a sphere of gender configurations less arcane than those of, say, André Gide's Symbolism or Vladimir Nabokov's Modernism. It gestures to the concerns of the "common" American male, whatever he may look like. Yet, as I have demonstrated in my unlikely pairing of Hesse and Williams in chapter 3, Narcissus constructs a space of reflection in which seemingly disparate subjects (here, post-Lacanian theory and drugstore thriller) are welded together by the sameness, the homeness, of their concerns. And, finally, Straub's *Ghost Story*, like the psychoanalytic theories I will discuss, is about storytelling. It takes as its focus the generating of narratives — their sources, their effects, their vicissitudes. In a tradition stretching as far back as Neoplatonism, that storytelling is narcissistic, and because it is narcissistic, it demonstrates the degree to which the postmodern moment — its Gothic tonality, its theoretical strata — is intransigently, disruptively queer.

"The Generation of Unpleasure"

An archetypal narcissistic narrative,[2] *Ghost Story* is actually many stories. (And since the plot is so Byzantine, I beg my reader's patience while I summarize it.) The novel centers on the Chowder Society, a group of old men in Milburn, New York, who meet regularly to tell ghost stories. The genesis of these stories is twofold: first, they arose to divert the men from thinking about the sudden and mysterious death of one of their members, Edward Wanderly; and, second, they were the direct response to the idle question, *"What was the worst thing you've ever done?"* John Jaffrey, one member of the society, responded, *"I won't tell you that, but I'll tell you the worst thing that ever happened to me...the most dreadful thing"* (1992, 11). The circumlocuted "worst thing you've ever done" turns out to be the society's murder of a woman named Eva Galli, with whom they had all been infatuated in their youth. The "most dreadful thing" to happen to them is Galli's ghostly return. She manifests herself as Ann-Veronica Moore to some members of the society, Anna Mostyn to others, Alma Mobley to others, and Angie Maule to others as she proceeds to ravage the small town. The two main characters, Ricky Hawthorne and Sears James (N.B.: Straub intends the names to resonate with American history, as does Nabokov with John Shade), enlist the help of Don Wanderly, Edward's nephew, whose brother David had died at the hand of Mobley. Don can help the Chowder Society fight the growing evil because he is an English professor and novelist whose successful book, *The Nightwatcher*, resembles in many ways the horror plaguing Milburn. Indeed it seems that Don is living out in Milburn the fictional events he created earlier in his novel. Finally, young Peter Barnes, whose mother was having an affair with Chowder member Lewis Benedikt before falling victim to the devastation of Milburn, rounds out the troupe. But what is most significant about the female ghosts they battle, what is most relevant to a history of literary narcissism, is their response to the male lovers' question about their identity: when pressed to reveal "Who are you?" by David/Edward/Don, and so on, Anna/Alma/Ann-Veronica invariably responds, "I am you." Clearly evil comes in female form, but it is a form that seems to gesture to some male narcissistic anxiety in late-twentieth-century America.

According to Stephen King, this narcissism is *the* central anxiety of contemporary horror fiction in America. In *Danse Macabre* (1983), King explores Straub's theme — "a very Jamesian theme" —

> that ghosts, in the end, adopt the motivations and perhaps the very souls of those who behold them. If they are malevolent, their malevolence comes from us. Even in their terror, Straub's characters recognize the kinship. In their appearance, his ghosts, like the ghosts James, Wharton, and M. R. James conjure up, are Freudian. Only in their final exorcism do Straub's ghosts become truly inhuman — emissaries from the world of "outside evil." (257)

Indeed, for King, the novel's references to Narcissus — including three prose poems on Narcissus that serve as the epigraphs to various chapters — constitute the novel's central trope: horror is our own face looking out at us from the ghostly mirror. And this fundamental narcissism, for King, has become the ruling symptom of our time. Following a critical article by John Park on Shirley Jackson's *The Sundial*, King argues that the haunted house or Bad Place in contemporary horror is no longer the womb of sexual anxiety but rather the self; it is haunted by the contemporary interest in and fear of the self, so that "the symbolic womb," says King, has become "the symbolic mirror" (1983, 281).

The privileged role accorded to Narcissus by King's survey and by Straub's novel certainly concurs with another treatment of the Narcissus myth, Christopher Lasch's *The Culture of Narcissism: American Life in an Age of Diminishing Expectations*. First published in 1979, the same year as *Ghost Story*, Lasch's book posits that the individual in the late twentieth century has been emptied of meaning, having given over his/her self-image to the proliferation of bureaucratic and mechanical specialists who then assume responsibility for that individual's life decisions. The politico-religious individualism of the nineteenth century in America called for the citizen to mold and shape the empty wilderness to his own design, a remolding articulated from the American Renaissance to John Shade (see chapter 4). But now such individualism has given way to a flat meaninglessness. The narcissistic optic that re-created nature (the phenomenon we saw in the Romantics in chapter 1) has become a flat mirror in which the individual can only reflect himself back to himself in a quest for grandiosity and self-definition. Thus, the "quest of nature and the search for new frontiers have given way to the search for self-fulfillment," Lasch maintains, so that individual therapy and a psychiatric ideal have replaced a more socially minded construction of the nation (1991, 25). After the failed revolutions of the 1960s, people have retreated into obsessive concern with self-improvement and psychic health, thereby losing their sense of place in a larger social and historical matrix. The kind of oedipal strength one gained from battling the wilderness has dispersed into a narcissistic insularity that merely feeds itself, indulging the destructive appetites of its own self-consumption. If Neoplatonism and Symbolism found narcissism useful for getting to the Truth, postmodern late capitalism finds it inescapable, implacable, ruefully omnipotent.

Lasch's worldview is replicated in Straub's novel, where the lawyers' professional responsibilities have been reduced to neighbors' petty wranglings over land borders, teenagers are unable to see beyond the immediate concerns of marrying their high school sweethearts, and the (allegedly inferior) Cornell is preferred to Yale because it is closer to home for weekend sojourns. Milburn, a town "too self-conscious about its status" (Straub 1992, 149), is bored, its only excitement being the occasional adulterous fling or nasty practical joke. As one resident puts it, "you live in this town long enough . . . you have to keep reminding yourself that the whole world isn't just one big Milburn" (274).[3] This narcissism, moreover, typifies America generally: nearby New York City is "wrapped in a self-absorbed cocoon of energy" (37), while a southeastern AM radio station blares out "a vast and self-conscious story, a sort of seamless repetitious epic" (14). One senses in the novel Lasch's point of an America soured, banalized by its own provincialism and psychological inbreeding. Its culture is narcissistic, and its narcissism is a synecdoche for the larger American condition where citizens "have erected so many psychological barriers against strong emotion, and have invested those defenses with so much of the energy derived from forbidden impulse, that they no longer remember what it feels like to be inundated with desire" (Lasch 1991, 11). Not surprising for either Lasch or Straub, this narcissistic insularity explodes into the Gothic: "People . . . cultivate more vivid experiences, seek to beat sluggish flesh to life, attempt to revive jaded appetites" (Lasch 1991, 11). Anna/Alma/Angie is terrifying because she is the living dead; she simply projects that fear of self-atrophy in an age of "diminishing expectations" that Lasch claims is the current state of the American nation. As Alma Mobley once told Don Wanderly, " 'You are a ghost.' You, Donald. You" (Straub 1992, 385).

Speculum of the Other Man

But if Alma Mobley, like Tennessee Williams's Sebastian Venable, acts as a synecdoche for a larger American narcissism, if the woman and the gay man are given the curiously fraught status of being both re-ceptacle and representative (metonym and metaphor) of American anxiety, then what kind of definition of gendered narcissism might we expect to find in the contemporary, postmodern Gothic? Amid the blatantly misogynistic narrative of *Ghost Story*, we can read the feminist discourses that were critiquing masculinity at the same time the novel was being written. In the few years prior to the 1979 pub-lication of *Ghost Story* and *The Culture of Narcissism*, Luce Irigaray was theorizing the gender implications of the mirror and how they relate to feminist praxis. Much of this theory has become too famil-iar to rehearse, but it is interesting to hold it up next to the concerns of a popular, conservative, "reactionary" novel.[4] That the Chowder Society should see in Anna Mostyn (and specifically in her bedroom mirror, which "reflects" monstrosities happening elsewhere in Mil-burn) a perfidious vampire would come as no surprise to Irigaray, who argues that the phallic order of masculine symmetry is constituted through a "*flat mirror* — which may be used for the self-reflection of the masculine subject in language, for its constitution as subject of discourse" (1985b, 129). Like Virginia Woolf, who argued that "Women have served all these centuries as looking-glasses possessing the magic and delicious power of reflecting the figure of man at twice its natural size" (1975, 37), Irigaray contends:

> Now woman, starting with this flat mirror alone, can only come into being as the inverted other of the masculine subject (his *alter ego*), or as the place of emergence and veiling of the cause of his (phallic) desire, or again as lack, since her sex for the most part — and the only historically valorized part — is not subject to specularization. (1985b, 129)

In *Ghost Story*, the mirror is both metaphorical and literal, in that Mostyn in seen in it but also seen through it. Whereas Bram Stoker's hyper-masculine Dracula cannot be reflected in a mirror, Mostyn is nothing but reflection, her ubiquitous "I am you" exposing with glar-ing clarity that she is a projection of masculine fears and masculine narratives. As "a reflecting screen and not as a reminder of the depths of the mother" (Irigaray 1985a, 28), the woman in male speculariza-tion can be made to halt the terrifying ambivalence she introduced into the male subject in "Leonardo" and momism, the ambivalence of founding his (heterosexual) otherness while collapsing him (homo-sexually) into her own desires. Straub's Eva Galli meets her Gothic end, then, in a narrative move that could have been written by Irigaray. Galli is drowned in a freezing, wintry pond; man "turn[s] her to ice in which he mirrors himself. . . . She is chilled just enough to prevent his being deformed in her waters" (Irigaray 1985a, 302).[5] Well, almost. By being frozen in Narcissus's pond, she exists eternally as a terrifying hallucination of patriarchal power and of patriarchal disempowerment.

This mirror distortion of the female other comes, for Irigaray, to constitute what she so troublingly calls the "hom(m)o-sexual monopoly" of the social matrix. Rooted in the male's narcissistic adoration of his own phallus, an adoration he commands women to imitate, *"the very possibility of a sociocultural order"* comes to require *"homosexuality* as its organizing principle" (1985b, 192). In 1978, the year before *Ghost Story,* Irigaray writes:

> The law that orders our society is the exclusive valorization of men's needs/ desires, of exchanges among men. What the anthropologist calls the passage from nature to culture thus amounts to the institution of the reign of hom(m)o-sexuality. Not in an "immediate" practice, but in its "social" mediation. From this point on, patriarchal societies might be interpreted as societies functioning in the mode of "semblance." The value of symbolic and imaginary productions is superimposed upon, and even substituted for, the value of relations of material, natural, and corporal (re)production.
>
> In this new matrix of History, in which man begets man as his own likeness,[6] wives, daughters, and sisters have value only in that they serve as the possibility of, and potential benefit in, relations among men. The use of and traffic in women subtend and uphold the reign of masculine hom(m)o-sexuality, even while they maintain that hom(m)o-sexuality in speculations, mirror games, identifications, and more or less rivalrous appropriations, which defer its real practice. Reigning everywhere, although prohibited in practice, hom(m)o-sexuality is played out through the bodies of women, matter, or sign, and heterosexuality has been up to now just an alibi for the smooth workings of man's relations with himself, of relations among men. (1985b, 171–72)

Women in her analysis are hopelessly abstracted into articles of exchange — both the exogamic exchange of marriage partners as discussed by "the anthropologist" Lévi-Strauss and in the exchange of signifiers of a phallogocentric discourse belonging only to men. As she puts it, "It is not as 'women' that they are exchanged, but as women reduced to some common feature — their current price in gold, or phalluses — and of which they would represent a plus or minus quality. . . . On this basis, each one looks like every other. They all have the same phantom-like reality" (1985b, 175).

Woman reflected in a flat (discursive) mirror, woman reduced to some common feature, matter, or sign, woman as having only a phantom-like reality: Is this not the woman of Peter Straub's *Ghost Story*? Eva Galli, dead yet returned as a ghost in Moore, Mobley, Mostyn, Maule, a being who exposes American male misogyny through her declaration that "I am you," a woman reduced to the common features of mere initials ("A. M." remains constant throughout her ghostly incarnations) and of castrating power, the phallic domination of the Milburn old boys' club. She is other but an other who, in Terry Castle's delightful phrase, *"looks like every other other"* (1995, 126). And lest his audience not see the degree to which Alma is precisely the projection of male definitions of the feminine, Straub shows his hand in a very telling scene near the end of the novel. Don Wanderly is watching a 1925 film, *China Pearl,* which features both the actor Eva Galli in a bit part and a soundtrack that had been added years after the film's completion. This soundtrack introduces Galli's character as "the notorious Singapore Sal. . . . Will she get to our hero?" (488). But Don knows that this superscription is misleading metanarrative: "Of course she was not the notorious Singapore Sal, that was an invention of whoever had written the inane commentary" (488). In this moment we are told what we, with Luce Irigaray, have known all along, that beneath the distortions of a monstrous femininity that almost destroys Milburn is a discursive invention of femininity, a virtual inscription of masculinist desire upon the flat mirror of woman, a desire whose bifurcating narcissism uncannily affiliates Straub's popular novel with Irigaray's academic theorizing. It is a discursive invention of woman, moreover, that founds the hom(m)osexual economy of the Chowder Society. "I won't tell you that [i.e., the worst thing I've ever done — I've murdered a woman], but I'll tell you the worst thing that ever happened to me [she came back to let me know she didn't care much for it]."

However, to argue that woman is the mirror against which man sees himself, to condemn her to the status of flat cipher in the specular economy, is to repeat that paradigm of repudiation that is as old as Pausanias. It is to inscribe woman in a reflection where man must be. This repudiation is, of course, Irigaray's revision of Jacques Lacan, whose theory of the specular ego both founds Irigaray's analysis and necessitates her resistances. According to Lacan, the ego's structuration proceeds from the now-famous "mirror stage" in which "the subject originally identifies himself with the visual *Gestalt* of his own body" (1977, 18), the image of his body in the mirror. Having inaugurated the structure of otherness by first seeing himself as reflection, the child (a male in Lacan's analytic language) is then doomed to seek in the other a confirmation of his self. Since that other is most often the mother, who appears with the child in the specular reflection, she becomes indelibly associated with the imperative to seek the other outside the self; to her is attributed in the child's fantasy "the images of castration, mutilation, dismemberment, dislocation, evisceration, devouring, bursting open of the body, in short, the *imagos* that I have grouped together under the apparently structural term of *imagos of the fragmented body*" (11) — the imagos at the heart of any psychology of aggression, the imagos of woman in Irigaray's and Straub's texts. But Lacan is clear that the primary image with which the "self" identifies — and that the "subject" will continually desire — is itself. The specular, where Irigaray will place the woman, is an "erotic relation, in which the human individual fixes upon himself an image that alienates him from himself," and that projected self is "the form on which this organization of the passions that he will call his ego is based" (19). That external, eroticized image, then, is not just partially but primarily the self. It is Narcissus.

Thus Irigaray can argue that "hom(m)o-sexuality is played out through the bodies of women, matter, or sign, and heterosexuality has been up to now just an alibi for the smooth workings of man's relations with himself, of relations among men," but such an argument depends upon eliding Lacan's notion that the male subject seeks the male object (his specular reflection) as the goal of its desire. And Irigaray is not really consistent here. As she slips from the "hom(m)o-sexual" to the "homosexual" — from the homosocial to the homoerotic — she both homophobically collapses the distinction between the gay and the straight (a collapse whose anxieties have been articulated by Leo Bersani) and opens up a space to return to the Lacanian imago, the imago of the self, the same-sex imago. If the hom(m)o-sexual economy arises from man's imperative to worship the phallus, that phallus signifies not only masculine power but masculine sexual desire. It places the male member at the heart of man's desire for self. Hence Lacan: "There is no need to emphasize that a coherent theory of the narcissistic phase clarifies the fact of the ambivalence proper to the 'partial drives' of scoptophilia, sadomasochism, and homosexuality, as well as the stereotyped, ceremonial formalism of the aggressivity that is manifested in them" (1977, 25). Nor is there a need to emphasize that such a coherent theory of narcissism may also go some distance to explain the anxiety and aggression of the "normal" heterosexual male. To the extent that the narcissistic imago is a Narcissistic one — a desired and desiring same-sex image — he surely causes trouble for the heteronormative specular economy.

Or he does so in *Ghost Story,* at any rate. For Straub, the "smooth workings of men" that characterize Irigaray's masculine economy are not so smooth after all. The novel's hom(m)o-sexual bond, so glorified at the end as the surviving Chowder Society members murder the last incarnations of the ghost, is disrupted and challenged through the very anxiety that caused the men to bond in the first place. *Ghost Story* is laden with resonating suggestions that it is precisely man's relation to himself and other men that is the problem. At a very basic level, it must trouble the society to learn that Alma Mobley attracts gay men. She tells Don Wanderly that her previous boyfriend, Alan McKechnie (note the initials), "was not very — physical. I began to think that what he really wanted to do was go to bed with a boy, but of course he was too whatever to do that" (1992, 202). Don is taken by Alma's "androgynous quality" (207) — indeed, "She could have been a pretty nineteen-year-old freckled boy" (215) — but the aesthetic begins to lose its appeal when he sees her "in the shadows beside a bar called The Last Reef; it was a place I would have hesitated to enter, since by repute it was a haunt for bikers and homosexuals looking for rough trade" (211). If, as Irigaray has argued, genital homosexuality is prohibited as an "immediate practice" while encouraged as a "social mediation," then perhaps it is the function of the Gothic to make the distinction impossible to sustain; its refracting mirrors take the *(m)* out of "hom(m)o-sexual."[7] Alma Mobley may be the fearful projection of misogynistic anxieties, but she is also the fearful projection of male homosexual affiliation: when Narcissus looks in the mirror, he sees not his sister-mother but himself.

Indeed, the fear of homosexual affiliation as immediate practice seems to run throughout *Ghost Story* and can allow us to tie together the Mobley plot with a seemingly gratuitous subplot involving two brothers named Gregory and Fenny Bate. First appearing in the ghost story told by Sears James, the Bates are a contemporary rewriting of Henry James's *The Turn of the Screw,* but they literalize what is only suggested in the earlier Gothic tale.[8] Gregory Bate has sodomized his younger brother, and the abuse has rendered young Fenny despondent, almost catatonic, and thus a disastrous student for the young teacher, Sears James. James attempts to rescue Fenny from the abusive brother, thus setting himself up as a "rival" for the child's affections (73), but Fenny and his sister Constance beat him to the punch by killing Gregory first. Gregory then returns to haunt Fenny and to seduce him to the "other side," luring him inexorably to death.

A typical ghost story, except that Fenny and Gregory return during Mostyn's reign of terror to become other figures in the mirror,
other projections of straight male fear/desire. Like Alma/Anna with
the Chowder Society, Fenny tells Peter Barnes, "I am you" (341), and
the mirror becomes a site of male-male blending, as Peter finds himself
indistinguishable from Fenny (306). Fenny and Gregory continually
haunt him (as well as Sears), inciting his fear of being invaded by another male; as Peter tells Don, "They *stink* — they're like rotten dead
things — I had to scrub and scrub. Where Fenny touched me." And
as for Gregory, "He let me *see* him. He was — he was nothing but
hate and death. . . . [H]e can make you do things. He can talk inside
your head. Like E.S.P. . . . He said he was *me*. . . . *He said he was me*. I
want to kill him" (360). Thus, what gets called the "hom(m)o-sexual
matrix" in the 1978 chapter of *This Sex Which Is Not One* gets Gothicized the next year to reveal what the American male actually feels
about his place within that matrix. To see one's self — one's self as
desiring, as touching, as touchable, as ghostly — is to go to the center
of what constitutes the masculine subject of discourse: it is to see the
phallic signifier in and as one's own reflected self.

What is most rich and disturbing about *Ghost Story,* then, is the
way it employs male narcissism and mirror reflection to complicate
the distinctions between straight and gay male subjectivity, to blur its
boundaries, and to play with fantasies of queer identification. Nor are
these fantasies always as loathsome as Peter Barnes's protests would
claim. In a final scene of mirror imaging, Ricky Hawthorne has entered the deserted bedroom of Anna Mostyn, the room where the
magic mirror hangs on the wall. When Ricky "[makes] the mistake
of looking directly" into this mirror, he begins a series of displace-
ments and substitutions that constitute what exactly is at stake in
self-replication in the novel. First, a "face appeared before him, a
face he knew, wild and lost" — it is his own face (402). But immediately it is replaced by the face of Elmer Scales, a farmer who has just
murdered his entire family: "Like the first apparition, the farmer was
splashed with blood; the jug-eared face had starved down to skin-
covered bone, but in Scales' fierce gauntness was something which
forced Ricky to think *he saw something beautiful — Elmer always
wanted to look at something beautiful*" (402). The elision is swift
but sure: "he" sees something beautiful, but the "he" who sees is
both Elmer, whose beautiful vision is male, "the most beautiful man
Elmer had ever seen" (412), and Ricky, who is looking at the desire in Elmer, the beauty in Elmer, and at the desire for male beauty
in himself as it is displaced and reflected through Elmer. And this

displacement/reflection of another's desire is repeated in the scene's third transformation. Here, "Elmer and his target blew away and he [Ricky] was looking at Lewis's back. A naked woman stood in front of Lewis. . . . The woman was not living, nor was she beautiful, but Ricky saw the lineaments of returned desire in the dead face and he knew he was looking at Lewis's wife" (402). The optic here is as sophisticated as it was in Schlegel and Coleridge; in fact, it is pure Magritte: Ricky is looking into a mirror where he sees the back of Lewis (cf. Hermann in Nabokov's *Despair*?), thus identifying him with Lewis; yet the face reflected to him in this mirror is that of Linda Benedikt, a Linda whose face is marked by "the lineaments of returned desire," a desire that is Lewis's for her, a desire that is Ricky's for Lewis, a desire that is Lewis's for either Linda or Ricky. If, as Lacan has argued, desire is the desire of the other that is at the same time the self, then this scene renders strikingly unclear who is the other being desired, and certainly includes in the range of possibilities Ricky's homoerotic desire that may itself be the reflection, the returned desire, of Lewis's homoerotic desire. And, finally, the figure in the mirror transforms into Peter Barnes, the bright young thing envied by all the Chowder boys. What Ricky sees in the mirror, a mirror that presumably reflects *him,* is a male figure looking longingly at Peter, a figure who, "Lion-like . . . [bites] into the boy's skin and [begins] to eat" (402). Like Eve Sedgwick's work on closet epistemologies, and in particular the Gothic paranoia of Daniel Paul Schreber, Straub's scene makes it impossible to sustain Irigaray's premise that relations among men are ever smooth. Instead, it traces the trajectories of men's desires for other men as issuing from a desire for the self, a desire encapsulated by mirror reflections and distortions. Straub redoubles his postmodern Gothic mirror by making the object of loathing and the object of desire — that which will constitute the "reactionary" stability at the end of the novel — into the same male, homoerotic, narcissistic object.

When Hawthorne looks into the mirror, a mirror that generates as many narcissistic images as did that of King Charles in *Pale Fire*, he sees the face of a murderous father who had recently become a poet; he sees the face of a woman desiring Lewis, whose striking good looks have never failed to impress the Chowder Society; and he sees a vampire in a story created by James (both Sears in a Chowder Society story and Henry in *The Turn of the Screw*) bite into the youthful object of his wistful longing, Peter Barnes. Both villains and victims here, as Irigaray well knows, are patriarchs: the American Gothic proceeds from those who created it to attack those who continue to narrate it. In this personalized attack on Hawthorne and

James we see what Christopher Lasch bemoans as the loss of "all forms of patriarchal authority and thus...the social superego, formerly represented by fathers, teachers, and preachers" (1991, 11). This decline of a social authority, he says, results in the strengthening of the individual superego, that which fears parental prohibition and represents parents as devouring monsters, and the weakening of the social superego, that post-oedipal voice that encourages the laudable virtues of altruism and social conscience. But for Jacques Lacan, the distinction between the individual and the social superego is difficult to sustain. Rather, in a child's fantasy — as in the postmodern Gothic of Peter Straub — it is precisely *language itself* that is the harbinger of horror. Lacan writes:

> The super-ego is at one and the same time the law and its destruction. As such, it is speech itself, the commandment of law, in so far as nothing more than its root remains. The law is entirely reduced to something, which cannot even be expressed, like the *You must,* which is speech deprived of all its meaning. It is in this sense that the super-ego ends up by being identified with only what is most devastating, most fascinating, in the primitive experiences of the subject. It ends up being identified with what I call *the ferocious figure,* with the figures which we can link to primitive traumas the child has suffered, whatever these are.
>
> In this very special case, we see, embodied there, this function of language, we touch on it in its most reduced form, reduced down to a word whose meaning and significance for the child we are not even able to define, but which nonetheless ties him to the community of mankind. (1988, 102–3)

Which brings us back to Irigaray and the generating of discourse: if women are merely signifiers meant to solidify the hom(m)o-sexual economy in their exchange, if generating signifiers reflects man back to himself, makes him the subject of discourse, or, in Lacan's words, "ties him to the community of mankind," then it also implicates him in a compulsory submission to the paternal law, the law of sameness, a phallicism that is as terrifying as it is comforting. And in Straub's Gothic that terror comes not only from a castrating authority figure but from the very possibility of one's own — and another's — phallic desire. The problem with the father in a culture of narcissism is that he can be what one wants to *have* every bit as much as he is what one wants to *be.*

But just as Freud's treatment of the phallic mother-vulture in "Leonardo" opened up the possibility for homoerotic desire that, as I argued in chapter 3, Freud avoids exploring, so does Lasch veer away from the possible homo-narcissistic cathexis on the dead father he mourns. Later in *The Culture of Narcissism* he singles out the "immature, narcissistic mother" for special attention. Caught between child-rearing discourses that demand her perfection and her own sense that she is doing it all badly, the mother in the America of the 1970s does nothing for her child but represent an ego ideal that she can never really be. To the degree that her overattentiveness "causes" homosexuality, as we saw Violet Venable "doing" in chapter 3, her impossibly idealistic, textbook maternity sets up a narcissistic crisis in the child, whose collapsing self-worth mirrors her own. And at one level, Peter Straub seems to agree: he clearly indicates that the object of fear and loathing in the novel is specifically matriarchal. This narcissistic mother, by implication, allows Straub the sleight of hand that connects maternal love with male homosexuality, the mamma's-boy-as-queer that America assumes from badly reading Freud. But what if this maternally inspired queerness stands not outside the "smooth workings" of the homosocial bond but actually establishes them? To explore these connections, to understand the confluence of this patriarchal figure with the phallic mother of Straub's text, and to reflect on how this might differ from Freud's treatment of the problem in "Leonardo," I want now to turn to another theorist of narcissism and the matriarchal, Julia Kristeva, whose 1980 *Powers of Horror* and 1983 *Tales of Love* place her as a contemporary of Straub and allow us to understand more fully how theories of narcissism can queer gender relations in the "me generation" period.

Peter Straub's Mysterious Mother

Readers of Kristeva will immediately recognize in Eva Galli and her ghostly descendants the phenomenon of the *abject*. A phobic object marked by disgust, defilement, and the profane, the abject in Kristeva's analysis is that which the child has had to jettison in order to constitute the ego but which, by its very status as structural other for the ego, must continually exert a seductive allure; it "draws me toward the place where meaning collapses," thus providing the space from which I recoil in order "to constitute myself and my culture" (Kristeva 1982, 2). In *Ghost Story,* the ghost returns to attack the self that each of the Chowder Society members has constructed since the murder of Eva, yet paradoxically the ghost also provides a demonic focus for the boredom, failure, and diminishment that Lasch has suggested frame the late-twentieth-century American. This paradoxical status that "simultaneously beseeches and pulverizes the subject" (Kristeva 1982, 5) is perhaps most clearly embodied in Christina

Barnes, Peter's mother, who was murdered by Gregory Bate and who continually returns to Peter in his dreams, even after the ghosts have been exorcised. Peter explains the problem to Don Wanderly: "I keep seeing my mother.... I mean, I dream about her all the time. It's like I'm back in Lewis's house, and I'm seeing that Gregory Bate grab her again" (1992, 490). Wanderly attempts to comfort Peter thus: "I think you're afraid that if you give up the horror and fear, that you'll also be giving up your mother. Your mother loved you. And now she's dead, and she died in a terrible way, but she put her love into you for seventeen or eighteen years, and there's a lot of it left" (490). Thus, Peter's knowledge that his mother had been having an affair with Lewis — his knowledge of his own dissolving family, the structuring principle of his identity, for which his mother is to "blame" — combines with the desire for his mother's love and projects the contradictory force that Kristeva calls abjection: Christina is continually resurrected in order to be vilified, continually vilified in order to be resurrected.

That Straub should locate this clear definition of abjection in the novel's primary mother figure is hardly surprising, given Kristeva's thesis that the "abject confronts us ... with our earliest attempts to release the hold of *maternal* entity even before ex-isting outside of her, thanks to the autonomy of language. It is a violent, clumsy breaking away, with the constant risk of falling back under the sway of a power as securing as it is stifling" (1982, 13). As I discussed in chapter 3, classic psychoanalytic thought sees the male child as basking in an oceanic primary narcissism with the mother until that oedipal moment when the dyad is ruptured by the father's prohibitive "no," his threat of castration should the child not relinquish the erotic cathexis on the mother. Hence the "ferocious figure" in Lacan's Symbolic. In Kristeva's theory, that bond is ruptured prior to the oedipal moment when the child learns that he is only a substitution for the object of his mother's desire, that the mother desires an object (the phallus) for which he stands but that he by definition is not. Thus, it is the recognition that the mother desires, and that she desires elsewhere or other, that necessitates abjection, the child's rejection of her into other that is the beginnings of his constitution of himself as a self. And this is precisely the moment that originates the horror in *Ghost Story*. Fifty years ago, Eva Galli moved to town and immediately captured the hearts of the fledgling Chowder Society. Ricky's memory of this experience is couched in extremely significant language: "We were in a sort of sexless, pre-Freudian paradise.... In an enchantment" (370). After Galli's fiancé committed suicide, the boys longed to visit her, to indulge in the "magical" and "poignant" character of an "ideal" friendship with her (371). But one afternoon, Eva visited *them,* " 'And she was *wild,*' Sears said. 'She was frightening. She came in like a typhoon.' " To which Ricky adds, "She wanted to drink and she wanted to dance, and she didn't care who was shocked" (371). Most shocked was Lewis, the youngest of the boys. As Ricky says, " 'Lewis was frozen stiff with horror. As if he had seen his mother begin to act this way.' 'His mother?' Sears asked. 'Well, I suppose. At least it tells you the depth of his fantasy about her — our fantasy, to be honest' " (373). What it tells us about the depth of the fantasy, of course, is not only that Eva Galli had sexual desires ("She tried to seduce Lewis" [372]), and not only that her desires were indiscriminate (she could direct them at one boy or another, making each interchangeable with another), but that they were metonymic, redirected from her desire for her dead fiancé (whom everyone suspects she killed) and not authentically fixed on the individual child himself. In a pseudo-oedipal legacy at least as old as Horace Walpole's 1767 *The Mysterious Mother* (1924),[9] the male child here is rendered substitute, a displacement of maternal desire rather than the object of it. And so, Eva Galli must "accidentally" be killed, rendered permanently filthy and abjectionable in memory, able only to return as ghost, the "phobic hallucination" that Kristeva locates in the mother's sexualized, abjected body.

As Luce Irigaray had written, "in the advent of a 'feminine' desire, [the] flat mirror cannot be privileged and symmetry cannot function as it does in the logic and discourse of a masculine subject" (1985b, 129). Thus Hermann Hesse's Eve, the Universal Mother, here gets placed into the Gothicized Eve-as-Alma, the "soul" (*alma*) whose malignancy is a clear projection of the child's need to abject her body. But the abjection of the mother's body has a greater significance for Kristeva than a mere disillusionment with the expectations for her love. In *Tales of Love* (1987), Kristeva argues that abjection is necessary in order for the child in primary narcissism to separate himself from the mother so that her love, which to this point he has merely replicated within him, can be metamorphosed into *desire:* in other words, she becomes other to the degree that the child can transfer his identification with her love (primary narcissism) into the identification with her need to love another (1987, 34). To explain this notion, Kristeva turns to Freud's notion of "the father in individual prehistory," from the 1921 "Group Psychology and the Analysis of the Ego." In the earlier "Leonardo," narcissistic desire became homosexual desire because the boy sought in the mother an image of his own phallus, the marker of sexual difference and of sexual power. The Egyptian mother-vulture became the perfect image for Freud, as it represented a unity and wholeness that situated the phallus (in the phallic mother) at the center of desire. In the same year, that phallus got relocated to the boy's own body: in the analysis of Schreber, object-relations arose from the child's cathexis on his own penis, heralding a narcissism that would underwrite the later "Some Neurotic Mechanisms of Jealousy, Paranoia, and Homosexuality." Mother was nowhere in sight. By 1921, that phallus has conflated the two previous narcissistic paradigms: prior to the Oedipus complex, says Freud, the male child develops an intense emotional bond with the father as well as the mother, a tie that makes of the father an ego ideal (1921, 105). The father's phallus in this scheme is not (only) his but (also) the mother's desire for it, her act of desiring elsewhere. Thus this phallus, as the nascent object of the child's desires, exists in "prehistory," that is, prior to the child's individuation and knowledge of sexual difference. Because of this "prehistory" or "preindividuation," the imaginary father cannot be understood as masculinity in any conventional (or even unconventional) sense. Rather, the father in individual prehistory is an undifferentiated "conglomerate" of father and mother (Kristeva 1987, 40), a unity that is "a coagulation of the mother and her desire" (41), her desire for the phallus, for completion, for wholeness. And this child's desire, Kristeva argues, has been predicated on the primary narcissism that establishes the child's series of transformations by reduplicating the mother's breast within the pre-self. In this way, she dramatizes a phenomenon whose manifestations I've been locating throughout this book: narcissism is not so much a deviation from the norm or a fixation in immaturity as it is a structural necessity for the human subject.

Kristeva insists that this reduplication, beginning with narcissistic incorporation and moving on toward the imitation of the m/other's desire, is not a phase through which one passes but actually a structure that underlies the psyche. This structure makes possible the dynamic of transference that Kristeva hopefully calls love and that she sees as the only possible salvation from an original narcissism that threatens to collapse into psychosis (where the other is never established) or to effect a "perverse dodge" (1982, 5) into homosexuality, the positing of otherness where what is desired is merely the same. By recognizing that the mother loves another — the father — the child initiates itself into a world of otherness, of "hetero"ness, where it is forced to construct its own subjectivity. Thus, Kristeva takes her place in a history at least as old as the classical *Anthologica Latina* of Pentadius (date uncertain), where Narcissus's "father was a river" and so "he looks for his father in the river" (quoted in Vinge 1967, 25). And in a curious way, Kristeva finds herself teamed with Christopher Lasch in calling for daddies: but whereas Lasch advocates a return to the oedipal father who can whip us back into shape, Kristeva pines for a pre-oedipal father whose status as both presubject and preobject of desire institutes the identity of the "lover" — that is, "the narcissist with an *object*" (1987, 33).

How might we read this desire for the father's phallus in a Gothic novel whose matrices of desire are as complex as those in *Ghost Story*? What are we to make of the seemingly laudable sexlessness of this father of individual prehistory, this phallus which is not one? And what purchase does Kristeva's repudiation of homosexuality as a "perverse dodge" offer us for reading the desired father in the contemporary Gothic? Let us return to the case study of Peter Barnes, who abjects his own mother in order to constitute his identity. If, as Kristeva suggests, the desire for the father's phallus is really a double-edged desire for the mother and for the object of her desire, then we might wonder what kind of anxiety is produced by the heterosexual male's recognition that he is identifying with his mother's desire, that he wants not only her but what she wants as well. In *Ghost Story*, the object of Christina's desire is Lewis Benedikt, the phallic presence who replaces the totally ineffectual and wimpy Walter Barnes. And Lewis, the man whose looks and sexual prowess the whole Chowder Society envies (what *is* the difference between envying another's sexuality and desiring it, between wanting to be it and wanting to have it?), certainly stands in a conflicted relation to the son of the woman he's sleeping with: "Peter . . . had very complicated ideas about Lewis Benedikt" (255); "From the bottom of his mind floated the image of himself leaping on Lewis, swinging at him with his fists, battering at the handsome face" (322).[10] A violent, masculine reaction to be sure, but these moments also give us leave to ask about the exact implications of the oedipal paradigm here: Does the son want to fight the father or fuck him? For it is this same son who is repeatedly effeminized in the novel: "His black hair seemed almost girlishly long to Ricky" (39); he is touched and invaded by Fenny and Gregory; and he is constantly called "Clarabelle" by his best friend, Jim Hardie. My point here is not to suggest that Peter's dislike of Lewis is really closet gayness; Peter's hallucinations are not those of a paranoid Schreber desiring Fleschig. Rather, Peter's avenging of his mother's death (or rather, his justification of her abjection) puts him in a dangerous, volatile relation to the sexual polymorphousness of his mother's desire. Lewis is not the father of Peter's individual prehistory, but he is the masculine phallic object of his (mother's) desire. And to that degree, Kristeva's psychonormalizing praise of bigendered "love" proceeding from primary narcissism invites as many psychic terrors for the adolescent male as it does consolations.

For Peter Straub, the origins of this panic/desire are as clearly narcissistic as they are for Julia Kristeva and as they were for Sigmund Freud. See, for example, Peter's looking into the mirror in Anna Mostyn's bedroom, that same mirror that gave Ricky Hawthorne such trouble. First, "His own face was fading to a pale outline and beneath the outline, on the other side of it, swimming up, was the face of a woman. He did not know her, but he took her in as if he were in love" (445). Pausanias's Narcissus, or Kristeva's subject whose ability to love is structured on the primary bond of maternal narcissism? "She touched all the tension in him, all the feeling he had, and he saw things in her face that he knew were beyond his understanding, promises and songs and betrayals he would not know for years" (Straub 1992, 445): a veritable semiotic *chora,* in which the mother becomes the receptacle of all bodily knowledge that remains outside the access to the Symbolic, of the language authorized only by a castrating, Lacanian father. "And, in a rush of tenderness, an enveloping nimbus of emotion, she was speaking to him" (445), calling him to become one of them, to enter the other, ghostly, m/otherly world, the world of a semiotic *jouissance* that can only be achieved if he knifes the Chowder Society to death. This Kristevan phallic mother loves, but threatens to swallow the child within her love to the exclusion of the outside world.

This primary transference between the mother and the son must be halted, smashed, lest the child collapse into psychosis or homosexuality; Kristeva is enough Lacan's daughter to insist that the child take up his place in the Symbolic order. And so, enter the loving father, Ricky Hawthorne, who breaks the mirror and the spell it has. An act of love, this destruction of the phallic, abjected mother is performed by a father whose "face and experienced eyes [were] so near to Peter's own face that Peter . . . trembled and embraced him" (446). Is this an Irigarayan moment, in which the hom(m)o-sexual bond triumphs over Woman? Or a Kristevan moment, in which the loving father heals the wound of abjection and constitutes the gender of the adolescent boy? Or is it somewhere in-between? After all,

> When they separated, Peter bent down to the two halves of the mirror and held his palm over one of the pieces. A delicious wind (*the one song which*

is my song)[11] lilted up from it. He felt or sensed Ricky stiffening beside him: half of a tender mouth glimmered in his hand, just visible. He drove his heel into the broken mirror, then brought it down again and again, splitting the silvery glass into a scattered jigsaw puzzle. (446)

That oughta do it, but the "it" it does is left rather ambiguous: Does Peter finish off the expulsion of the mother who has tried to seduce him back to her body, her *chora,* beseeching him in order to pulverize him? To whom does that "half of a tender mouth" (one of Irigaray's two lips?) in the mirror belong? Peter? Or is it Ricky, whom Peter can feel "stiffening" beside him and who leans over him like the Schlegelian sonneteer or Camille seeing Teleny in the glass? In one way, the scene promotes the reactionary, misogynistic reading that sees hom(m)o-sexuality triumph over the feminine; the maternal *chora,* the "song which is my song," is silenced, its "mouth" destroyed. Yet the evocation of the desired paternal phallus also foregrounds a prohibited male-male desire that has troubled Peter all along — one that Irigaray leaves ambiguous in her shuttle between the "hom(m)o-sexual" and the "homosexual" and one that Kristeva's male homophobia never allows her to address adequately.[12] Her model of the abjected mother completed by the loving father may satisfy the bourgeois demand for compulsory heterosexuality, but in the novel it does little (perhaps thankfully) to arrest the panic that identifying with the mother's desire might invoke in the straight boy.

While Straub may use Peter and Ricky to flirt with the complexities of father-son desire, of a loving father whose salvational otherness is also erotic sameness (the hetero is homo to Narcissus), he analyzes the problem much more fully in the character of Don Wanderly and his relation to Alma Mobley. Don met Alma at Berkeley. He was an adjunct English professor, she a Ph.D. student writing on Virginia Woolf. They fell in love, or at least in lust, and began a torrid affair that can best be described as narcissistic. Don lost all interest in literature, students, and lectures, spending all of his time having sex with Alma.[13] But this complete and self-enclosed sexual union is soon triangulated by Alma's stories of "Tasker Martin," a previous lover who died some years ago. As a ghostly presence who does nothing but hang around and "approve" of Don's relationship with Alma, Tasker seems to contain all the elements of Kristeva's imaginary father: "He was older — a lot older" (214); he is always present when they are making love; and unlike the phallic, oedipal father, Tasker is not in erotic competition for Alma; rather, "he just *likes* you, Don. He'd be a good friend of yours if he were alive" (214). Indeed, like the Kristevan loving father who is a conglomerate of the mother and her love for another, Alma implores Don to "just think about Tasker as though he were a part of me" (215), as if this should make Don feel better about having a ghostly former boyfriend peep in on his lovemaking. But in a curious way, it does. Like the Kristevan father, Tasker gradually siphons Don off the symbiotic, narcissistic consumption of the mother-son bond. Don reflects, "In part, I was fascinated by all this. . . . But also it was creepy. . . . I wanted to make love to her, and I also felt a separation from her" (215). Unlike others who come into contact with her, Don has escaped with his life. No castrating monster or Symbolic prohibitor, the imaginary father intervenes here to rescue the subject from narcissistic psychosis and to wean the child from its complete identification with the maternal body.

While Tasker Martin seems to function as the Dead Father who is a loving, imaginary third party, he also raises problems that Kristeva's optimistic theory does not address.[14] For if, as we have seen earlier, the figure in the narcissistic mirror is a male who reflects back some form of homosexual desire, then what might be implied in the search for the imaginary father, not only for the mother but for the model of her desire for the male? Straub's answer is clear, at least in the trajectories of Don's psyche. While Alma is telling him of the benevolent, triangulating Tasker, "I looked across the table at Alma, who was regarding me with a kindly expression of expectancy, and thought: she does look androgynous. She could have been a pretty nineteen-year-old freckled boy" (215). Don quickly realizes what this androgyny means: the "beautiful marriage" Alma proposes will be between "You and me and Tasker." Moreover, Tasker's willingness to share Don's bed may fulfill the promise of another of Alma's lovers, Alan McKechnie, whose failed sexuality—both hetero and homo— I noted earlier. And lest the sodomitic panic underlying the whole Tasker fantasy is still not clear, Straub completes the scene with Don's reflection: "On the way to the lecture theater I remembered the man I had seen her with [at the gay bar], the Louisianian Greg Benton with his dead ferocious face, and I shuddered" (215). And no wonder: to love the mother-father, to reduplicate the mother's desire for the father, as Kristeva argues we must do, is to desire the father erotically. It is to open up a morass of identifications whose eventual objects are by no means clear or heterosexually othered. If, as Kristeva suggests, the metaphor of transferential love subtends or gives way to the metonymies of sexual desire, then Alma's metaphorical "I am you" can be seen to lay bare Don's desire not just for the imaginary father but for the erotic presence of another man.

Tales of Lovers

For Irigaray, the woman is a narcissistic *"flat mirror* — which may be used for the self-reflection of the masculine subject in language, for its constitution as subject of discourse" (1985b, 129). For Kristeva, the curiously liminal status of primary narcissism — in which a not-yet-ego reduplicates, imitates, and incorporates a not-yet-object — establishes in the child the possibility of subject-object relations. It makes possible the formation of an ego that can later be distinguished from its objects. In so doing, Kristeva breaks from Lacanian theory, which sees such structuration as occurring only at the later mirror stage and which posits the ego as the product of the father's castrating symbolic "no." For her, the structure of self-other is generated by the child's primary narcissistic repetition of the mother's breast within itself and of itself in relation to the mother's breast, a repetition that begins in the semiotic, pre-Symbolic affiliation and only later moves through the Symbolic. The mother with whom the child identifies is not a metonymic object of desire, a signifier of the phallus, as Lacan suggests, but a metaphorical object, a reduplicated, incorporated self with which the child identifies (1987, 29): "The object of love is a metaphor for the subject — its constitutive metaphor, its 'unary feature,' which, by having it choose an adored part of the loved one, already locates it within the symbolic code of which this feature is a part" (30). This early metaphoric identification/incorporation later becomes abjection when the child recognizes that he himself is not the metaphor for the mother, not the fulfilling complement of her desire. Rather, he recognizes that whatever the mother wants, it is "not I," and "it is out of this 'not I' . . . that an Ego painfully attempts to come into being" (41). The pain of this recognition leads the child to identify with the father in his individual prehistory, the father/phallus that will satisfy the mother as a way of overcoming the narcissistic emptiness and potential sterility of primary love. In this move, Kristeva says, signification is born:

> If narcissism is a defense against the emptiness of separation, then the whole contrivance of imagery, representations, identifications, and projections that accompany it on the way toward strengthening the Ego and the Subject is a means of exorcising that emptiness. Separation is our opportunity to become narcists or narcissistic, at any rate subjects of representation. The emptiness it opens up is nevertheless also the barely covered abyss where our identities, images, and words run the risk of being engulfed. (42)

Thus primary narcissism creates the system of repetition and difference that, in the Symbolic order, will become the metonymic order of signification and of desire.

How might such a trajectory from incorporation to desire, from metaphor to metonymy, affect the events of *Ghost Story*? Profoundly. Indeed, the "sexless, pre-Freudian paradise" that described the relation between the Chowder boys and Eva Galli marked each of them as ciphers in a kind of metaphoric substitution: the description of this utopia carries no recognition of competition, envy, or proprietariness, none of the symptoms of the desiring subject. Rather, libido is oceanic and undifferentiated, both in the boys' relation to Galli and in their relation to one another. With her murder, however, the society sets up a certain relation to discourse, to the Symbolic order, that the novel is bent on exploring. "The worst thing you ever did" is metonymically rerouted into "the worst thing that has ever happened to me," and the story of Eva Galli's murder/abjection becomes distorted, reinvented, and made into fictional narratives that the society members tell one another for recreation. Galli's story then *becomes* the ghost in this novel in at least two ways. First, the abjected Eva Galli returns in spectral form to haunt the very men who refuse to name her, to tell stories about her. Indeed, their literary productions take on a performative dimension in constituting horror: "I know who killed [John Jaffrey]," cries Molly, the doctor's former housekeeper and lover, "It was you. You — you Chowder Society. You killed him with your terrible stories. You made him sick — you and your Fenny Bates!" (181). Ricky Hawthorne agrees: "when all of us were joined by Don, the forces, whatever you want to call them, were increased.... [We] invoked them. We by our stories, Don in his book and in his imagination" (289). And, second, the society gradually learns that Don Wanderly's next novel, still unwritten, is providing the events for the ghost's haunting of them. The novel makes explicit that the characters are living inside another novel, a novel that was generated subconsciously from Don's rejection of Alma Mobley.

But if the Chowder Society is trapped by the Symbolic order, then they can use that order to advantage: "I think in stories we make [our ghosts] manageable," Don tells the men, "the stories at least show that we can destroy them" (379). Writing has a curiously paradoxical status here, as it does in Julia Kristeva. On the one hand, writing is the attempt to cover up the emptiness of primary narcissism, to speak through the void that always necessarily underlies the human psyche as it exists in relation to the abjected mother. An echo of Lawrence Kubie, the psychoanalyst who told Tennessee Williams that writing would simply indulge his narcissistic illness by eternally returning him to himself, the theory of writing in Kristeva suggests a deflection from the primary rupture and thus a forgetting of it. But elsewhere in

Kristeva and her contemporaries, narcissism can also serve another, more therapeutic purpose. According to Christopher Lasch, aligning himself with Heinz Kohut,

> The mere act of writing already presupposes a certain detachment from the self; and the objectification of one's own experience, as psychiatric studies of narcissism have shown, makes it possible for "the deep sources of grandiosity and exhibitionism — after being appropriately aim-inhibited, tamed, neutralized — to find access" to reality. (1991, 17)

Similarly for Kristeva, the writer objectifies the experience in a dialogism that she likens to the pregnant mother, in that the writer produces a self that is simultaneously part of the mother yet also clearly and inexorably other, with a significance of its own. Without writing, the narcissist is sterile, caught in a fleeting and failed self-image that refuses to signify meaningfully. Through writing, Narcissus siphons himself off to otherness and begins the process of healthy reconnection to the world.

Yet this process is itself a compulsory narcissism: by replicating the self, the writer fashions an otherness that is at the very heart of the signifying process. Just think of Don Wanderly, whose first novel had inscribed himself by displacing him (a homographesis) into his character "Saul Malkin."[15] And to therapeutic effect. After Alma left him to become affianced to his brother David, a union resulting in David's fatal fall from an Amsterdam hotel window, Don turned to writing:

> Two years before the world had gathered itself in this ominous way, had been slick and full of intent — after the episode of Alma Mobley, after his brother had died. In some fashion, literally or not, she had killed David Wanderly: he knew that he had been lucky to escape whatever it was that took David through the Amsterdam hotel window. Only writing had brought him back into the world; only writing about *it*, the horrid complicated mess of himself and Alma and David, writing about it as a ghost story, had released him from it. He had thought. (26)

Poetic writing, Kristeva says, consciously indulges figuration and image in a way that both narcissistically projects ourselves into image and reminds us that the image is an image, a fake, a fabrication, something that can lead to Truth but must be rejected as Truth — a Truth that is, among other things, the narcissistic void at the heart of our being (1987, 127). Writing, Kristeva and Lasch have maintained, is an initial step in negotiating one's self and an other — the other as reader, the other as self inscribed in signifiers. Writing here is a narcissism, a salvational distantiation that both inscribes oneself within horror and removes oneself from the center of that horror.

Or so Don had thought. According to Kristeva, it is precisely this shuttle, through writing, between love and abjection that constitutes the healthy subject. She calls this imagistic play of seduction without incorporation a semiotics of *love,* a mother tongue that is "more iron-ically than mythically narcissan: decentered as it is, it opens a space of thought to the labyrinthian and muddy canals of undecidable sail-ing, of game playing with fleeting meanings and appearances, with images" (1987, 136). But these fleeting images and appearances are also ghosts. Thus, in a novel (and a novelistic, political, and gendered history) where such narcissan sailing takes us into queer ports with queer ghosts — did I mention that Gregory Bate is a sailor? — it should not surprise us to find a queer content performatively established by Don's very act of writing. In his attempt to figure out who or what Alma Mobley is ("I am you" is a circular locution about as illuminating, and narcissistic, as Yahweh's "I am that I am"), Don writes in his journal: "the oddest feeling, the feeling that makes the adrenaline go, is that I am about to go inside my own mind: to travel the territory of my own writing, but this time without the comfortable make-believe of fiction. No 'Saul Malkin' this time; just me" (232). In that self-exploration, in that compulsorily narcissistic indulgence, Don will discover the full implications of his nagging intuition that "David had been the miss-ing element in the book I'd tried to write" (231). David has been the central figure metonymically embodied in Alma; David is the figure who has triangulated and inflected Don's desire for her.

Which explains Don's repeated Schreber-esque hallucinations, his fear — his fantasy — that the woman whom he desires is not only himself but David, the figure behind the screen of his desires, a fig-ure who may itself have been displaced into the fantasy of Tasker Martin. Shortly after David's death, Don began to hallucinate him: "teaching a Henry James novel [!] to my section of the survey class, I had seen on one of the chairs not the red-haired girl I knew was there, but — again — David" (230). Nor is this the only transformation of a woman into David. When Angie ("I am you") Maule catapults him into a hallucination of New York, he dines with a "stylish sun-tanned anonymous woman" who turns into "his brother David, his face crumbled and his body dressed in the torn and rotting clothing of the grave" (31). The erotic Alma becomes David again in the novel's epilogue (500), continuing Don's archaic fear that the ostensibly fe-male object of his erotic desires is indistinguishable from his brother, a fear of transpositional collapse that he shares with the other mem-bers of the Chowder Society. And like Narcissus, that woman/man/ desired other is indistinguishable from the self: early in the novel,

Don hallucinates David's grave and is panicked by the feeling that the tombstone "was for him. And that if he were to . . . dig up the coffin, within it he would find his own putrefying body" (27). What Don's novel *The Nightwatcher* seems to have missed, then, is not a thorough understanding of Alma per se but an understanding of the psychic content of Don's narcissistic fantasies. If narcissism is an attempt to cover over the emptiness of maternal abjection by cathecting on the self, then the self to be desired is same-sexual: homoeroticism is both required and prohibited. And as a writer, Wanderly seems to have employed the Symbolic to inscribe a hetero-normative tale of desire and fear, but by doing so he has abjected — consigned to the realm of the unthinkable, which is also the realm of the attractive, the seductive, the necessary — a homo-disruptive matrix that underlies his hetero-desire. As Judith Butler has helped us to see, what is repudiated in the constitution of the subject becomes eroticized precisely because it must be repudiated. And what is repudiated here (and for the last two hundred years of men's Gothic sexuality) is Narcissus.

Nor is Straub alone in his sense that the author is somehow prone to homosexual panic by virtue of the fact that he is an author. I have argued elsewhere that it is an idée fixe for Stephen King, currently the world's most popular horror author, that his male protagonists be authors and that their status as author render them susceptible to an emasculation that is coded queer (see Bruhm 1996b): Ben Mears, the writer in *'Salem's Lot,* is continually gendered female in a subtle parallel with the homosexual vampire Barlow, with whom he shares some physical similarities; Jack Torrance of *The Shining* is going through a writer's block that seems to have at its heart Jack's tortured relation to George Hatfield, a beautiful young man from his former college;[16] Thad Beaumont in *The Dark Half* is persecuted by a pseudonym that he had used to write horror novels and who has taken on a life of its own, a pseudonym whose relationship to Thad is as erotic as it is scripted; finally, Paul Sheldon of *Misery,* perhaps the most butch of the lot, continually likens himself to Sheherazade as he is forced to compose a new novel for his phallic mother/captor, Annie Wilkes. In that essay I argue that the act of writing, the exchange of signifiers, appears to draw its tropology from the Lacanian image of the phallus-as-signifier — the initiator of the Symbolic — and the signifier-as-phallus, that material projection that is intended to represent and embody the self while at the same time destabilizing and displacing that self. While Lacan is clear that this phallus-signifier affiliation is not metaphoric (they are not equivalent), I insist that in Lacan's work and King's Gothic the affiliation is at least metonymic, that the act of writing and speaking between men carries with it a specter of the penis that panics the man insistent on straight self-identification. The exchange of phallic signifiers that constitutes American society — Irigaray's hom(m)o-sexual matrix — is haunted by Lacan's thesis that language is a *demand:* the demand for attention, for emotion, for identification of the listener with the speaker, of one man with another. Judith Butler has argued that Lacan's treatment of the phallus-as-signifier depends for its signification on the phallus-as-penis, thereby obfuscating the difference within the very material organ that is to signify difference and making of it a ghostly signifier that holds melancholically onto its roots in the physical. By this definition, and in this psychic economy, the stories that the postmodern Gothic hero is obliged to tell psychically engage him with phallic, that is, *penile* play, play with one's own phallus, play with another's. He uses this phallic play to constitute his hom(m)o-sexual matrix, but in so doing invokes ghosts, ghosts that are stories, stories that are the ghostly form of his own phallus-penis, the phallus-penis of the other man.

But in a Kristevan system, that penile play exists even prior to the enforced regime of the Symbolic, even prior to the oedipal configuration of gender, even prior to the assumption (or "perverse dodge") of heterosexed object-choice. In my (admittedly abusive) reading of Kristeva through the narrative economies of *Ghost Story,* the primary narcissism that subtends language and storytelling — that subtends any construction of the self — is inevitably queer because Narcissus *will* return to the image of the man in the pool. As I have noted, language for Kristeva is primarily an act of transference, an act of *love,* that is initiated within primary narcissism and that continues throughout psychic life. (Indeed, it is what makes therapy possible. The verbally structured bond of love between analyst and analysand, the transference and countertransference through amorous language, can do much to counteract the castrating, prohibitive, symbolic father.) This primal, archaic language is not only metaphorical; it is *metaphor:* when I speak, when I am spoken to, when I tell you my story, when I listen to yours, "I am you" in an act of loving transference. Writes Kristeva:

> When the object that I incorporate is the speech of the other — precisely a nonobject, a pattern, a model — I bind myself to him in a primary fusion, communion, unification. An identification. For me to have been capable of such a process, my libido had to be restrained; my thirst to devour had to be deferred and displaced to a level one may well call the "psychic," provided one adds that if there is repression it is quite primal, and that it lets one hold on to the joys of chewing, swallowing, nourishing oneself... with

words. In being able to receive the other's words, to assimilate, repeat, and reproduce them, I become like him: One. A subject of enunciation. Through psychic osmosis/identification. Through love. (1987, 26)

By this logic, Narcissus is not merely a literary *figure;* he is literary *figuration* whose imaginary phallus *is* the object of desire through the fantastically, phantasmatically elusive necessity of self-imaging, homo-imaging.

That is why to chew, to swallow, to nourish oneself with the words of the other takes on a particularly Gothic tone in a novel whose ghosts are blood-sucking vampires, whose abjected men are cannibals conjured out of the American literary canon and out of the stories men tell one another. A Kristevan reading of *Ghost Story* (and certainly not only *Ghost Story*) suggests that the nourishment of another's words might somehow be homologous to the oral attractions of male homo-eros. That somehow, to desire the discourse of the other man and to be penetrated by it accesses some archaic fantasy or fear of homo-erotic bonding. That somehow, the signifiers we seek from the father, whether symbolic or imaginary, are rendered eroticized by our own compulsory narcissism, by our desire for our own phallic image. A queer Narcissus drives the novel, then, not by some political or sexual project; its chapters are not those of Queer Nation rising up among the New England set. Rather, the psychodynamics of metaphor in *Ghost Story* register that terrifying ambivalence by which men's nar-ratives for one another slide among the homosocial, the homoerotic, the self-constituting, and the self-destructive. Narcissus's signification (which is to say, *all* signification) invokes desires among men it refuses to fulfill, and such refusal abjects men into the perennial desire for other men's stories. Language in the novel — the stories men tell one another — is necessary to constitute a hom(m)o-sexual monopoly, but it also predicates the very panic beneath that monopoly.

The Incoherence of Gothic Conventions

> *Narcissus, gazing at his image in the pool, wept. When his friend, passing by, enquired the reason, Narcissus replied, "I weep that I have lost my innocence."*
> *His friend answered, "You should wiser weep that you ever had it."*
> — STRAUB, *Ghost Story*

A final historical-theoretical reflection: in 1978, the year of the hom(m)o-sexual, the year before *Ghost Story*, Roland Barthes's *A Lover's Discourse* appeared in America. In it, Barthes celebrates Nar-cissus as the perfect queer figure: Narcissus makes meaning, but that meaning cannot be read in either a purely Imaginary (maternal) or a purely Symbolic (paternal) register. The lover (always a Narcissus) is simultaneously a Mother (concerned for the other, the loved one) and "an insufficient Mother" whose "identification is imperfect" (51) and who always remains outside a narcissistic union with the other, thus assuring him his status *as* other. For Barthes, the simultaneity of this in/not-in is precisely what constitutes the queer pleasure of the text. On the one hand,

> A long chain of equivalences links all the lovers in the world. In the theory of literature, "projection" (of the reader into the character) no longer has any currency: yet it is the appropriate tonality of imaginative readings: reading a love story, it is scarcely adequate to say I project myself; I cling to the image of the lover, shut up with this image in the very enclosure of the book. (131)

But, on the other hand,

> Writing is dry, obtuse; a kind of steamroller, writing advances, indifferent, indelicate, and would kill "father, mother, lover" rather than deviate from its fatality (enigmatic though that fatality may be). When I write, I must acknowledge this fact (which, according to my Image-repertoire, lacerates me): there is no benevolence within writing, rather a terror: it smothers the other, who, far from perceiving the gift in it, reads there instead an assertion of mastery, of power, of pleasure, of solitude. Whence the cruel paradox of the dedication: I seek at all costs to give you what smothers you. (78–79)

Enclosed by the book, engulfed by the other, smothered (mothered? othered?) by a text that terrorizes us while it loves us, or loves us while it terrorizes: this is the ambivalence of Narcissus. This is the Barthesian lover who is located in the space of the other — "This is how it happens sometimes, misery or joy engulfs me, without any particular tumult ensuing: nor any pathos: I am dissolved, not dismembered; I fall, I flow, I melt" (10). This too is the Barthesian lover who recognizes in other moments that he in no way inhabits the space of the other — "For me as an amorous subject . . . it is becoming a *subject,* being unable to keep myself from doing so, which drives me mad. *I am not someone else:* that is what I realize with horror" (121).

Horror yes, but nothing of the kind that plagues the men of *Ghost Story,* for just as Barthes recognizes that his subjectivity keeps him from full union with his desired other, so too does he seek to re-store the *I* who loves, the *I* who utters the lover's discourse. Barthes's narcissistic lover is as aware that the other, the image, constitutes him as he is that he invents that other and invests him with his own eros. In Barthes, we see what has become the familiar presentation of the poststructuralist, posthumanist subject; we see him write into presence and write into absence a queer subjectivity whose ancestors we find in Tennessee Williams's Sebastian Venable and Ovid's Narcissus himself. We see a lover whose "innocence" has been radically abandoned for a utopian ideal of consciousness constituted upon the plethora of Image, "the abolition of the manifest and the latent, of the appearance and the hidden" (61). And this is in contradistinction to the Narcissus of Peter Straub's narrative. For him, innocence is lost to the horrors of self-knowledge, those apocalyptic realizations when the repressed returns. Yet Straub also seems to suggest that innocence should be gleefully abandoned for something approaching recognition, awareness, a psychoanalytic truth. This is not a knowledge of "self" such as the moralists sought for the Ovidian Narcissus — that is, a defined, articulated, stabilized, phallic self — but a knowledge of, and a dissolution of, what has been repressed to form the self, what possibilities for desire have been given up to take on the identity of the male. That Straub's characters reject such knowledge constitutes in them a queer panic at the level of their discourse; that Barthes does not constitutes a queer pleasure in his.

If Christopher Lasch is to be believed, we are in a culture of narcissism, inexorably compelled to search our psyches for some vestige of identity among the technological postmodern fragments. And if Peter Straub is to be believed, that narcissism is intensely Gothic. It creates a seemingly omnipotent hall of fun house mirrors where even fictional writing eventually leads us back to our selves, to the mechanisms and contents of our own buried fantasies. But that such narcissism should be Gothicized is less a reason to despair than it is to hope, to see the possibilities for intervention in social and psychic economies that still deploy Narcissus in the service of antiqueer regulation. Roland Barthes's Gothic tropes — enclosing, engulfing, lacerating, mastery, power, solitude — not only engage the Gothic's commitment to exposing the buried, and to returning us to what has been repressed, but also convey the lure of self-destruction that, in queer aesthetics, generates possibilities rather than closing them off. These tropes align with Leo Bersani's in calling for a smashing of the hegemonically constructed self, an internment of the ego in the "grave" of anal pleasure. The Gothic can offer us queer pleasure not just because it provides a deliciously nasty critique of the universalized norms of contemporary culture but because it emblematizes possibilities for narcissistic self-destruction into new forms of pleasure. The Gothicism of our culture is terrifying because it threatens to destroy certain constructions of the self. The narcissism of our culture is promising for exactly the same reason.

Conclusion

REJECTING NARCISSUS

The project of this book has been to read Narcissus's privatizing, minoritizing impulse together with his synecdochic, universalizing one. I've tried to show how white Western culture since the late eighteenth century draws on both classical/early modern texts and psychonormalizing theories to make narcissism compulsory at the same time as regulating and compartmentalizing it. More specifically, culture mutes the narcissistic eros that it simultaneously depends upon for introspection's epistemological, ethical, and analytical work. In a broad range of discourses from Neoplatonic Romanticism to Modernism, from the most arcane of poststructuralist theories to the most popular Gothic best-sellers, Narcissus comes to figure stably as an emblem of instability; he occupies both sides of those familiar binaries structuring our culture: self/other, surface/depth, active/passive, masculine/feminine, soul/body, inside/outside, sanity/psychosis. And in that figuration he comes to look like the rather predictable product of another historically specific intellectual moment: the postmodern. Narcissus as I have traced him here is *the* trope of undecidability, hanging suspended between the "that" and the "not-that," a giddy wonderland queen who deconstructs as many as six impossible epistemes before breakfast. Narcissus always brings us to the abyss of meaning. If we're straight, he throws us over the edge; if we're queer, he offers his hand for a dance along the precipice, like Jacques Derrida and Paul de Man in the famous Mark Tansy canvas.

To the degree that Narcissus is a central trope in the current queer moment — and it's been one of the purposes of this book to bring together queer theory's tacit or explicit uses of Narcissus — he draws a line between those who advocate the postmodern ludic possibilities of his gender transgression (Judith Butler, Lee Edelman, Earl Jackson) and those who are suspicious of a self-deluding danger in such transgressive, ludic play (Donald Morton, David Savran, at times Leo Bersani). But it is now left to ask where we go from this stonewall, this battle between playful undecidability and the diagnostic impulse of materialist or psychoanalytic criticism. Is there a place from which to read Narcissus that does not determine in advance what we will think of him? Perhaps the real question here is about the direction of queer intellectual critique in the wake of its second wave: Who will take it up, how, with what agenda, and through what optic? Will this taking up be a self-proclaimed "political" use, and, if so, what then are we to do with the multiple significations of Narcissus, significations that we might say generate desire yet might be seen to undermine the coherence we deem necessary for any group to undertake political action?

Let me state the problem another way. In *The Psychic Life of Power* (1997), Judith Butler argues that subjectivity is constituted by subjection and that the subject, in order to be a subject, must cathect on that which subjects or oppresses: "To desire the condition of one's own subordination," she maintains, "is thus required to persist as oneself" (9). However, for the heteronormative subject to take up his or her place in culture, s/he must not recognize that something is being lost in the formation of subjectivity, that certain desires are rendered unavailable from the start. Those desires, Butler maintains, are homoerotic, and the inability to recognize them as lost — an inability based on the fact that they were culturally prohibited to begin with — institutes in the heteronormative subject a sense of melancholy. Echoing arguments made in *Gender Trouble* (1990) and *Bodies That Matter* (1993), Butler then suggests the omnipresence of a *"heterosexual melancholy"* where

> a masculine gender is formed from the refusal to grieve the masculine as a possibility of love; a feminine gender is formed (taken on, assumed) through the incorporative fantasy by which the feminine is excluded as a possible object of love, an exclusion never grieved, but "preserved" through heightened feminine identification. In this sense, the "truest" lesbian melancholic is the strictly straight woman, and the "truest" gay male melancholic is the strictly straight man. (1997, 146–47)

Significantly, this melancholia is to be found only in straights. While gays in the age of AIDS are presented more emphatically than ever with the loss of same-sex objects whom they love, we appear in Butler's version to be free from melancholy. We mourn — and the Names Project Quilt is evidence of our mourning — but we recognize what we have lost. We are not plagued by a melancholy that, according to Freud, is at base a narcissistic condition. Homosexuality in this reading repudiates melancholia by repudiating repudiation. We are always already desublimated and thus seemingly outside the regulatory regimes of melancholy's construction of gender.

Butler's treatment of melancholia here provides her queer readers a safe space, a stable subject-position that her rigorous skepticism elsewhere denies. (Indeed, it was the project of *Bodies That Matter* to undo the sartorial manifesto of queer drag that she saw readers of *Gender Trouble* to be advocating with a classical humanist assumption of "self" performing the subversive drag.) "Negative narcissism," the self's "engaged preoccupation with what is most debased and defiled about it" (1997, 50), is the lever by which we may jubilantly crack open straight melancholia, a melancholia from which our speech-acts of coming out may save us. I do not take such an optimistic stand, nor do I believe Butler does either, generally. Rather, I cite this problem to ask, with Butlerian logic, what happens to queer critique and queer subjectivity when we (narcissistically) withdraw ourselves from a Freudian logics of narcissism. What happens when we repudiate repudiation? And where might it get us to reject that repudiated repudiation?

If there is a utopian impulse governing Narcissus, an impulse we can detect in Ovid and Marcuse, in Butler and Earl Jackson, it is an impulse that is tautological in nature: it imagines a perfect original to which it then wants to return. As we saw in André Gide's "Le traité du Narcisse" in chapter 2, human perfectibility is predicated upon division or separation, where such division opens up and makes possible the desire for perfection. But what are the effects on queer Narcissus when the "original" is not desirable, when it signifies more pain than pleasure? Such is the question that seems to underlie the poetry of Reginald Shepherd, an out gay African American whose two published collections, *Some Are Drowning* (1994) and *Angel, Interrupted* (1996), compulsively return to the figure of the desiring Narcissus. But unlike the homoerotic white men whose reflected images have comprised my entire analysis so far, Shepherd renders Narcissus a figure of abjection, of an unspeakable personal and political history signifying rejection, self-loathing, silence, and slavery. Like Gide, Shepherd imagines a paradise that might escort him to a state of healed pleasure, but this paradise depends less upon Narcissus's desire for himself than on his desire for a racial and cultural other. That other is the white male as the sexual object of desire. In "Paradise," from *Some Are Drowning,* Shepherd articulates a desire for "a man / who doesn't look like me" (10), the "antonym[] of my own face" (1994, 9). Elsewhere, in *Angel, Interrupted,* this desire culminates in a "Searching for the body's hidden paradise" where the black man "cuts off his face to spite his skin, cuts off / his black skin and calls it love" (1996, 17). In that white face the speaker sees himself "turning from the summary glance, a little / light captured in the momentary retina, but / reversed" (1996, 53). The white other is the black man's reflection, but also his opposite. Repeating a text that psychoanalysis has written exhaustingly, Narcissus despises himself.

However, the white lover in "Paradise" is not only the speaker's antonym but also the man "who looks like me / if I could speak my name, / if I could stop / the repetitions of oppressive beauties / not my own" (1994, 10). White beauty, beauty-as-whiteness, is historically responsible for "oppressions"; yet, paradoxically, it is the very means by which Shepherd can imagine a way out of cultural and erotic disempowerment. These paradoxes are fascinating precisely for the danger they suggest. What Narcissus imagines and desires is not enslavement to the oppressive beauty of whiteness; the white boys that haunt the pages of Shepherd's poetry as erotic chimeras are objects of desire not because they oppress, not because they objectify the black male body — although they do both of these — and not because the poet needs the oppressor to guarantee him the subjectivating comforts of oedipal tyranny, the interlockings within power that Foucault and Butler say constitutes the modern subject. Rather, for Shepherd the white boy is the phallus-as-signifier, the image of what it can mean to have some degree of self-possession, narrative, a language that constructs (even fictitiously) a history other than that of enslavement. And that signifier is a narcissistic signifier exactly as it shuttles between the registers of sameness (he is what I am, a queer male pleasuring subject, an object of the other's desire) and difference (he represents a power and entitlement to which I aspire and that will give me a sense of self that is not defined by him). The white male makes narcissism both impossible (he has taught me to hate myself) and inevitable (he makes me recognize my blackness and imagine what I might become, and on my own terms). Shepherd does not want to be enslaved by his white lover, nor does he want to be his white lover — he wants to have what his white lover has, while, and after, he is having the white lover. As Shepherd says elsewhere, "Having nothing / I can pretend to everything" (1996, 11).

I close with this brief discussion of Reginald Shepherd not to complete or fix the story of Narcissus but to suggest aesthetic and political directions in which he has yet to take us. Shepherd's poetry, it seems to me, retains the imperative to claim subjectivity, a claim that a decade of queer theorizing has made difficult to hold to without the embarrassing name-calling of essentialism or totalizing. Shepherd imagines identity, but it is an identity that exists in the future tense: as he will become, rather than as he is at present described. He can come to an articulation of this future-oriented queer subjectivity by deploying Narcissus not only as the static, compulsive desirer but as the subject of a metamorphosis; Narcissus is he who changes. This change is real and possible, yet never idealized: Shepherd remains constantly aware of the degree to which Narcissus is an abject figure, seeking an impossible goal, desiring a utopian return that he can never effect because the utopia never existed. But most important, I think, is Shepherd's revision of politically dangerous desires that are desires precisely because they are politically dangerous. He asks us to imagine further dissolutions of political and somatic boundaries, boundaries that desire simultaneously creates and penetrates, boundaries that affirm and shatter identity. Shepherd makes racial the refusal to repudiate desires while at the same time laying bare the vicissitudes of that repudiation. His poetry shows us that we need new thinking on how to have promiscuity in an epidemic — not just an epidemic of HIV but of identity correctness, of the regulation of desire, of the fear of being narcissistic. If there is a "use" in Narcissus, it is in his dangers. Narcissus, who is said to aspire to that which is the same, is continually destroying the political safety promised by sameness.

NOTES

Introduction

1. Gregory W. Bredbeck notes "the way in which the progression of sexology (especially as it culminates in Freudian psychoanalysis) increasingly consolidates inversion, narcissism, and homosexuality" (1994, 70).

2. While Näcke used the word *Narcismus,* Freud, in his discussion of Schreber, uses *Narzissmus,* which he found more euphonious than the technically correct *Narzissismus* (1911, 60).

3. For Bredbeck, this explanation allows Freud to use narcissism to ground a heterosexual, binaristic narrative of desire: "both narcissism and inversion become, first, ensnared by an anaclitic division that replicates the *form* of heterosexual union, and thereby both narcissism and inversion seem to make that form inevitable and universal. Second, . . . the *difference* of narcissistic and inverted cathexis is erased by rewriting the potentiality for both as a universalized subject" (1994, 65–66).

By positing that inverts mimic the heterosexual desire for otherness, homosexual desire *as* difference can be made to fit "a socialized and reproductive tale" that denies sexual difference at the same time that it pathologizes it.

4. One of the earliest and still most famous examples of female narcissism is John Milton's depiction of Eve in book 4 of *Paradise Lost.* She tells Adam:

> I thither went
> With unexperienc't thought, and laid me down
> On the green bank, to look into the clear
> Smooth Lake, that to me seem'd another Sky.
> As I bent down to look, just opposite,
> A Shape within the wat'ry gleam appear'd
> Bending to look on me, I started back,
> It started back, but pleas'd I soon return'd,
> Pleas'd it return'd as soon with answering looks
> Of sympathy and love; there I had fixt
> Mine eyes till now, and pin'd with vain desire,
> Had not a voice thus warn'd me, What thou seest,
> What there thou seest fair Creature is thyself,
> With thee it came and goes; but follow me,
> And I will bring thee where no shadow stays
> Thy coming, and thy soft imbraces, hee
> Whose image thou art, him thou shalt enjoy
> Inseparably thine, to him shalt bear
> Multitudes like thyself, and thence be call'd

> Mother of human Race: what could I do,
> But follow straight, invisibly thus led?
> Till I espi'd thee, fair indeed and tall,
> Under a Platan, yet methought less fair,
> Less winning soft, less amiably mild,
> Than that smooth wat'ry image; back I turn'd . . .
>   (1962, lines 456–80)

But not for long, of course. As soon as Adam identifies her as "My other half" (line 488), Eve yields and heterosex is born. But the ironies here are many, among them the following: God is the original narcissist, creating humanity in his own image; Eve the woman is the reflection of that narcissism, since she was made in God's image; and Eve is to become the next narcissist by creating multitudes like herself.

5. I have corrected the exact wording and punctuation of the Freud quotation to reflect the original Strachey translation.

6. Another example in Jackson's arsenal: "The gay male spectator accesses a network of 'inappropriate' or transgressive identifications, structured by the anti-Oedipal mutuality of identification and desire. In his multiple or shifting identifications, the gay male spectator transgresses the gendered dichotomies and disrupts the Cartesian unity of self that are part of the subject effect intended in the dominant cultural representational institutions to which the anaclitic subject submits" (1995, 139). We might read this reclamation of homosexual narcissism against Gregory Bredbeck's essay, "Narcissus in the Wilde: Textual Cathexis and the Historical Origins of Queer Camp" (1994). Whereas Jackson maintains the distinction between the anaclitic/straight subject and the narcissistic/gay one, Bredbeck argues that sexological discourse in general and Freud's work in particular increasingly sacrifice the idea of narcissism to anaclisis and object-relations, so that the homosexual subject in Freudian theory eventually becomes an anaclitic subject, thus privileging a heterosexual model in its figuration of homosexual subjectivity.

7. Lesbian film theory is now beginning to think more about lesbian narcissism and its relation to the cinematic image. For examples of this discussion, see Jackie Stacey (1987), Teresa de Lauretis (1994), and Kaja Silverman (1988).

1. No Exit

1. To this list from *Civilization and Its Discontents* (1930), Pamela A. Boker adds "an overestimation of subjective mental processes, an intensification of the critical conscience, a preference for isolation, a pervading feeling that life is empty and meaningless, a tendency toward incestuous impulses, and a fascination with beauty" (1992, 3).

2. The Schlegels were so much a source for British Romanticism that there is a long debate over the degree to which Coleridge plagiarized August. For a summary and treatment of this problem, see Thomas McFarland (1969, 256–61). See also Norman Fruman (1971), chapter 14, as well as G. N. G. Orsini (1964), and Oswald Doughty (1981).

3. My thanks to Goran Stanivukovic, Peter Schwenger, and Robert K. Martin for translating this sonnet.

4. The only exception to this statement is Herbert Read's *The True Voice of Feeling* (1947). Read draws on the work of psychoanalyst Trigant Burrows to argue in Percy Shelley a primary identification with the mother. This identification results in autoerotism, a condition that Burrows argues is "precisely homosexuality" (quoted in Read 1947, 248). Read concludes: "Shelley belonged to a definite psychological type — a type whose consciousness is incompletely objectified, which is therefore evidently narcissistic, and unconsciously homosexual. Such unconscious homosexuality gives rise to a psychosis of which Shelley shows all the normal symptoms."

5. As G. N. G. Orsini points out, chapter 9 of Coleridge's *Biographia Literaria* refers to the "illustrious Florentine" whom Coleridge had read at least as early as 1780 (1969, 9–10).

6. This passage is also quoted in Vinge 1967, 124–26.

7. Vinge also cites the *Phaedrus* as the source of Philostratus's use of the Narcissus myth (1967, 31). Plato may not discuss the mythic character by name, but he certainly provides a mirror by which the narcissistic comes to be reflected.

8. See Peter Thorslev for other uses of the hermaphrodite section of the Aristophanes myth; see also Caroline Franklin (1992, 222–23) and Diane Long Hoeveler (1990, 140). Loren Glass (1995) offers a more diversifying reading of narcissism but strictly within a heterosexual register.

9. Compare Shelley's *On Love,* previously quoted, to his translation of Aristophanes' tale, and in particular the description of same-sex love. Shelley records in his translation: "These are they who devote their whole lives to each other, with a vain and inexpressible longing to obtain from each other something they know not what; for it is not merely the sensual delights of their intercourse for the sake of which they dedicate themselves to each other with such serious affection; but the soul of each manifestly thirsts for, from the other, something which there are no words to describe, and divines that which it seeks, and traces obscurely the footsteps of its obscure desire" (quoted in Notopoulos 1969, 432). Shelley will of course interpret this desire as "Platonic" in the conventional sense, seeming not to notice that the qualifier "merely" to refer to the sensual delights is not a negation of sensuality but its incorporation.

10. For a complete discussion of Greek thought and the necessity of physical desire, see Michel Foucault (1985) and David Halperin (1990).

11. Louis Crompton (1985) traces the history of translations of Plato's *Symposium,* notably that of Floyer Sydenham in 1761 and 1767. Sydenham changed all the pronoun references and much of the other language of the Greek text to heterosexualize Plato and the type of desire being discussed. This bowdlerization was to be amended by Percy Shelley's translation, but it too was subject to sanitization. When Mary Shelley tried to publish it in 1840, Leigh Hunt convinced her to change words like "lover" into "friend," "men" into "human beings," and so forth. Moreover, it omitted the speech of Alcibiades altogether. The full work was not published in English until James Notopoulos did so in 1949. Crompton also notes that "Scholars writing on the history of Greek studies have noted the almost total disappearance of Plato from the British educational curriculum in this period" (285). And, finally, Crompton gives the statistics for the drastic rise in persecution of sodomites in the early nineteenth century.

12. In 1749, Richard Spencer was convicted, according to G. S. Rousseau, "for merely *hoping* 'to commit the horrible Crime of Sodomy'" (1985, 147; emphasis in original). This conviction is significant, in that it marks a change from the persecution of sodomitical behavior to the persecution of sodomitical desire and thus begins to construct the internal, private site of desire as a juridical field that one had to police and protect. It made the contents of one's closet, rather than one's external behaviors, a subject of critical investigation.

13. And here Anne Mellor's feminist analysis can be read with that of Barbara Schapiro, whose *The Romantic Mother* (1983) argues that Romantic narcissism always has at origin a repudiation of the mother who is abjected, idealized, and/or despised.

14. We might contrast this with Blake, whose mirror is actually a window he can look through; see "A Vision of the Last Judgement" (1982). Coleridge holds no such radical hope that one can see through; rather, we are always narcissistically reflected back upon ourselves.

15. For a more complete discussion of Coleridge's fascination with the image of the mirror, see Kathleen Coburn. Coburn argues that "The mirror, the looking-glass of Narcissus, is in obvious and also in less obvious ways connected with the search for the self" (1965, 417). One of the "less obvious ways" is Coleridge's depiction of the maternal breast as a mirror. This breast, which both nurtures and poisons, "reflects" both metaphysical principles of idealism and Coleridge's own sense of himself as alienated or abjected. Writes Coburn, "The mirror reflects the image of the inward self. It also distances the self from the self. The intervention of a reflecting surface, whether warm, animate, or cold and inanimate, asserts the essential severance of the self from the other, from the image even, and inspires, with whatever fear and awe it is capable, the need to bridge the gap, whether by philosophy or poetry, between the percipient and the perceived" (433).

16. This letter and others to Thomas Poole are also quoted in Wayne Koestenbaum, *Double Talk: The Erotics of Male Literary Collaboration* (1989). In a letter of 6 May 1799, also quoted by Koestenbaum, Coleridge's language to Poole is thoroughly indebted to the Socratic pederast's: "O my God! how I long to be at home — My *whole Being* so yearns after you, that when I think of the moment of our meeting, I catch the fashion of German Joy, rush into your arms, and embrace you" (Coleridge 1956, 490).

17. For a related discussion of homosexuality-as-death, see James Holt Mc-Gavran (1995, 163). McGavran reads the "Nightmare Life-In-Death" figure of the *Ancient Mariner* as a terrifying drag queen.

18. This "pressure of the thrilling hand" also stands nicely with one of Coleridge's letters to Poole, which I have already quoted in part (6 May 1799). After telling Poole that "My *whole Being* so yearns after you," Coleridge writes, "when I think of the moment of our meeting, I catch the fashion of German Joy, rush into your arms, and embrace you — methinks, my *Hand* would swell, if the whole force of my feeling were crowded there. — Now the Spring comes, the vital sap of my affections rises, as in a tree" (1956, 490). For a lovely analysis of this letter, see Koestenbaum (1989, 71–72). For more on the erotics of hand-holding, see the discussion of *Teleny* in the next chapter.

19. Miller writes of secrecy: "I have had to intimate my secret, if only *not to*

tell it; and conversely, in theatrically continuing to keep my secret, I have already rather *given it away.* But if I don't tell my secret, why can't I keep it better? And if I can't keep it better, why don't I just tell it? I can't quite tell my secret, because then it would be known that there was nothing really special to hide, and no one really special to hide it. But I can't quite keep it either, because then it would not be believed that there *was* something to hide and someone to hide it.... More precisely, secrecy would seem to be a mode whose ultimate meaning lies in the subject's formal insistence that he is radically inaccessible to the culture that would otherwise entirely determine him" (1988, 194–95).

20. Rank writes, "The stage of development from which paranoids regress to their original narcissism is sublimated homosexuality, against the undisguised eruption of which they defend themselves with the characteristic mechanism of projection" (1971, 74). This projection, he argues, takes the form of the doppelgänger (85).

21. For a more complete discussion of this pairing in Shakespeare's *Troilus and Cressida,* see chapter 1 of Gregory W. Bredbeck, *Sodomy and Interpretation* (1991).

22. As Samuel Chew noted in 1915, "With the second scene of the play the mood is changed. Arnold no longer *wishes;* he has acquired all his desires save love" (Chew 1964, 147). For Daniel P. Watkins, this change of mood heralds the downfall of a play that was conceived during Byron's increased Republicanism of 1821. Because of his political concerns, Byron "wrote the drama with even less patience and precision than usual, allowing his ego and impulse toward autobiography to obscure other interests" (1983, 27). In other words, the play is vague for Watkins because Byron was unusually narcissistic at the time of its composition. I would suggest the opposite: the play is fascinating because Byron is narcissistic, and his narcissism does not work at odds with the political Republicanism that captures Watkins's attention, but rather is part of it.

23. Caesar is, among other things, the beloved of the Bithynian king Nicomedes, as mentioned in Jeremy Bentham's 1785 essay on pederasty; or he is Byron's "Caesar of sexuality," a phrase that describes his pederastic relation with Nicolo Giraud (quoted in Christensen 1993, 61–62; see Byron 1973b, 14).

2. Reverse of the Mirror

1. Of course, not all the reviews of Oscar Wilde's decadent sexuality were damning. In a much more positive light, poet Marc-André Raffalovich includes a chapter on Wilde in *L'Uranisme.*

2. Here is Dollimore's summary of the now-famous incident in which Gide met Wilde in Algiers in 1895 and Wilde continued his efforts to deprogram Gide's prudery: "[Gide] is taken by Wilde to a café. It is there that 'in the half-open doorway, there suddenly appeared a marvelous youth. He stood there for a time, leaning with his raised elbow against the door-jamb, and outlined in the dark background of the night.' The youth joins them; his name is Mohammed; he is a musician; he plays the flute. Listening to that music, 'you forget the time and place, and who you were.' ... Now, as they leave the café, Wilde turns to Gide and asks him if he desires the musician. Gide writes: 'how dark the alley was! I thought my heart would fail me; and what a dreadful effort of courage it needed to

answer: "yes," and with what a choking voice!' " Wilde arranges something with their guide, rejoins Gide, and then begins laughing: "a resounding laugh, more of triumph than of pleasure, an interminable, uncontrollable, insolent laugh" (Dollimore 1991, 49–50; he is quoting Gide 1935, 280–85).

3. Regenia Gagnier has this to say about *Dorian Gray:* "Wilde insisted on the 'moral' of the story, a constant moral throughout his prose fiction: that an exclusive preoccupation with the physical and material surfaces of life would result in the attrition of human creativity. But simultaneously his prose insisted on ornate description of material conditions and an obsession with physical beauty. Indeed, to a great extent, *Dorian Gray* is about *spectators,* from spectators of the beauty of others such as Basil of Dorian's or Dorian of Sybil Vane's to 'spectators of life,' as Wilde called Wotton. Similarly, critics of what was considered Wilde's aristocratic pose and immorality could not see the moral of the novel because of their own preoccupation with its physical and material representations. Both Wilde and his critics argued for spirit; both sides' energy was directed toward externals. Both sides were situated in the context of public images and self-advertisement: the journalists posing as gentlemen guardians of public morality, Wilde advertising himself as the subtle dandy-artist of higher morality, thinking himself within the Symbolist ranks that Arthur Symons [in *The Symbolist Movement in Literature*] called the 'revolt against exteriority, against rhetoric, and against a materialist tradition' " (1986, 56–57).

4. This fantastically lucid definition of art comes so close to the definition of Symbolist art that one is left to wonder what Nordau thought separated him from the Symbolists whom he so roundly condemned. Indeed, one thinks here of Eve Kosofsky Sedgwick's analysis of Nietzsche, whom she holds up against Wilde to demonstrate the ways in which Nietzsche was implicated in precisely the kind of dandyism that he was denouncing. Nietzsche, she argues, was panicked by his own sentimental relationship to figures like Wagner and channeled that panic through a renunciation of the sentimental (see Sedgwick 1990, chap. 3). While a similar analysis of Nordau is beyond my scope here, the similarities between Nietzsche and Nordau might be very illuminating.

5. Nordau's condemnation of the narcissist and its possible self-contestations can most easily be glimpsed in his discussion of Wilde's dandiacal dress. Offering no proof, Nordau argues that "The adornment of the exterior has its origin in the strong desire to be admired by others — primarily by the opposite sex — to be recognised by them as especially well-shaped, handsome, youthful, or rich and powerful" (1968, 318). Wilde's queer clothing perverts this desire as it offends those who see it (especially women, presumably?) and thus keeps him out of the (heterosexual) arena. Moreover, "The fool who masquerades in Pall Mall does not see himself, and, therefore, does not enjoy the beautiful appearance which is supposed to be an aesthetic necessity for him" (318). One is not sure here whether the dandiacal Wilde is being too narcissistic or not narcissistic enough, since he is not able to see himself either for his own pleasure or for his own edification.

6. So does it in Dollimore. In his list of binary oppositions that Dollimore argues distinguish Wilde's definition of desire from that of Gide, Dollimore pairs "narcissism" with "maturity," even though other elements in the Wilde list in-

clude "surface," "lying," "difference," and "style/artifice" (in Gagnier 1991, 57). I take this pairing as instructive of the degree to which our culture has entrenched narcissism in a model of regression and infantilization that is related to but exclusive of other characteristics.

7. Conversely, Valéry's own work on Narcissus, the sonnet "Narcisse parle," came too quickly. Writes Valéry to Gide on 1 February 1891, "I took up my pen, and here I am in the throes of anguish. For the only way my long-imagined *Narcisse* should be written is scrupulously, in short periods of time. And I suffer from feeling it grow almost *easily,* and I am very moved for I see the Work ungratefully becoming separate from me and enticing the dream of myself as a solitary ephebus" (Mallet 1966, 39). An interesting anxiety, both deconstructive and classical: Narcissus is mine yet constantly gets away from me, making me in my active search for him a passive lover-in-training, and all of this is caused by the very act of writing that separates me from what I write.

8. Patrick Pollard, however, does not detect the same kind of sexual energy in the treatise: "For Gide Plato's (and Peladan's) original hermaphrodite is not the symbol of sexual excess but the image of the Absolute. It is Narcisse who, when he is self-regarding, is self-complete" (1991, 303). Indeed, "It seems unlikely that Gide knew of the exclusively homosexual versions of the legend of Narcissus recorded by the Greek writer Conon" (461). Be that as it may, the Ovidian version is itself a "homosexual" version, and it is only its history of repudiation, as I discussed in the previous chapter, that constitutes its idealism and/or its heteronormativity. But if Butler's discussion of the logic of repudiation is to be believed, "the image of the Absolute" is always troubled by the presence of "sexual excess," and it seems to me that the presence of Adam in the treatise makes precisely that point.

9. While Gregory Bredbeck refers to "The Disciple" as Wilde's "brief tribute to Narcissus" (1994, 66), I find Wilde's work to be obsessed with the image. We find it not only in the obvious places, *Dorian Gray* and *Teleny* (if the latter was written by Wilde), but also in narcissistic moments, mirror reflections, and various deployments of the trope in the poem "The Burden of Itys" and in the short stories "The Birthday of the Infanta," "The Star-Child," "The Young King," and "The Nightingale and the Rose."

10. Jeffrey Berman (1990, 149) lists the following discussions of Oscar Wilde and narcissism, many of which use *Dorian Gray* as a testing ground: Alexander Grinskin (1973), Jerome Kavka (1975), Bernard A. Green (1979), and Ellie Ragland-Sullivan (1986).

11. There is some debate as to whether Wilde wrote major sections of *Teleny* or had any hand in its editing. Regenia Gagnier asserts that "it is fairly certain that he was neither the author nor a major collaborating author" of *Teleny* (1986, 60). Conversely, John McRae, the editor of the Gay Men's Press edition of *Teleny,* argues that the novel "certainly reflects many of the aesthetic, moral, and sexual concerns of Wilde; it certainly contains more than just echoes, touches, or influences of Wilde" (Wilde et al. 1986, 15). Absolute authenticity is not my concern here. I do think that Wilde had a hand in the writing of the novel, and I find convincing McRae's stylistic analyses. However, my concern in this chapter is to discuss the historical moment that saw the construction of the homosexual

as narcissist and to use the constellation of Wildean words and identities as a test case. That Wilde may have "influenced" more of *Teleny* than he composed is not germane to my argument.

12. Such sexual sameness takes on an almost ludicrous and parodic mystique in the novel. At one point in the novel, Teleny sires a child who, straining medical credibility as pornography often does, turns out to look not like the father Teleny but like the father's lover Camille (Wilde et al. 1986, 84).

13. Another version — less violent but equally insidious — of narcissism's destruction of the other appears in Lord Henry's musings on influence: "There was something terribly enthralling in the exercise of influence. No other activity was like it. To project one's soul into some gracious form, and let it tarry there for a moment; to hear one's own intellectual views echoed back to one with all the added music of passion and youth; to convey one's temperament into another as though it were a subtle fluid or a strange perfume: there was real joy in that" (Wilde 1987, 35). Henry's projection of self onto another obliterates that other, a narcissistic projection that has much to do with the dangerous solipsism of the novel.

14. It is this refusal to relinquish the reflection of the other that Herbert Marcuse finds in the fin de siècle's fascination with the Narcissus figure. In *Eros and Civilization* (1966), Marcuse defines narcissism in the works of Paul Valéry and André Gide as the "refusal to accept separation from the libidinous object (or subject). The refusal aims at liberation — at the re-union of what has become separated" (154). Ultimately, this "Great Refusal" in late-nineteenth-century aesthetics seeks to liberate the pleasure principle from the tyranny of the reality principle, a liberation that Earl Jackson effects in narcissism as well.

15. Wilde wrote to Ralph Payne about *Dorian Gray:* "I am so glad that you like that strange coloured book of mine; it contains much of me in it. Basil Hallward is what I think I am: Lord Henry what the world thinks of me: Dorian what I would like to be — in other ages, perhaps" (1962, 352).

16. As quoted by Lucien Dällenbach, here is the full context of Gide's definition from the original journal entry: "In a work of art, I rather like to find thus transposed, at the level of the characters, the subject of the work itself. Nothing sheds more light on the work or displays the proportions of the whole work more accurately. Thus, in paintings by Memling or Quentin Metzys, a small dark convex mirror reflects, in its turn, the interior of the room in which the action of the painting takes place. Thus, in a slightly different way, in Valásquez's *Las Meninas.* Finally, in literature, there is the scene in which the play is acted in *Hamlet;* this also happens in many other plays. In *Wilhelm Meister,* there are the puppet shows and the festivities in the castle. In *The Fall of the House of Usher,* there is the piece that is read to Roderick etc. None of these examples is absolutely accurate. What would be more accurate, and what would explain better what I'd wanted to do in my *Cahiers,* in *Narcisse* and in *La Tentative,* would be a comparison with the device from heraldry that involves putting a second representation of the original shield 'en abyme' within it" (1989, 7).

17. Interestingly, Krafft-Ebing uses the image of the "sympathetic man" to discuss the sexual partner that the homosexual seeks out (1965, 308). Once again regulatory psychological discourse gets translated into homoerotic union.

18. The mother plot also establishes a kind of family romance that reminds us of the "normal" sexuality to which we should always be attracted. This family romance obviously forecasts Freud's normalizing thesis that homosexual males are homosexual because of a bond with the mother, a bond that has moved from heteronormative desire to homosexual identification — although the fact that the mother's desire for Teleny comes so long after Camille's interrupts the psychogenetic theory of mother-as-origin (more on the presence of the mother in the next chapter).

19. Wilde himself attempted to exploit the medicalization of homosexuality to get him out of prison. In 1896, he twice petitioned the courts for a discharge from Reading by referring to his "offenses" as "forms of sexual madness . . . recognized as such . . . by modern pathological science" (Wilde 1962, 402) and to his "absolute madness — the insanity of perverted sensual instinct" (411). However, unlike his psychiatric counterparts, Wilde does not believe his own diagnosis. In a letter to Robert Ross in 1898, he refused to suggest "that Uranian love is ignoble. I hold it to be noble — more noble than other forms" (1962, 705). Rather, Wilde may have been employing the strategies of homosexual emancipators like Karl Heinrich Ulrichs, who find the medicalization of homosexuality a convenient means of moving beyond religious moralizing.

3. Sons and Lovers, Birds and Johns

1. A discussion of the primacy of the mother in narcissistic desire seems to beg for extended reference to the theories of Julia Kristeva. And so it shall, but not here. In the interests of connecting literary texts to theoretical approaches circulating in the same historical period, I am holding off on Kristeva until the final chapter when I discuss the Gothic novel at the end of the 1970s.

2. As James Strachey's note to this discussion makes clear, Freud's entire analysis of the "vulture" is specious, as Freud mistranslates the Italian word *nibio*, meaning "kite," as "vulture." For a complete discussion of this mistranslation and its long history among Freud's disciples, see Alan Bass (1985).

3. Here I part from Earl Jackson's reading of sublimation, which seems to take the concept at face value. For Jackson, sublimation is the means by which the male homosexual can be assimilated "into the privileged 'indifference' of phallocentric patriarchy" (1995, 85), and it is in the desublimating narcissistic identifications of artists like Wilde and Derek Jarman that iconoclastic strategies emerge (88). Says Jackson, "The desublimation effected by the narcissistic subject . . . can liberate the identificatory processes and demystify the theological appurtenances of Truth" (90). As I stated in my introduction, I find Jackson's empowerment of "gay" subjectivity both attractive and too categorical, as in this move to equate the political gay with the desublimated one. What follows in my discussion is a deconstruction of Freud's definition of sublimation to demonstrate the ways in which the very process of sublimation causes queer trouble in gender configuration.

4. Freud writes: "When we consider that inquisitive children are told that babies are brought by a large bird, such as the stork; when we find that the ancients represented the phallus as having wings; that the commonest expression in German for male sexual activity is '*vögeln*' ('to bird': '*Vogel*' is the German for

'bird'); that the male organ is actually called *'l'uccello'* ['the bird'] in Italian — all of these are only small fragments from a whole mass of connected ideas, from which we learn that in dreams the wish to be able to fly is to be understood as nothing else than a longing to be capable of sexual performance. This is an early infantile wish" (1910, 125–26).

5. Eugene L. Stelzig notes that the sparrow-hawk is the totem symbol of the Gnostic god Abraxas, who figures largely in Sinclair's quest (1988, 144). According to Pistorius, the novel's stand-in for Hesse's psychotherapist Josef Lang, Abraxas is a combination of the godly and the devilish and is absolutely crucial to one's journey of self-awareness. For a Jungian symbolic reading of Hesse's novels, see Theodore Ziolkowski (1967).

6. There is a long critical debate over whether Freud or Jung was more important to Hesse's aesthetic program. For various treatments of this issue, see Mileck (1978), Stelzig (1988), and Brink (1974). For more on Hesse's debt to German Romanticism, see Stelzig (1988).

7. Hesse's biography, most fully documented by Ralph Freedman in *Hermann Hesse, Pilgrim of Crisis* (1978), is a dream come true for the psychoanalytic critic. He was sent away to school early because his parents could not cope with his difficult behavior at home (29–30). When he attempted suicide in his teens, his mother went immediately to his side (46–47). When away from home, he wanted to be there; when he was there, he found it "forbidding and hostile" (48). He was especially angry at his parents, particularly his father, for having labeled him mentally ill after his suicide attempt (49). When he became depressed at school in Cannstatt, his mother again rushed to his side (51–52) and remained protective of him all his young life. The two were estranged, however, after Hesse published his first book (79).

8. Goldmund does finally carve his Eternal Mother, but he takes her image from Lydia, the first woman he had slept with, and does not seem to satisfactorily bring to a conclusion his search for the mother in the novel. Thus, I disagree with the tendency in criticism of the novel to reify the abstract Eternal Mother as the fulfillment of Goldmund's quest.

9. Nor was the language of homoeros free from Hesse's sessions with Lang. Ralph Freedman describes these sessions with reference to the few extant notebooks of Josef Lang: "The third entry, of October 26, 1917, contains the most vivid and significant image. Dr. Lang refers to the psyche as a mine shaft: 'I hammer within my mine shaft that encloses me and gives me no light that I do not radiate myself. You hear my hammering in the roaring within your ear. Your heartbeat is the hammering of my arms that long to be freed.' In the final entry cited by [Hugo] Ball, of October 28, 1917, Dr. Lang hammered in the patient's mine shaft: 'Some time you will understand and chisel out the rocks of your soul, the primordial signature of men which you must teach them: the tablets of the Law of what is to come.' The therapist identified with the patient, the friend with the friend: their souls were compared to mine shafts in which they worked separately but through which they could meet if they managed to break down with gigantic hammers the walls that separated them. The strikingly physical way of portraying a mental state owes a good deal of its power to psychoanalytic energy and imagination. It is the type of imagery that began to filter into Hesse's work

as he sought to portray inner experience in pictorial and dramatic terms" (1978, 187–88).

10. Ronald Hayman writes: "Sebastian inherits not only Tennessee's predatory interest in boys, but also his diffidence.... Sebastian resembles Williams closely. Fed up with dark boys, he feels famished for blonds. 'That's how he talked about people — as if they were — items on a menu. "That one's delicious looking, that one is appetizing" or "that one is not appetizing" — I think because he was really nearly half-starved from living on pills and salads.' Ten years earlier, after two months in Italy, Tennessee had told Donald Windham he was tired of dark Romans and building up an appetite for northern blonds" (1993, 174–75).

11. That Sebastian should offer his body in divine sacrifice places him in a history of Narcissus as Christ-figure. Louise Vinge tells us that in the 1650s Jacobus Masenius, a German Jesuit, figured Narcissus as "a kind of image of God who was seized with love for men and became flesh" (1967, 189). In Juana Inés de la Cruz's seventeenth-century play *El Divino Narciso*, Christ is a "Divine Narcissus" who is tempted by Echo but remains true to his own image as the savior of a lost mankind that he sees reflected in the well (Vinge 1967, 245). And then of course there is the even more ancient, original act of narcissism: "Then God said, 'Let us make man in our image, after our likeness.... So God created man in his own image, in the image of God he created him; male and female he created them" (Genesis 1:26–27; RSV).

12. Donald Spoto sees these obsessions in the play: "*Suddenly Last Summer,* written quickly, in something like a confused trance of guilt and remorse, was the most creative result of [Tennessee Williams's] psychoanalysis. With his doctor he felt confined and restricted; in the study at the new apartment on East 65th Street, he produced a confessional drama that dealt with his demons not by avoiding them, not by reducing that guilt to insignificance or by denying it, but by *asserting* that guilt and working through it: confession to begin the creative process" (1985, 219–20).

13. Lyle Leverich's biography of Williams quotes a journal entry from 1941: "The cold beautiful bodies of the young! They spread themselves out like a banquet table, you dine voraciously and afterwards it is like you had eaten nothing but air" (1995, 424).

14. Williams had done this earlier as well, in the characters of Amanda and Tom Wingfield in *The Glass Menagerie.* By wanting so passionately to have Tom at home, Amanda drives him to the theater, a site that, as we know from "Hard Candy" and "The Mysteries of the Joy Rio," is awash in gay sex. Moreover, this score off the mother is one that Edwina, Williams's own mother, didn't understand. She could not see that Amanda *was* her, even though the stage character used all of Edwina's most common expressions. Narcissus could not recognize herself in the pool. For more on Edwina's relationship to Amanda and *The Glass Menagerie,* see Leverich 1995, 559–60.

15. Sebastian's alleged chastity is part of a chain of associations connecting him to Freud's Leonardo. Like Violet's Sebastian, Freud's Leonardo "represented the cool repudiation of sexuality" (1910, 69). In both artists this repudiation proceeded from a devotion to work, and in both it gestured to religious fascination, a kind of existential anxiety. Sebastian is, of course, looking for God when he finds

the vultures and sea turtles at the Encantadas, a search he shares with Leonardo. Freud quotes Edmondo Solmi's biography of Leonardo: "But his insatiable desire to understand everything around him, and to fathom in a spirit of cold superiority the deepest secret of all that is perfect, had condemned Leonardo's work to remain for ever unfinished" (1910, 73); to which Freud adds, "When, at the climax of a discovery, he could survey a large portion of the whole nexus, he was overcome by emotion, and in ecstatic language he praised the splendour of the part of creation that he had studied, or — in religious phraseology — the greatness of his Creator" (1910, 75). Compare this to Violet's description of Sebastian's Mosaic descent from the crow's nest on page 19.

16. Gross indicates that we have no reason to believe Catharine when she makes the claim that Violet procured for Sebastian. But why would she lie? And, moreover, why would we place more faith in Violet's construction of the past than in Catharine's?

17. While I will not expand on Williams's relationship to his mother, Edwina, Lyle Leverich's biography gives some very rich anecdotes about her overprotectiveness and fussing in regard to her son's welfare. Also, for a materialist reading of the play within the social forces of 1950s America, see Bruhm, 1991.

18. We may find here a source for Williams's alchemical language to describe art: his notion, which I quoted earlier, that art is a "distillation" of the best of the artist is a language he shares with his therapist. In 1962 Kubie wrote, "The primary derivation [of the term 'sublimation'] is from that chemical process by which solids are heated until they vaporize, the vapor then being cooled until it recondenses. But what does it then become? It becomes a purified version of itself all over again, freed from impurities perhaps but otherwise unaltered" (1962, 75–76). However, Kubie, who rejected the theory of sublimation, also rejects this notion of alchemical art; Williams, who rejected Kubie, rejects his rejection and employs the image of sublimation as an apt metaphor.

19. While Williams thought *Orpheus Descending* was panned mostly for its subject matter (Spoto 1985, 212), he also suggests that critics were out to get him for his self-aggrandizing narcissism: "In New York they put [*Orpheus Descending*] down with a vengeance. . . . I suspect it was a cabal to cut me down to what they thought was my size" (Williams 1972, 173). Moreover, this narcissism, as in Kubie's interpretation of homosexuality, is directly linked to Williams's repetitious indulgence of his own neuroses. As Hayman records, Williams told the *New York Herald-Tribune* in May 1957, "Maybe, I thought, they'd had too much of a certain dish, and maybe they don't want to eat any more" (1993, 170). Given that the next play Williams would write is about the cannibalizing of a gay artist, I suspect his gustatory metaphor here is not accidental.

20. Much of this resistance got translated into the preface to *Sweet Bird of Youth* (1975b), the play written directly after *Suddenly Last Summer* and whose very title raises questions about birds, phalluses, and sublimation.

21. For a full discussion on the geography of New Orleans, see Thomas J. Richardson (1977).

22. David Savran has argued that works such as *Moise and the World of Reason* and the short story "One Arm" explore a "symmetry of writing and

sexuality, pencil and penis, page and anus" that "announces an erotics of writing and reading" (1992, 156–57). Writing in these works is for Savran equivalent to homosexuality because it inscribes a Barthesian "pleasure of text."

23. In "Blond Ambition: Tennessee Williams's Homographesis" (1996a), I relate this dynamic to Lee Edelman's notion of "homographesis," the use of language to simultaneously inscribe and de-scribe (or displace) homosexual identity. Edelman's theory is especially important for discussion of a politics of writing, and so I have decided to hold it until the next chapter, which will deal explicitly with the problems of queerness, writing, and politics as they all figure the narcissistic paradigm.

24. In Robert F. Gross's reading of a gay sublime in *Suddenly Last Summer,* Sebastian rends and dismembers his body in a Christlike act of sacrifice precisely because he cannot render his experience poetically. For Gross, the absent mother results in Sebastian's writer's block, and so Sebastian renders himself a poetic text on the blank white wall of Cabeza de Lobo. The "block . . . caused by the loss of the Mother" is transformed into a "grisly realism" where "[t]he poet's body becomes the Sublime body — necessarily dismembered" (1995, 249). Gross argues that the dismemberment encodes a gay aesthetic of pleasure by paying homage to Hart Crane. Crane's own bodily dismemberment at sea becomes a kind of intertextual *jouissance* for Williams, and so, in a revision of Harold Bloom, Gross proffers a kind of erotics of influence where Williams and Crane dismember together, and Williams finds in the literary *father* an inspiration Sebastian could not find due to the absence of the literary *mother* (249). Thus, Gross sees the possibility of a homoerotically inspired text, even if this text sublimates the anxiety he sees in the loss of the mother. While I find this intertextual reading fascinating, I am troubled by the emphasis on anaclitic investments (Sebastian and mother, Williams and "father") to the derogation of narcissistic ones. Not only does the reading reinscribe the (hetero)normativity of queer-as-mamma's-boy, but it also cannot find in narcissism a creative productivity.

4. Queer Queer Vladimir

1. Caroline A. Jones argues that this paranoia was not only the property of right-wing government but even permeated artistic circles: she locates a "paranoid talk of a 'homointern' among the aggressively masculinist painters of abstract expressionism" in 1950s New York (1993, 652).

2. Significantly, this description of homoerotic narcissism was, by Nabokov's own admission, "an important passage which had been stupidly omitted in more timid times" — that is, in the Russian version of the novel published in 1932 (quoted in Grayson 1977, 78–79). Nor was this the only addition Nabokov would make to the later English publication. The fantasy of brother Felix sucking Hermann's big toe was another such addition, suggesting an increasing fascination with the erotics of narcissistic male relations.

3. Nabokov was not the only person to detect narcissism within fascism. As Ellis Hanson has made clear, "[Theodor] Adorno saw in the psychoanalytic concept of narcissism, and the pre-oedipal in general, both a way of describing the authoritarian personality and a position from which to launch a critical assault on fascism; that is, he found in narcissism a theory of fascist propaganda as well as a

theory for its subversion. Adorno collapses the distinction between the narcissist and the authoritarian subject whose position is secured through a repression of narcissism" (1992, 25).

4. For a bibliography of this debate, see Porter (1987, 246–48).

5. Another symptom of this need to construct resemblances is Kinbote's supposed similarities to Hazel Shade, John's daughter who commits suicide. Kinbote compares Hazel's love of wordplay to his own and concludes that "Hazel Shade resembled me in certain respects" (Nabokov 1962, 193). Another of these respects, apart from the wordplay, is the sexual queerness that defines the two. Each of them is outside traditional, successful, heterosexual paradigms.

6. The most important thinker about narcissism as an adaptive strategy is Heinz Kohut in his *The Analysis of the Self: A Systematic Approach to the Psychoanalytic Treatment of Narcissistic Personality Disorders* (1971). For a Kohutian reading of Nabokov's *Lolita*, see Jeffrey Berman's *The Talking Cure: Literary Representations of Psychoanalysis* (1985, 235–36).

7. *Pale Fire* presents numerous similarities between Kinbote and Nabokov. For example, the scene in which Kinbote pushes Shade's car down the icy driveway parallels Nabokov's helping his philosopher/neighbor Max Black push his car out of the snow (Boyd 1991, 359). Moreover, Black contended that the view from Shade's and Goldsworth's houses was taken from the surroundings of his and Nabokov's house in Ithaca (the New Wye of the novel being New York, and Wordsmith University being Cornell).

8. Given my discussion of Symbolism in chapter 3 and of phallic/maternal birds in chapter 4, it is interesting to read Nabokov's explanation for his choice of the pseudonym "Sirin" for his early Russian fiction. He says in *Strong Opinions:* "In modern times *sirin* is one of the popular Russian names of the Snowy Owl, the terror of tundra rodents, and is also applied to the handsome Hawk Owl, but in old Russian mythology it is a multicolored bird, with a woman's face and bust, no doubt identical with the 'siren,' a Greek deity, transporter of souls and teaser of sailors. In 1920, when casting about for a pseudonym and settling on that famous fowl, I still had not shaken off the false glamour of Byzantine imagery that attracted young Russian poets of the Blokian era. Incidentally, circa 1910 there had appeared literary collections under the editorial title of *Sirin* devoted to the so-called 'symbolist' movement, and I remember how tickled I was to discover in 1952 when browsing in the Houghton Library at Harvard that its catalogue listed me as actively publishing Blok, Bely, and Bryusov at the age of ten" (1973c, 161).

9. For an anthology of Nabokov's dismissals of Freud, see Shute 1995, 412–20.

10. This phobia can be tracked through Nabokov's torturous attempts to publish *Lolita*, another novel of forbidden love. While the novel did eventually become a best-seller and made Nabokov famous, it was first turned down by Simon and Schuster; Viking; New Directions; Farrar, Straus, and Giroux; and Doubleday. Finally, it was published by the European Olympia Press, whose aesthetic and moral credentials were not beyond reproach, before being picked up G. P. Putnam's Sons in 1958. Upon its release, a critic for the *New York Times* slammed it as "highbrow pornography," and it faced the con-

tinued threat of legal persecution. For more on the history of *Lolita*, see Boyd 1991.

11. Nor should we forget what Nabokov thought we might miss altogether — that Kinbote, Shade, and Gradus are themselves all fantasy-projections of Veselav Botkin, a disaffected scholar in the Russian department of New Wye (Boyd 1991, 443). In the search for a single, unified consciousness in this novel, we are constantly displaced into another act of splitting.

12. One model of this multiplication of self as a queer aesthetic is Oscar Wilde, whose representation of Dorian Gray on the canvas mirrors the replication of the Modernist self through art. For Wilde, self-replication is "a method by which we can multiply our personalities" in order to experience more fully "myriad lives and myriad sensations" (1987, 142–43). As a nine-year-old, Nabokov read Wilde in his father's library.

13. Kinbote's jaded response to Shade's optimism suggests a moment from *Speak, Memory*. Nabokov writes: "I see again my schoolroom in Vyra, the blue roses of the wallpaper, the open window. Its reflection fills the oval mirror above the leathern couch where my uncle sits, gloating over a tattered book. A sense of security, of well-being, of summer warmth pervades my memory. That robust reality makes a ghost of the present. The mirror brims with brightness; a bumblebee has entered the room and bumps against the ceiling. Everything is as it should be, nothing will ever change, nobody will ever die" (1966b, 76–77). While the child's voice echoes that of the young John Shade, the autobiographer's distance from this scene (which is, after all, prerevolution, pre–the death of his father, etc.) aligns him more clearly with Kinbote. The childlike voice is the phallically centered, whereas the mature, knowing voice is the queerly displaced, one always conscious that it is another.

14. For the context of this textual quotation, see "Solus Rex" in Nabokov's *A Russian Beauty and Other Stories* (1973b).

15. We might detect in Hermann Hesse a similar suspicion of psychoanalytic imagery and its political implications. At the end of *Demian*, Emil Sinclair has a vision of the great Mother that has a specifically political meaning: "A great town could be seen in the clouds and out of it poured millions of men who spread in hosts over vast landscapes. In their midst strode a mighty, godlike form with shining stars in her hair, as huge as a mountain but having the features of Frau Eva. The ranks of men were swallowed up into her as into a gigantic cave and vanished from sight. The goddess crouched on the ground, the 'sign' shone on her brow. She seemed to be in the grip of a dream. She closed her eyes and her great countenance was twisted in pain. Suddenly she called out, and from her forehead sprang stars, many thousands of them which leaped in graceful curves across the dark heavens. One of the stars shot straight towards me with a clear, ringing sound; it seemed to be seeking me out. Then it burst into a thousand sparks, bore me aloft and cast me down to the ground again; the world was shattered above me with a thundrous roar" (Hesse 1969, 153–54). The "Mother" — that Freudian-Jungian symbol of wholeness and unity — has become the First World War, her strength a deadly bomb. And it was Germany's increasing tendency to swallow everything up into itself that gradually disillusioned Hesse and resulted in his eventual emigration to Switzerland.

16. See also Shade's discussion of IPH, the Institute of Preparation for the Hereafter, where he notes that "Among our auditors were a young priest / And an old Communist. Iph could at least / Compete with churches and the party line" (lines 635–37), soon followed by: "to fulfill the fish wish of the womb, / A school of Freudians headed for the tomb" (lines 643–44).

17. It is interesting for our purposes that Lenin himself deployed the image of Narcissus, the "self-infatuated Narcissus," to condemn what he saw as liberal weakness in the intellectual left (1937, 354).

18. Nabokov's use of the term "pederast" is interesting here. Haegert also uses it, as do Julie Bader (1972, 33) and Andrew Field (1967, 320). While "pederast" can refer to any man who has sex with other men, it of course etymologically signifies man-boy love. Thus, it is usually used to invoke child-invasion as a way of upping the stakes of homophobic persecution. Now like Kinbote with Shade's poem, I ransack the novel looking for evidence of pederasty and can only find Charles's sexual attraction to university students. Surely these critics cannot equate such students with children. Could they be thinking of *Lolita* instead?

19. Sergey was not the only victim of a man whose theoretical poses could not seem to make their way into domestic policy: Vladimir's favorite nanny, an English woman named Miss Norcott, was dismissed, much to the boy's heartache, on the grounds of lesbianism (Boyd 1990, 52). Nabokov's widely documented homophobia has a long history of trouble spots in which queers in his immediate sphere fall victim to persecution.

20. Perhaps, but one cannot miss the irony that in *Pale Fire* the invasion of privacy is conducted at the hands of the gay man Kinbote, who spies on Shade's house. Significantly, he trains his binoculars on the mirror in Shade's study.

21. As I noted in chapter 2, the term *mise en abyme* originally referred to "a comparison with the device from heraldry that involves putting a second representation of the original shield 'en abyme' within it" (Dällenbach 1989, 7). An extended discussion of Nabokov's interest in heraldry (as in *Bend Sinister*) is outside my project, but may deliver some fascinating reflections on his connections with Gide.

22. Narcissus's life is often based on a misprint. As I outlined in chapter 3, Freud insists on translating the Italian *nibio* as "vulture" when it really means "kite." Moreover, an entire critical enterprise then grew up around defending that translation. See chapter 3 note 2. Granted, the *"nibio"* is a mistranslation rather than a misprint, but the two instances highlight the slipperiness of signifiers in constituting the "meaning" of Narcissus.

23. I do not want to suggest here any watering down of Nabokov's hatred of what the Soviet Union had become and of communism in general. As Brian Boyd points out, in 1957 Nabokov befriended the FBI agent assigned to rout out communism at Cornell — investigating, among others, Roman Jakobson — and declared that he would have been proud to have his son join the FBI in the same capacity (1991, 311).

5. The Gothic in a Culture of Narcissism

1. Narcissus invaded the popular Gothic imagination in the 1970s. Other examples include Stephen King's 1975 *'Salem's Lot,* where the homosexual vam-

pire Kurt Barlow doubles the hero, Ben Mears; the 1977 *Twins,* the novel by Bari Wood and Jack Geasland that later gave us David Cronenberg's *Dead Ringers* (1988); and Dean Koontz's 1981 *Whispers,* with scenes like the following: "Now [Bruno] stood in front of the mirror that was fixed to the door of Sally's bathroom, and he stared with fascination at the reflection of his penis, wondering what difference Tammy had sensed when she'd felt his pulsating erection in that massage parlor cubicle, five years ago. After a while, he let his gaze travel upward from his sex organs to his flat, hard, muscular belly, then up to his huge chest, and farther up until he met the gaze of the other Bruno in the looking glass. When he stared into his own eyes, everything at the periphery of his vision faded away, and the very foundations of reality turned molten and assumed new forms; without drugs or alcohol, he was swept into a hallucinogenic experience. He reached out and touched the mirror, and the fingers of the other Bruno touched his fingers from the far side of the glass. As if in a dream, he drifted closer to the mirror, pressed his nose to the other Bruno's nose. He looked deep into the other's eyes, and those eyes peered deep into his. For a moment, he forgot that he was only confronting a reflection; the other Bruno was real. He kissed the other, and the kiss was cold. He pulled back a few inches. So did the other Bruno. He licked his lips. So did the other Bruno. Then they kissed again. He licked the other Bruno's open mouth, and gradually the kiss became warm, but it never grew as soft and pleasant as he had expected. In spite of the three powerful orgasms that Sally-Katherine had drawn from him, his penis stiffened yet again, and when it was very hard he pressed it against the other Bruno's penis and slowly rotated his hips, rubbing their erect organs together, still kissing, still gazing rapturously into the eyes that stared out of the mirror. For a minute or two, he was happier than he had been in days" (Koontz 1981, 390–91). It needn't be added that Bruno is the stalking, murderous, misogynistic villain of the novel.

2. The section title, "The Generation of Unpleasure," is from Freud 1914, 85.

3. And Fenny Bate, about whom we will hear more later, actually thinks Milburn is the entire world, and that nothing else exists outside it.

4. This evaluation of the novel is King's: "The bare situation is enough to delineate the conflict in *Ghost Story;* in its way it is clearly a conflict between the Appollonian and Dionysian as Stevenson's *Dr. Jekyll and Mr. Hyde,* and its moral stance, like that of most horror fiction, is firmly reactionary. Its politics are the politics of the four old men who make up the Chowder Society — Sears James and John Jaffrey are staunch Republicans, Lewis Benedikt owns what amounts to a medieval fiefdom in the woods, and while we are told that Ricky Hawthorne was at one time a socialist, he may be the only socialist in history who is so entranced by new ties that he feels an urge, we are told, to wear them to bed. All of these men — as well as Don Wanderly and young Peter Barnes — are perceived by Straub as beings of courage and love and generosity (and as Straub himself pointed out in a later letter to me, none of these qualities run counter to the idea of reactionism; in fact, they may well define it). In contrast, the female revenant (all of Straub's evil ghosts are female) is cold and destructive, living only for revenge" (1983, 261).

While I agree that Republicanism is the driving political ideology in the old boys, I also want to suggest that the degree to which that Republicanism is troubled makes the novel a more ambivalent and interesting register of anxiety, rather than clear party doctrine.

5. Ellis Hanson quotes these lines as well (1992, 40).

6. Earlier, Irigaray cited Marx, who argued that "History is the process by which man gives birth to himself" (Irigaray 1985b, 126).

7. Hanson reads Irigaray as sympathetic to gay men who are themselves victims of patriarchal power: "She includes repressed male homosexuality in the patriarchal exclusion of the feminine," he says (1992, 38), and her term "hom(m)o-sexual" relates only to "the 'pretense' of homosexuality, the homo-erotic social ties of man to man which are first established with the patriarchal family and which, paradoxically, rely on the repression and vilification of actual genital acts between men" (41). Perhaps, but I am still troubled by Irigaray's premise that it is the man's adoration of his own phallus — and she intends at least something of a biological meaning here — that constitutes the hom(m)o-sexual, for by this logic the homosexual is not outside of patriarchy but rather is its most flagrant example. In any event, what interests me more is precisely the shimmers of the term "hom(m)o-sexual," for it articulates the strange male moment after Stonewall when men are forced into greater consciousness of their social position vis-à-vis other men, the penis, and the phallus. Irigaray may or may not try to separate gay men from straight men, but what she does do is demonstrate the slipperiness within male fantasy of allegiances to the phallus and to the organ that supposedly underlies it but is displaced by it.

8. In the Henry James story, the narrator, the governess, fears that the ghostly Peter Quint may "seduce" her young charge, Miles, into the world of the ghosts. In *Ghost Story,* the seduction is literalized as sexual, and, whereas Miles dies before capitulating (which itself may be a capitulation), Fenny dies in order to go to the other world. Note here how the governess is replaced by the male Sears James, a transposition that raises the stakes in the complex representation of gender.

9. Near the end of Walpole's 1767 tragedy, the Countess of Narbonne reveals to her son Edmund that, upon hearing of the death of her husband, she went mad with despair. Then,

> Guilt rush'd into my soul — my fancy saw thee
> Thy father's image —
> . . . .
> I took the damsel's place [i.e., the one Edmund was about to bed]; and
>   while thy arms
> Twin'd, to thy thinking, round another's waist,
> Hear, hell, and tremble! — thou didst clasp thy mother! (1924, 248)

This history is significant both for its echo of the narcissistic transpositions within the oedipal triangle — I saw you to look exactly like your father and I desired you for that resemblance — and for its difference from *Ghost Story.* Whereas Walpole makes clear that the child was a substitute, the Chowder Society's narrative is that Eva probably caused the death of her fiancé, Stringer Dedham, and so her sexual desire for them was not a rerouting at all, but rather just another bead in the string of her destructions. What this difference seems most strongly to suggest is the investment that Straub's boys have in projecting any sexual desire onto the woman by representing all female desire as by definition murderous.

10. *Symplegma,* a Latin term that may adequately describe this fantasy, refers to a group of persons who are either embracing or wrestling. The inability to tell the difference, either on our part or Peter's, may designate the complexity of Peter's feelings about Lewis.

11. This is a line from a song that Peter often hears when he has fallen under the spell of Anna Mostyn and her sort. But, moreover, it connects to the kind of music that Kristeva sees as part of the semiotic *chora,* which engages all the physical senses and is not tyrannized by the specular/audial of the father's symbolic Law.

12. The debate around Kristeva's usefulness in antihomophobic analysis has focused on lesbian eros only. In *Gender Trouble* (1990), Judith Butler critiques Kristeva's assumptions about female homosexuality (79–93), while Elizabeth Grosz attempts in *Jacques Lacan: A Feminist Introduction* (1990) to salvage Kristeva for lesbian analysis.

13. Anne Williams has suggested to me that Don Wanderly's name undoubtedly puns "Don Juan," which opens up a whole history of psychoanalytic readings of his compulsive (hetero)sexuality. I thank her for this suggestion.

14. One problem, obviously, is the notion that the father is loving, that the mother loves him, and that the child picks up on this love. The first two of these questions belong more properly to feminism, and I leave them there. The third seems to be answered only by psychoanalytic leaps of faith about what the pre-oedipal child does and does not experience.

15. The *OED* provides the following definitions for "malkin": (1) a female personal name; applied typically to a woman of the lower classes; (2) the proper name of a female specter or demon; (3) an untidy female, especially a servant or country wench; a slut, slattern, drab, a lewd woman; (4) an effeminate man. For more on the gender transposition of names, see note 8 to this chapter.

16. For a more complete reading of Torrance's relation to Hatfield and its homoerotic basis in Lacanian psychoanalysis, see my "Picture This: Stephen King's Queer Gothic" (1999).

WORKS CITED

Alexandrov, Vladimir E., ed. 1995. *The Garland Companion to Vladimir Nabokov*. New York: Garland.

Anderson, Benny, Björn Ulvaeus, and Stig Anderson. 1979. "Does Your Mother Know." On *ABBA Gold: Greatest Hits*. Polar Music International.

Bader, Julie. 1972. *Crystal Land: Artifice in Nabokov's English Novels*. Berkeley: University of California Press.

Barthes, Roland. 1978. *A Lover's Discourse: Fragments*. Translated by Richard Howard. New York: Hill and Wang.

Bass, Alan. 1985. "On the History of a Mistranslation and the Psychoanalytic Movement." In *Difference in Translation,* edited by Joseph F. Graham, 102–41. Ithaca, N.Y.: Cornell University Press.

Bentham, Jeremy. 1978. "Offences against One's Self: Paederasty, Parts 1 and 2." Edited by Louis Crompton. *Journal of Homosexuality* 3:389–405; 4:91–107.

Berman, Jeffrey. 1985. *The Talking Cure: Literary Representations of Psychoanalysis*. New York: New York University Press.

———. 1990. *Narcissism and the Novel*. New York: New York University Press.

Bersani, Leo. 1988. "Is the Rectum a Grave?" In *AIDS: Cultural Analysis/ Cultural Activism,* edited by Douglas Crimp, 197–222. Cambridge, Mass.: MIT Press.

———. 1995. *Homos*. Cambridge, Mass.: Harvard University Press.

Bieber, Irving, et al. 1962. *Homosexuality: A Psychoanalytic Study*. New York: Basic Books.

Blake, William. 1982. *The Complete Poetry and Prose of William Blake*. Edited by David V. Erdman. New York: Anchor Books.

Boker, Pamela A. 1992. "Byron's Psychic Prometheus: Narcissism and Self-Transformation in the Dramatic Poem *Manfred.*" *Literature and Psychology* 28:1–37.

Boone, Joseph, and Michael Cadden, eds. 1990. *Engendering Men: The Question of Male Feminist Criticism*. New York: Routledge.

Boyd, Brian. 1990. *Vladimir Nabokov: The Russian Years*. Princeton, N.J.: Princeton University Press.

———. 1991. *Vladimir Nabokov: The American Years*. Princeton, N.J.: Princeton University Press.

Bredbeck, Gregory W. 1991. *Sodomy and Interpretation: Marlowe to Milton*. Ithaca, N.Y.: Cornell University Press.

———. 1994. "Narcissus in the Wilde: Textual Cathexis and the Historical Origins of Queer Camp." In *The Politics and Poetics of Camp,* edited by Moe Myer, 51–74. New York: Routledge.

Brink, A. W. 1974. "Hermann Hesse and the Oedipal Quest." *Literature and Psychology* 24:66–79.

Bruhm, Steven. 1991. "Blackmailed by Sex: Tennessee Williams and the Economics of Desire." *Modern Drama* 34:528–37.

———. 1996a. "Blond Ambition: Tennessee Williams's Homographesis." *Essays in Theatre* 14, no. 2:97–105.

———. 1996b. "On Stephen King's Phallus; or, The Postmodern Gothic." *Narrative* 4, no. 1:55–73.

———. 1999. "Picture This: Stephen King's Queer Gothic." In *Companion to the Gothic,* edited by David Punter, 269–80. Oxford: Blackwell.

Butler, Judith. 1990. *Gender Trouble: Feminism and the Subversion of Identity.* New York: Routledge.

———. 1993. *Bodies That Matter: On the Discursive Limits of "Sex."* New York: Routledge.

———. 1997. *The Psychic Life of Power: Theories in Subjection.* Stanford, Calif.: Stanford University Press.

Byron, Lord George G. 1973a. *Byron's Letters and Journals.* Edited by Leslie A. Marchand. Vol. 1. Cambridge, Mass.: Belknap.

———. 1973b. *Byron's Letters and Journals.* Edited by Leslie A. Marchand. Vol. 2. Cambridge, Mass.: Belknap.

———. 1978. *Byron's Letters and Journals.* Edited by Leslie A. Marchand. Vol. 8. Cambridge, Mass.: Belknap.

———. 1980–91. *Byron: The Complete Poetical Works.* Edited by Jerome J. McGann. Oxford: Clarendon.

Capote, Truman. 1976. *Other Voices, Other Rooms.* New York: Penguin Books.

Case, Sue-Ellen. 1988–89. "Toward a Butch-Femme Aesthetic." *Discourse* 2, no. 1:55–83.

Castle, Terry. 1993. *The Apparitional Lesbian.* New York: Columbia University Press.

———. 1995. *The Female Thermometer: Eighteenth-Century Culture and the Invention of the Uncanny.* New York: Oxford University Press.

Chauncey, George, Jr. 1983. "From Sexual Inversion to Homosexuality: Medicine and the Changing Conceptualization of Female Deviance." In *Homosexuality: Sacrilege, Vision, Politics,* edited by Robert Boyers and George Steiner, 114–46. Saratoga Springs, N.Y.: Skidmore College Press.

Chew, Samuel. 1964. *The Dramas of Lord Byron: A Critical Study.* New York: Russell and Russell.

Christensen, Jerome. 1993. *Lord Byron's Strength: Romantic Writing and Commercial Society.* Baltimore: Johns Hopkins University Press.

Coburn, Kathleen. 1965. "Reflections in a Coleridge Mirror: Some Images in His Poems." In *From Sensibility to Romanticism: Essays Presented to Frederick A. Pottle,* edited by Frederick W. Hilles and Harold Bloom, 415–37. New York: Oxford University Press.

Cohen, Ed. 1987. "Writing Gone Wilde: Homoerotic Desire in the Closet of Representation." *PMLA* 102:801–13.

Coleridge, Samuel Taylor. 1956. *Collected Letters of Samuel Taylor Coleridge.* Edited by Earl Leslie Griggs. Vol. 5. Oxford: Clarendon.

————. 1957. *The Notebooks of Samuel Taylor Coleridge.* Edited by Kathleen Coburn. 4 vols. London: Routledge and Kegan Paul.

————. 1969. *Poetical Works.* Edited by Ernest Hartley Coleridge. Oxford: Oxford University Press. First published as *The Poems of Samuel Taylor Coleridge* (London: Oxford University Press, 1912).

————. 1987. *Biographia Literaria.* Edited by George Watson. 1975. Reprint, London: Dent.

Crompton, Louis. 1985. *Byron and Greek Love: Homophobia in 19th-Century England.* London: Faber and Faber.

Cronenberg, David, director. 1988. *Dead Ringers.* Morgan Creek Productions.

Dällenbach, Lucien. 1989. *The Mirror in the Text.* Translated by Jeremy Whitely. Chicago: University of Chicago Press.

De Lauretis, Teresa. 1994. *The Practice of Love: Lesbian Sexuality and Perverse Desire.* Bloomington: Indiana University Press.

Dollimore, Jonathan. 1991. "Different Desires: Subjectivity and Transgression in Wilde and Gide." In *Critical Essays on Oscar Wilde,* edited by Regenia Gagnier, 48–67. New York: Macmillan.

Doughty, Oswald. 1981. *Perturbed Spirit: The Life and Personality of Samuel Taylor Coleridge.* Rutherford N.J.: Fairleigh Dickinson University Press and Associated University Press.

Dowling, Linda. 1994. *Hellenism and Homosexuality in Victorian Oxford.* Ithaca N.Y.: Cornell University Press.

Dynes, Wayne, ed. 1990. *Encyclopedia of Homosexuality.* New York: Garland.

Edelman, Lee. 1994. *Homographesis: Essays in Gay Literary and Cultural Theory.* New York: Routledge.

Ellis, [Henry] Havelock. 1897. *Studies in the Psychology of Sex.* Vol. 1. London: University Press.

————. 1928. *Studies in the Psychology of Sex.* Vol. 7. Philadelphia: F. A. Davis.

Ellmann, Richard. 1973. *Golden Codgers: Biographical Speculation.* New York: Oxford University Press.

————. 1988. *Oscar Wilde.* Markham, Ont.: Penguin.

Ficino, Marsilio. 1985. *Commentary on Plato's Symposium on Love.* Translated by Jayne Sears. Dallas: Spring Publications.

Fiedler, Leslie. 1960. *Love and Death in the American Novel.* New York: Criterion.

Field, Andrew. 1967. *Nabokov: His Life in Art.* Toronto: Little, Brown and Co.

Field, George Wallis. 1970. *Hermann Hesse.* Boston: Twayne.

Foster, John Burt, Jr. 1993. *Nabokov's Art of Memory and European Modernism.* Princeton, N.J.: Princeton University Press.

Foucault, Michel. 1978. *The History of Sexuality.* Vol. 1, *An Introduction.* Translated by Robert Hurley. 3 vols. New York: Random House.

————. 1985. *The History of Sexuality.* Vol. 2, *The Use of Pleasure.* Translated by Robert Hurley. 3 vols. New York: Vintage.

Fowlie, Wallace. 1979. "Sexuality in Gide's Self-Portrait." In *Homosexualities and French Literature: Cultural Contexts/Critical Texts,* edited by George Stambolian and Elaine Marks, 243–61. Ithaca, N.Y.: Cornell University Press.

Franklin, Caroline. 1992. *Byron's Heroines*. Oxford: Clarendon.

Freedman, Ralph. 1978. *Hermann Hesse, Pilgrim of Crisis*. New York: Pantheon Books.

Freud, Sigmund. 1905. "Three Essays on the Theory of Sexuality." In *The Standard Edition*, translated by James Strachey, 7:125–245. London: Hogarth.

———. 1908. "The Sexual Theories of Children." In *The Standard Edition*, 9:205–26.

———. 1910. "Leonardo da Vinci and a Memory of His Childhood." In *The Standard Edition*, 11:59–137.

———. 1911. "Psychoanalytic Notes on an Autobiographical Account of a Case of Paranoia (Dementia Paranoides)." In *The Standard Edition*, 12:3–82.

———. 1913. "Totem and Taboo." In *The Standard Edition*, 13:ix–xv, 1–162.

———. 1914. "On Narcissism: An Introduction." In *The Standard Edition*, 14:69–102.

———. 1920. "The Psychogenesis of a Case of Homosexuality in a Woman." In *The Standard Edition*, 18:145–72.

———. 1921. "Group Psychology and the Analysis of the Ego." In *The Standard Edition*, 18:67–143.

———. 1922. "Some Neurotic Mechanisms in Jealousy, Paranoia, and Homosexuality." In *The Standard Edition*, 18:221–32.

———. 1923. "The Ego and the Id." In *The Standard Edition*, 19:3–66.

———. 1930. *Civilization and Its Discontents*. In *The Standard Edition*, 21:59–145.

Fruman, Norman. 1971. *Coleridge: The Damaged Archangel*. New York: George Braziller.

Fuss, Diana. 1993. "Freud's Fallen Woman: Identification, Desire, and 'A Case of Homosexuality in a Woman.' " In *Fear of a Queer Planet: Queer Politics and Social Theory*, edited by Michael Warner, 42–68. Minneapolis: University of Minnesota Press.

Gagnier, Regenia. 1986. *Idylls of the Marketplace: Oscar Wilde and the Victorian Public*. Stanford, Calif.: Stanford University Press.

———, ed. 1991. *Critical Essays on Oscar Wilde*. New York: Macmillan.

Galef, David. 1985. "The Self-Annihilating Artists of *Pale Fire*." *Twentieth-Century Literature* 31:421–37.

Garrett, Siedah, and Glen Ballard. 1987. "Man in the Mirror." On *Michael Jackson: Bad*. Produced by Quincey Morris. MCA Music Publishing.

Gide, André. 1935. *If It Die . . . an Autobiography*. Translated by Dorothy Bussy. New York: Random House.

———. 1950. *Corydon*. New York: Farrar, Straus, and Giroux.

———. 1953. "Narcissus: A Treatise on the Theory of Symbolism." In *The Return of the Prodigal*, translated by Dorothy Bussy, 1–15. London: Secker and Warburg.

Glass, Loren. 1995. "Blood and Affection: The Poetics of Incest in *Manfred* and *Parisina*." *Studies in Romanticism* 34:211–26.

Grayson, Jane. 1977. *Nabokov Translated: A Comparison of Nabokov's Russian and English Prose*. Oxford: Oxford University Press.

Green, Bernard A. 1979. "The Effects of Distortions of the Self: A Study of *The Picture of Dorian Gray.*" *Annual of Psychoanalysis* 7:391–410.

Grinskin, Alexander. 1973. "On Oscar Wilde." *Annual of Psychoanalysis* 1:345–62.

Gross, Robert F. 1995. "Consuming Hart: Sublimity and Gay Poetics in *Suddenly Last Summer.*" *Theatre Journal* 47:229–51.

Grosz, Elizabeth. 1990. *Jacques Lacan: A Feminist Introduction.* New York: Routledge.

Haegert, John. 1984. "The Author as Reader in Nabokov: Text and Pretext in *Pale Fire.*" *Texas Studies in Literature and Language* 26:405–20.

Halperin, David M. 1990. *One Hundred Years of Homosexuality, and Other Essays on Greek Love.* New York: Routledge.

Hamilton, Paul. 1983. *Coleridge's Poetics.* Oxford: Basil Blackwell.

Hanson, Ellis. 1992. "Narcissism and Critique." *Critical Matrix: Princeton Working Papers in Women's Studies* 6:23–45.

Hayman, Ronald. 1993. *Tennessee Williams: Everyone Else Is an Audience.* New Haven, Conn.: Yale University Press.

Hesse, Hermann. 1969. *Demian.* Translated by W. J. Strachan. London: Panther.

———. 1971. *Narziss and Goldmund.* Translated by Geoffrey Dunlop. Markham, Ont.: Penguin.

———. 1974. *My Belief: Essays on Life and Art.* Translated by Denver Lindley. New York: Farrar, Straus, and Giroux.

———. 1990. *Steppenwolf.* Introduction by Joseph Mileck. New York: Henry Holt and Co.

———. 1991. *Soul of the Age: Selected Letters of Herman Hesse.* Edited by Theodore Ziolkowski. Translated by Mark Harman. New York: Farrar, Straus, and Giroux.

Hirsch, Foster. 1979. *A Portrait of the Artist: The Plays of Tennessee Williams.* Port Washington, N.Y.: Kennikat.

Hoeveler, Diane Long. 1990. *Romantic Androgyny: The Woman Within.* University Park: Pennsylvania State University Press.

Hutcheon, Linda. 1980. *Narcissistic Narrative: The Metafictional Paradox.* Library of the Canadian Review of Comparative Literature, vol. 5. Waterloo, Ont.: Wilfrid Laurier University Press.

Huysmans, Joris Karl. 1969. *Against the Grain (A Rebours).* Introduction by Havelock Ellis. New York: Dover.

Hyde, H. Montgomery, ed. 1948. *The Trials of Oscar Wilde.* London: William Hodge.

Irigaray, Luce. 1985a. *Speculum of the Other Woman.* Translated by Gillian C. Gill. Ithaca, N.Y.: Cornell University Press.

———. 1985b. *This Sex Which Is Not One.* Translated by Catherine Porter. Ithaca, N.Y.: Cornell University Press.

Jackson, Earl, Jr. 1995. *Strategies of Deviance: Studies in Gay Male Representation.* Bloomington: Indiana University Press.

Jacobus, Mary. 1995. "Russian Tactics." *GLQ: A Journal of Lesbian and Gay Studies* 2, nos. 1–2:65–79.

James, Henry. 1965. *The Turn of the Screw.* In *The Henry James Reader,* edited by Leon Edel, 255–356. New York: Charles Scribner's Sons.

Jones, Caroline A. 1993. "Finishing School: John Cage and the Abstract Expressionist Ego." *Critical Inquiry* 19:628–65.

Jung, Carl Gustav. 1966. *The Collected Works of C. G. Jung.* Edited by Herbert Read, Michael Fordham, and Gerhard Adler. Vol. 15. Princeton, N.J.: Princeton University Press.

Katz, Jonathon Ned. 1976. *Gay American History.* New York: Thomas Y. Crowell.

Kavka, Jerome. 1975. "Oscar Wilde's Narcissism." *Annual of Psychoanalysis* 3:397–408.

Kessler, Edward. 1979. *Coleridge's Metaphors of Being.* Princeton, N.J.: Princeton University Press.

King, Stephen. 1975. *'Salem's Lot.* New York: Signet.

———. 1978. *The Shining.* Toronto, Ont.: Penguin.

———. 1983. *Danse Macabre.* New York: Berkley Books.

———. 1988. *Misery.* Scarborough, Ont.: New American Library.

———. 1990. *The Dark Half.* Toronto, Ont.: Penguin.

Koestenbaum, Wayne. 1989. *Double Talk: The Erotics of Male Literary Collaboration.* New York: Routledge.

———. 1990. "Wilde's Hard Labor and the Birth of Gay Reading." In *Engendering Men: The Question of Male Feminist Criticism,* edited by Joseph Boone and Michael Cadden, 176–79. New York: Routledge.

———. 1993. *The Queen's Throat: Opera, Homosexuality, and the Mystery of Desire.* Toronto: Poseidon.

Kohut, Heinz. 1971. *The Analysis of the Self: A Systematic Approach to the Psychoanalytic Treatment of Narcissistic Personality Disorders.* New York: International University Press.

Koontz, Dean R. 1981. *Whispers.* New York: Berkley Books.

Krafft-Ebing, Richard von. 1965. *Psychopathia sexualis: A Medico-Forensic Study.* Translated by Harry Wedeck. Introduced by Ernest van der Haag. New York: G. P. Putnam.

Kristeva, Julia. 1982. *Powers of Horror: An Essay on Abjection.* Translated by Leon S. Roudiez. New York: Columbia University Press.

———. 1987. *Tales of Love.* Translated by Leon S. Roudiez. New York: Columbia University Press.

Kubie, Lawrence. 1961. *Neurotic Distortion of the Creative Process.* New York: Noonday.

———. 1962. "Fallacious Misuse of the Concept of Sublimation." *Psychoanalytic Quarterly* 31:73–79.

Lacan, Jacques. 1977. *Écrits: A Selection.* Translated by Alan Sheridan. New York: W. W. Norton.

———. 1988. *The Seminar of Jacques Lacan, Book I: Freud's Papers on Technique, 1953–54.* Translated by John Forrester. New York: W. W. Norton.

Lait, Jack, and Lee Mortimer. 1951. *Washington Confidential.* New York: Crown.

Lasch, Christopher. 1991. *The Culture of Narcissism: American Life in an Age of Diminishing Expectations.* New York: W. W. Norton.

Lenin, V. I. 1937. *Selected Works.* Edited by J. Fineberg. Vol. 7. London: Lawrence and Wishart.

Leverich, Lyle. 1995. *Tom: The Unknown Tennessee Williams.* New York: Crown.

Lowes, John Livingston. 1927. *The Road to Xanadu: A Study in the Ways of the Imagination.* Boston: Houghton Mifflin.

Mallarmé, Stéphane. 1951. "Hérodiade." In *Poems,* translated by Roger Fry, 62–77, 304–7. New York: New Directions.

Mallet, Robert. 1966. *Self-Portraits: The Gide/Valéry Letters, 1890–1942.* Translated by June Guicharnaud. Chicago: University of Chicago Press.

Marcuse, Herbert. 1966. *Eros and Civilization: A Philosophical Inquiry into Freud.* 1955. Reprint, Boston: Beacon.

Martin, Robert K. 1986. *Hero, Captain, Stranger: Male Friendship, Social Critique, and Literary Form in the Sea Novels of Herman Melville.* Chapel Hill: University of North Carolina Press.

McFarland, Thomas. 1969. *Coleridge and the Pantheist Tradition.* Oxford: Clarendon Press.

McGavran, James Holt. 1995. "Glossing Over the Ancient Mariner: Perversion, Panic, and Collage-Texts." *The Wordsworth Circle* 26, no. 3:162–64.

Mellor, Anne K. 1993. *Romanticism and Gender.* New York: Routledge.

Melville, Herman. 1964. *Moby-Dick; or, The Whale.* Edited by Charles Feidelson Jr. New York: Bobbs-Merrill.

Mileck, Joseph. 1978. *Hermann Hesse: Life and Art.* Berkeley: University of California Press.

Mileur, Jean-Pierre. 1982. *Vision and Revision: Coleridge's Art of Immanence.* Berkeley: University of California Press.

Miller, D. A. 1988. *The Novel and the Police.* Berkeley: University of California Press.

Milton, John. 1962. *Paradise Lost.* Edited by Merritt Y. Hughes. Indianapolis: Odyssey.

Modiano, Raimonda. 1985. *Coleridge and the Concept of Nature.* Tallahassee: Florida State University Press.

Moore, Doris Langley. 1961. *The Late Lord Byron: Posthumous Dramas.* London: John Murray.

Morton, Donald. 1993. "The Politics of Queer Theory in the (Post)Modern Moment." *Genders* 17:121–50.

Nabokov, Vladimir. 1959. *The Real Life of Sebastian Knight.* Norfolk, Conn.: New Directions.

———. 1962. *Pale Fire.* New York: Vintage.

———. 1966a. *Despair.* New York: G. P. Putnam.

———. 1966b. *Speak, Memory: An Autobiography Revisited.* New York: G. P. Putnam.

———. 1970. *The Annotated Lolita.* Edited by Alfred Appel Jr. New York: McGraw-Hill.

———. 1973a. *Bend Sinister.* New York: McGraw-Hill.

————. 1973b. *A Russian Beauty and Other Stories*. New York: McGraw-Hill.

————. 1973c. *Strong Opinions*. Toronto: McGraw-Hill.

Nordau, Max Simon. 1968. *Degeneration*. Introduction by George L. Mosse. Lincoln: University of Nebraska Press.

Notopoulos, James A. 1969. *The Platonism of Shelley: A Study of Platonism and the Poetic Mind*. New York: Octagon.

Orsini, Gian Napoleone Giordano. 1964. "Coleridge and Schlegel Reconsidered." *Comparative Literature* 16, no. 2:97–118.

————. 1969. *Coleridge and German Idealism*. Carbondale: Southern Illinois University Press.

Ovid. 1986. *The Metamorphoses of Ovid*. Translated by A. D. Melville. Oxford: Oxford University Press.

Park, John G. 1978. "Waiting for the End: Shirley Jackson's 'The Sundial.'" *Critique: Studies in Modern Fiction* 19, no. 3:74–88.

Pater, Walter. 1873. *Studies in the History of the Renaissance*. London: Macmillan.

Pausanias. 1971. *Guide to Greece*. Translated by Peter Levi. Vol. 1. Baltimore: Penguin.

Plato. 1985. *Phaedrus and Letters VII and VIII*. Translated by Walter Hamilton. Markham, Ont.: Penguin.

————. 1987. *The Symposium*. Translated by Walter Hamilton. Markham, Ont.: Penguin.

Plotinus. 1966. *Porphyry on the Life of Plotinus and the Order of His Books; and Enneads I.1–9*. Translated by A. H. Armstrong. Cambridge Mass.: Harvard University Press.

Poe, Edgar Allan. 1956. "William Wilson." In *Selected Writings of Edgar Allan Poe,* edited by Edward H. Davidson, 112–30. Boston: Houghton Mifflin.

Polidori, John William. 1994. *The Vampyre and Ernestus Berchtold; or, The Modern Prometheus*. Edited by D. L. Macdonald and Kathleen Scherf. Toronto: University of Toronto Press.

Pollard, Patrick. 1991. *André Gide: Homosexual Moralist*. New Haven, Conn.: Yale University Press.

Porter, Roy. 1987. *The Social History of Madness: Stories of the Insane*. London: Weidenfeld and Nicholson.

Proffer, Carl. 1968. "From *Otchaiane* to *Despair.*" *Slavic Review* 27:258–67.

Ragland-Sullivan, Ellie. 1986. "The Phenomenon of Aging in Oscar Wilde's *Picture of Dorian Gray*: A Lacanian View." In *Memory and Desire,* edited by Kathleen Woodward and Murray M. Schwartz, 114–33. Bloomington: Indiana University Press.

Rajan, Balachandra. 1985. *The Form of the Unfinished: English Poetics from Spenser to Pound*. Princeton N.J.: Princeton University Press.

Rank, Otto. 1971. *The Double: A Psychoanalytic Study*. Translated by Harry Tucker Jr. Chapel Hill: University of North Carolina Press.

Read, Herbert. 1947. *The True Voice of Feeling: Studies in English Romantic Poetry*. London: Faber and Faber.

Richardson, Thomas J. 1977. "The City of Day and the City of Night: New Orleans and the Exotic Unreality of Tennessee Williams." In *Tennessee*

Williams: A Tribute, edited by Jac Tharpe, 631–46. Jackson: University Press of Mississippi.

Robinson, Charles E. 1970. "The Devil as Doppelgänger in 'The Deformed Transformed': The Sources and Meaning of Byron's Unfinished Drama." *Bulletin of the New York Public Library* 74:177–202.

Rogin, Michael. 1984. "Kiss Me Deadly: Communism, Motherhood, and Cold War Movies." *Representations* 6:1–36.

Rousseau, G. S. 1985. "The Pursuit of Homosexuality in the Eighteenth Century: 'Utterly Confused Category' and/or Rich Repository?" *Eighteenth Century Life* 9, no. 3:132–68.

Savran, David. 1992. *Communists, Cowboys, and Queers: The Politics of Masculinity in the Work of Arthur Miller and Tennessee Williams.* Minneapolis: University of Minnesota Press.

Schapiro, Barbara. 1983. *The Romantic Mother: Narcissistic Patterns in Romantic Poetry.* Baltimore: Johns Hopkins University Press.

Schlegel, August Wilhelm von. 1971. "Narcissus." In *Sämmtliche Werke.* Vol. 1, *Poetische Werke,* edited by Erster Theil, 332. New York: Georg Olms Verlag.

Schlegel, Friedrich. 1971. *"Lucinde" and the Fragments.* Translated by Peter Firchow. Minneapolis: University of Minnesota Press.

Schreber, Daniel Paul. 1955. *Memoirs of My Nervous Illness.* Edited by Ida Macalpine and Richard Hunter. Cambridge, Mass.: Robert Bentley.

Sedgwick, Eve Kosofsky. 1985. *Between Men: English Literature and Male Homosocial Desire.* New York: Columbia University Press.

———. 1990. *Epistemology of the Closet.* Berkeley: University of California Press.

Shaffer, Elinor S. 1968. "Iago's Malignity Motivated: Coleridge's Unpublished 'Opus Magnum.'" *Shakespeare Quarterly* 19:195–203.

Shelley, Percy Bysshe. 1969. "Discourse on the Manners of the Ancient Greeks Relative to the Subject of Love." In James A. Notopoulos, *The Platonism of Shelley: A Study of Platonism and the Poetic Mind,* 404–13. New York: Octagon.

———. 1977a. *Epipsychidion.* In *Shelley's Poetry and Prose,* edited by Donald Reiman and Sharon B. Powers, 371–88. New York: W. W. Norton.

———. 1977b. *On Love.* In *Shelley's Poetry and Prose,* 473–74.

Shepherd, Reginald. 1994. *Some Are Drowning.* Pittsburgh: University of Pittsburgh Press.

———. 1996. *Angel, Interrupted.* Pittsburgh: University of Pittsburgh Press.

Shute, Jenefer. 1995. "Nabokov and Freud." In *The Garland Companion to Vladimir Nabokov,* edited by Vladimir E. Alexandrov, 412–20. New York: Garland.

Silverman, Kaja. 1988. *The Acoustic Mirror: The Female Voice in Psychoanalysis and Cinema.* Bloomington: Indiana University Press.

Sofer, Andrew. 1995. "Self-Consuming Artifacts: Power, Performance, and the Body in Tennessee Williams' *Suddenly Last Summer.*" *Modern Drama* 38: 336–47.

Spoto, Donald. 1985. *The Kindness of Strangers: The Life of Tennessee Williams.* Boston: Little, Brown and Co.

Stacey, Jackie. 1987. "Desperately Seeking Difference." *Screen* 28, no. 1:48–61.

Steiner, George. 1963. *The Death of Tragedy.* New York: Alfred A. Knopf.

Stelzig, Eugene L. 1988. *Hermann Hesse's Fictions of the Self: Autobiography and the Confessional Imagination.* Princeton, N.J.: Princeton University Press.

Stoller, Robert. 1968. *Sex and Gender: On the Development of Masculinity and Femininity.* New York: Science House.

Straub, Peter. 1992. *Ghost Story.* London: Warner.

Tharpe, Jac, ed. 1977. *Tennessee Williams: A Tribute.* Jackson: University Press of Mississippi.

Thorslev, Peter. 1965. "Incest as Romantic Symbol." *Comparative Literature Studies* 2:41–58.

Trumbach, Randolph. 1989. "The Birth of the Queen: Sodomy and the Emergence of Gender Equality in Modern Culture, 1660–1750." In *Hidden from History: Reclaiming the Gay and Lesbian Past,* edited by Martin Duberman et al., 129–40. Markham, Ont.: Penguin.

Valéry, Paul. 1971. *Poems.* Translated by David Paul. Princeton, N.J.: Princeton University Press.

Vinge, Louise. 1967. *The Narcissus Theme in Western European Literature to the Early 19th Century.* Translated by Robert Dewsnap. Lund: Gleerups.

Walpole, Horace. 1924. "The Mysterious Mother." In *Constable's Edition of the "Castle of Otranto" and the "Mysterious Mother."* Edited by Montague Summers. London: Chiswick Press for Constable and Co.

Warner, Michael. 1990. "Homo-Narcissism; or, Heterosexuality." In *Engendering Men: The Question of Male Feminist Criticism,* edited by Joseph Boone and Michael Cadden, 190–206. New York: Routledge.

Watkins, Daniel P. 1983. "The Ideological Dimensions of Byron's 'The Deformed Transformed.' " *Criticism* 25:27–39.

Watson-Williams, Helen. 1967. *André Gide and the Great Myth.* Oxford: Clarendon.

Weiskel, Thomas. 1976. *The Romantic Sublime: Studies in the Structure and Psychology of Transcendence.* Baltimore: Johns Hopkins University Press.

Whitman, Walt. 1990. *Leaves of Grass (1892).* Toronto: Bantam.

Wilde, Oscar. 1962. *Letters.* Edited by Rupert Hart-Davis. London: Rupert Hart-Davis.

———. 1980. *Complete Shorter Fiction.* Edited by Isobel Murray. New York: Oxford University Press.

———. 1987. *The Picture of Dorian Gray.* Edited by Isobel Murray. New York: Oxford University Press.

———, et al. 1986. *Teleny.* Edited by John McRae. London: Gay Men's Press Publishers.

Williams, Tennessee. 1958a. *Orpheus Descending.* In *Tennessee Williams: Four Plays,* 129–44. New York: New American Library.

———. 1958b. *Suddenly Last Summer.* In *Tennessee Williams: Four Plays,* 1–93.

———. 1970. *The Glass Menagerie.* New York: New Directions.

———. 1972. *Memoirs.* New York: Doubleday.

———. 1975a. *Moise and the World of Reason.* New York: Simon and Schuster.

———. 1975b. *Sweet Bird of Youth*. New York: New Directions.

———. 1976–77. *Tennessee Williams' Letters to Donald Windham, 1940–1965*. Edited by Donald Windham. New York: Holt, Rinehart and Winston.

———. 1978. *Where I Live: Selected Essays*. Edited by Christine R. Day and Bob Woods. New York: New Directions.

———. 1990. *Five O'Clock Angel: Letters of Tennessee Williams to Maria St. Just, 1948–1982*. New York: Alfred A. Knopf.

Woolf, Virginia. 1975. *A Room of One's Own*. 1945. Reprint, Markham, Ont.: Penguin.

Wylie, Philip. 1955. *Generation of Vipers*. New York: Rinehart.

Yarlott, Geoffrey. 1967. *Coleridge and the Abyssinian Maid*. London: Methuen.

Ziolkowski, Theodore. 1967. *The Novels of Hermann Hesse: A Study in Theme and Structure*. Princeton, N.J.: Princeton University Press.

INDEX

Steven Bruhm is associate professor of English at Mount St. Vincent University, Halifax, Canada. He is the author of *Gothic Bodies: The Politics of Pain in Romantic Fiction,* as well as numerous articles on the contemporary gothic.